The Quest for Reality

For Julia, because . . .

This is how philosophers should salute each other:
"Take your time!"

—L. Wittgenstein

Preface

This book deals with a huge metaphysical enterprise. No one could treat it exhaustively in a single book—or lifetime—and I do not try to. I concentrate on drawing attention to what I think are some of its distinctive features and exploring one or two of them far enough to draw some tentative morals. I do not expect agreement from many philosophers, but I do hope even those with little sympathy towards what they find here are encouraged to look again at the task of reaching intelligible and reliable metaphysical conclusions.

I write out of the conviction that philosophy is extremely difficult. That would perhaps go without saying, did not so much recent philosophizing seem to me to proceed otherwise. I find it is especially true of treatments of some of the topics I try to investigate here.

One source of the difficulty is that responses to philosophical questions tend to start too late. J. L. Austin is reported to have observed that in works of philosophy it is usually all over by the bottom of page one. I think that is right and can be confirmed by more or less random reading. What really matters is off the page and settled in the mind before the author's announced task has even begun. Here I try to go into the sources of some of the questions I take up, but without supposing that I get far enough to avoid the inveterate tendency in my own case.

Another conviction out of which I write is that philosophy is one subject and that progress in one place depends on the resolution of issues that lie elsewhere. One is led eventually into almost all other areas and questions. This is certainly true of the work of the great philosophers of the past. Against that high standard, the current professional fixation on distinct "fields" or areas of academic "specialization" and "competence" looks like no more than a bad joke. It would be more amusing if it were not having such disastrous effects on philosophy and on intellectual life generally.

These convictions express part of my sense of the special character of philosophical problems and doctrines and of the difficulty of recognizing that character and describing or explaining it in the right way. Many philosophers do not pay much attention to this. Either they think they understand it well enough already, or they recognize no significant difference between philosophy and other efforts to get to know something. In any case, they are too busy trying to answer their philosophical questions to spend much time on where they come from.

Investigating the philosophical quest for reality as I do here is one way of pursuing the question of what philosophy is meant to do, at least if it takes the form of philosophical doctrine or theory. The very notion of a philosophical theory or thesis or doctrine is something I wish to understand better than I do. We cannot simply define the idea of the philosophical at the outset and then look for views or doctrines that fulfill that definition. No form of words alone can serve to identify a remark or a thought as philosophical. We must understand the task or question those words or thoughts are a response to and how they are meant to be taken for the particular philosophical purpose at hand.

I do think there is something that philosophy aspires to which needs to be identified and described and understood. Or, rather, I think there is something human beings aspire to which finds its expression in philosophy. We seek a certain kind of understanding of ourselves and of reality that will make intelligible to us in general terms the relation in which we stand to that reality—or perhaps the relation in which we really stand to it. But to describe the goal in this shorthand way is to make essential use of the very idea of reality that I want to explore. Can we get any independent understanding of it? Our grasp of the idea probably cannot be separated from our ability to understand and carry out the kind of project I am interested in. The quest for reality and the goal of philosophy are too closely connected for one of them to be much help in explaining the other.

Obviously, I cannot take up the quest wherever it has made its appearance. After identifying some of its general features, I concentrate on one particular area and hope that it will serve as an instructive example. What I have to say, if found plausible, might eventually encourage the suspicion that, at least within the area I consider, there might never be a philosophical theory or doctrine that could fully satisfy our philosophical desire to understand. That is not something I ar-

first half of this book the kind of careful reading and insightful criticism that one can normally only dream of in one's readers. Gabriele Mras has been especially helpful through many of my rewritings, understanding so well what I am up to and giving me good advice, most of which I have even followed.

There is by now simply no way to begin to identify all those who have had some effect in one setting or another on what appears here, but I know that I have gained directly from comments, criticisms, or suggestions from Robert Adams, Rogers Albritton, Carl Anderson, Michael Ayers, Annette Barnes, Jonathan Bennett, Simon Blackburn, Tyler Burge, John Carriero, Thompson Clarke, Donald Davidson, Ronald de Sousa, Keith Donnellan, Ronald Dworkin, Robert Fogelin, Dagfinn Føllesdal, Philippa Foot, Allan Gibbard, Hannah Ginsborg, John Heil, Julie Jack, Martin Jones, Michael Jubien, Jeff King, Saul Kripke, Ed McCann, John McDowell, Colin McGinn, Francisco Miro Quesada, Thomas Nagel, Derek Parfit, Christopher Peacocke, David Pears, Eduardo Rabossi, Joseph Raz, John Searle, Ernest Sosa, Galen Strawson, Nicholas White, David Wiggins, Bernard Williams, Crispin Wright, and Linda Zagzebski. I have been talking about these things for a long time. A list of philosophers from whom I am equally certain I have gained nothing might have been shorter.

From all these and other unmentioned friends, collaborators, and critics, I single out for special thanks Rogers Albritton, Thompson Clarke, Donald Davidson, Thomas Nagel, and Bernard Williams. In different ways, their (often even unwitting) encouragement has meant the most to me.

Contents

The Quest for Reality

1

Introduction

The Philosophical Project

It is always difficult to know where to begin in philosophy. No doubt it is best to begin at the beginning, but a major part of philosophy as I understand it is the attempt to find out where that is.

What I am calling the quest for reality has been part of Western philosophy since before Socrates was born. It is perhaps even definitive of philosophy. It involves a very general way of thinking that continues to exert great power. But I believe that where the inquiry starts and how it is meant to proceed are still not well enough understood. Its application to one particular area is the concern of the chapters that follow. I want to try it out there, not just survey its alleged results in the abstract. My aim is to develop from the inside a rich sense of what it takes to engage in the enterprise in the right way and to see what sorts of conclusions can be reached. That is finally the best test of whether we can make the project intelligible to ourselves and of the validity of whatever we find in carrying it out.

It would be best simply to describe the goal or point of the project, at least in general terms, and then get down to investigating it in detail. But I find that there is simply no saying in a few unambiguous words what it amounts to. The most I can do by way of introduction is to circle around it and distinguish what I have in mind from more familiar inquiries which it is not. I want to try to bring out how abstract and unfamiliar—in a word, how strange—this philosophical project really is.

It is meant to be a quest whose goal is the nature of reality—what the world is really like, or how things really are. And it involves distinguishing what is really so from what only appears to be so, or

separating reality as it is independently of us from what is in one way
or another dependent on us and so misleads us as to what is really there.
That is the general idea, but this way of describing it does not succeed
in bringing out the special philosophical character of the project. Philosophical questions about reality can look and sound exactly like familiar ordinary or scientific questions about reality. They can be expressed
in the very same words. But the two must be distinguished, however
difficult it is to say what the difference is. Not every question as to what
is so is part of the philosophical quest for reality.

Sometimes a failure to distinguish philosophical questions from
similar-sounding ordinary or scientific questions can make ordinary or
scientific thinking look worse than it is. That happens, I believe, in the
philosophical investigation of human knowledge. A philosophical question is raised about knowledge in general; we are unable to give a satisfactory answer that explains how human knowledge of the world is
possible; the investigation and its unsatisfactory outcome are taken to
have the same significance as they would have in science or everyday
life; so we feel forced to conclude that we do not really know anything
in science or in everyday life.

In the present case, failure to distinguish the two can have the opposite effect: it can make the philosophical investigation of reality look
more familiar and more straightforward than it turns out to be. It can
even make it look as if there is nothing at all special or problematic
about the project. I have said that it is a question about reality: the attempt to discover how things are, or what the world is like. But any attempt to understand or find out anything fits that description. A physicist wants to find out how matter behaves, a psychologist how human
beings behave, an economist how the market behaves, and so on. Even
someone who simply asks where the book she was reading yesterday is
now or what time the next flight leaves for London is asking what is so,
how things are, or what is true. Talk of truth here is nothing lofty, abstract, or metaphysical. It is the straightforward concern with what is
so or with the way things are that is inseparable from having or seeking beliefs about anything. It could equally be called a concern with
what the world is like. But not every question about what is so or what
the world is like amounts to the philosophical quest for reality that I
have in mind.

That is not because ordinary investigations do not try to distinguish
what is so from what only appears to be so. They sometimes do. But
when that distinction is at issue, our everyday questions about reality
vs. appearance are not to be understood in any special philosophical
way. For example, in a wax museum I might wonder whether the uni-

formed gentleman standing by the door is real or not. I give him a discreet nudge with my elbow on the way out, and then I know. I might wonder whether there really is a flat, shiny lake on the horizon of this otherwise barren desert. I find that it keeps getting farther away as I approach, so I do not continue in that direction in search of water. The page of the book I am reading in bright sunlight shows a sickly, yellowish tinge, but I remember that I am wearing new sunglasses. I can take them off and find out whether the paper is really yellow or only looks that way through these glasses.

These are all questions about reality, in fact about appearance and reality, but they are perfectly familiar questions of the kind we raise and answer every day. They, too, are just questions about what is so, even about what is really so. We answer them by further investigation or inquiry, just as physicists or psychologists or economists answer their questions, when they do, by further, if more elaborate, investigation of the appropriate kind. They are questions about what is really so or how things really are, but they are not for that reason philosophical—unless we absurdly declare all questions to be philosophical. They are not what is at stake in the philosophical quest for reality. That quest is not a search simply for what is true or what we should believe in physics or psychology or economics, or in the wax museum or the desert. None of those inquiries needs any help from philosophy.

There are, of course, familiar philosophical questions about what we know or what we should believe and whether we have reason to believe anything. Philosophers have asked completely general questions about the possibility of any knowledge at all, in physics or psychology or economics or everyday life or wherever else it might be thought to be available. The questions are not directly about the way things are but about our knowledge of the way things are. Epistemological inquiries of this kind cannot be separated completely from the quest for reality I have in mind, but here I focus on theories or investigations of reality rather than on theories or investigations of our knowledge of it. I think even questions about knowledge, when they are philosophical, turn out to be questions about what is so in reality: "Do we really know the things we think we know?" How things really are is perhaps always what is at issue in philosophy. The conception of reality that is presupposed or put to work in such philosophical inquiries is what I would like to understand. I want to explore the means by which any such conception of reality is reached.

What is at stake in the philosophical quest for reality is not only the way the world is, or even really is, but also the relations in which we human beings stand to that world. We want to form a conception of the world as a whole, and we seek the right kind of understanding of ourselves as part of it. We want to understand, in general, how we fit into the world as we know it or believe it to be. But not just any relations between human beings and the world they live in would give us what we want in the philosophical project.

We know that the world contains many physical things, for example, and we know that we ourselves are among those physical things. So we know that we fit into the world simply as parts of it, as physical constituents. The laws of physics apply to us just as they do to all other physical things. But the philosophical question is not simply how one physical part of the world is related to other physical parts of the world.

It gets closer to say that we are philosophically interested not just in the relations between physical things in the world, and not just in the relations between human beings and the rest of the world, but rather in the relations between human beings' responses, perceptions, thoughts, and beliefs about the world and the way the world really is. That takes us closer, but it is still not enough. We know that our responses, perceptions, thoughts, and beliefs are caused by things that happen in the world; if the objects around us were not as they are, we would not respond and believe as we now do. But acceptance of that causal relation does not alone give us what we want.

We want to understand not only what gives rise to our perceivings and believings but also whether *what* we perceive or believe or come to think about the world represents it as it really is. In which respects does the world correspond to the ways we think it is, and in which not? The philosophical quest for reality is an attempt to answer some such question. It is a question not only about the world, and not only about our perceptions, thoughts, and beliefs about it, but also about the relation between them.

We can begin to get a better idea of the question from some of the answers philosophers have given to it. For example, in the fifth century B.C. Parmenides held that the real, or what is, is a single, enduring, indivisible plenum, in which therefore no change and no motion are really possible. However clearly the world might appear to be otherwise, he gave what seemed to be impeccable logical reasons for thinking that that must be what is really so. One of several responses to the challenge of Parmenides' indivisible One was atomism. It held that there are an indefinitely large number of very little indivisible Ones, all moving around in otherwise empty space, colliding, joining, and separating from each other in ways that make things happen as they do in the world we are all familiar with.

This, too, was a grand, speculative metaphysical picture of reality, on all fours in that respect with other bold conjectures with which it is apparently in conflict. It was intended to be less paradoxical than Parmenides' story. It would fly less in the face of the obvious facts. Not only would it allow for change and motion, which seem such obvious features of the world we experience, but it would even explain how they are possible, as Parmenides had argued that they are not. But it, too, finds a gap between what is or what is real, on the one hand, and what is not real but only appears to be so, on the other. Considerably less material is assigned to mere "appearance" in the atomist picture than on Parmenides' account, but still there is a significant contrast. The world presented to human beings in their daily lives diverges from, and appears to be a much richer place than, that austere reality described by the atomists.

Democritus, for example, declared: "by convention colour, by convention the sweet, by convention the bitter, but in truth, atoms and the void".[1] This is a claim about how the world is; all that is real are indivisible atoms of various shapes and sizes moving through parts of otherwise empty space. That is the positive story. With details of the sizes and shapes and motions of the atoms filled in, that would be the whole truth about reality. But Democritus' atomism also consigns a great deal of what we take to be part of the world to another source—to what he here calls "convention" (*nomoi*). What holds "by convention" has a human source, or is valid only in those circles in which those "conventions" hold, as contrasted with what has its source in the nature of things and so is valid everywhere and independently of human participation. This distinction between "nature" and "convention", between what holds in the nature of things and what is a consequence of the human or subjective contribution to our conception of things, was given wide currency by the Greeks. It has been central in one form or another to most of Western philosophy.

Plato and Aristotle, each for different reasons, rejected the atomist hypothesis. It was resuscitated, at least in broad outlines, in the seventeenth century. Democritus had envisaged atomistic explanations of everything that happens. If all that exists are impenetrable atoms of different shapes and sizes, variously moving, then everything that happens must be nothing more than a matter of certain kinds of atoms coming together or separating or moving at various speeds. The world seems to

---

1. As translated and quoted by Kurt von Fritz in his "*Nous, Noein, and Their Derivatives in Pre-Socratic Philosophy*," in A. Mourelatos (ed.), *The Pre-Socratics: A Collection of Critical Essays*, Garden City, N.Y., 1974, p. 75.

us to be full of coloured, or sweet or bitter, or warm or cold things. But that is only so for human beings, constituted as we are. We, too, are nothing but combinations of variously moving atoms, and the atomic thesis is meant eventually to explain why the world appears to us in those ways, even though no such qualities belong to anything that exists. The "appearances" are just a result of the atoms that we are made of being affected in certain ways by other atoms.

This way of drawing a distinction between "appearance" and "reality"—and so accounting for the richness of human experience in terms of an independent but comparatively austere "nature"—was given enormous impetus in the seventeenth century with the emergence of the new science. A serious science with precise mathematical laws that would compute the effects of the comings and goings of its fundamental entities promised to complete the programme Democritus had only envisaged. Many details of the earlier atomic hypothesis had to be changed, but in general it seemed that an independent and mathematically describable physical world had been found, and that a purely mechanical science of its operations had been established.

That new physical science was thought to reveal the bankruptcy of the Aristotelian scheme of final causes and of the idea of full conformity between an inquiring human mind's conception of the world and what is so in the world it investigates. As in Democritus, there remained a huge gap between the way the world really is in itself and the way it happens to present itself to scattered organisms on the surface of one of the planets of the solar system. Galileo, for example, held that: "If the ears, the tongue, and the nostrils [of those perceiving beings] were taken away, the figure, the numbers and motions [of bodies] would indeed remain, but not the odours or the tastes or the sounds, which, without the living animal, I do not believe are anything else than names".[2] Physical science can describe every aspect of the figure or shape and the number and motions of the bodies that make up the world. We have words for what we think of as the colours, odours, and tastes of those objects as well, but those words stand for nothing that exists in reality. In that sense, they are nothing but empty words. "If the animal were removed", Galileo said, "every such quality would be abolished and annihilated".[3] The world as it is in itself—without the responses of "the animal", as it were—contains objects with only those

---

2. Galileo, *Il Saggiatore*, as translated and quoted by E. A. Burtt, *The Metaphysical Foundations of Modern Physical Science*, London, 1950, p. 78.
3. Galileo, *Il Saggiatore*, p. 75.

qualities that physical science deals with, the size, shape, number, and motion of bodies.

Some such distinction between the size, shape, and motion of things (what came to be called their "primary" qualities) and the colours, smells, and feel of things (their "secondary" qualities) came to seem like nothing more than scientifically enlightened common sense. It has remained so or has once again become so in our own day, when the details of the physical sciences have changed almost out of all recognition from those of the seventeenth century. This suggests that what a particular physical science actually says about the world is not what really serves to distinguish appearance from reality in this philosophical way. The mere possibility of any successful explanatory physical science would seem to be enough.

Descartes did not agree with everything in Galileo's physics, but he accepted the negative point about colours, smells, tastes, and sounds. He thought that "there is no way of understanding what sort of things" colours could be if we think of them as existing outside our minds, on the physical objects that surround us.[4] But the mathematically describable features of objects are fully intelligible to us as they are independently of us. Descartes thought the only way we can understand or have a clear and distinct conception of colours is to regard them "merely as sensations or thoughts" in the mind.[5] This banishes colours from the world of "real things existing outside our minds".[6] Colours, like tastes and smells and pains, are nothing more than "sensations" produced in us by objects with only those qualities attributed to them by mathematical physical science. Those are the only qualities objects have "in reality", despite what they "appear" to have because of the way they affect us. We are confused if we think otherwise. We are too closely tied to the senses, and have not fully escaped what Descartes calls certain "preconceived opinions of childhood".[7]

Locke was one of the first to use the terms 'primary' and 'secondary' qualities to make this distinction. The terms might have been coined by his scientific mentor, Robert Boyle, a thoroughgoing corpuscularian. Locke expressed his view not in terms of names, as Galileo did, but in terms of ideas. We have ideas of those qualities dealt with in atomist

---

4. R. Descartes, *Principles of Philosophy* I, 68, in *The Philosophical Writings of Descartes*, vol. I (tr. and ed. J. Cottingham, R. Stoothoff, and D. Murdoch), Cambridge, 1985, p. 217.

5. Descartes, *Principles of Philosophy*, I, 68 (p. 217).

6. Descartes, *Principles of Philosophy*, I, 68 (p. 217).

7. Descartes, *Principles of Philosophy*, I, 71 (pp. 218–219).

physical science—the bulk, figure, number, and motion of the bodies around us—and we have ideas of such things as their colours, tastes, sounds, and smells as well. Locke held that these first, "the *Ideas of primary Qualities* of Bodies, *are Resemblances* of them, and their Patterns do really exist in the Bodies themselves; but the *Ideas, produced* in us *by* these *Secondary Qualities, have no resemblance* of them at all".[8] In the case of colours, tastes, sounds, and smells, "There is nothing like our *Ideas*, existing in the Bodies themselves".[9] Clearly echoing Galileo, Locke says: "Take away the Sensation of them; let not the Eyes see Light, or Colours, nor the Ears hear Sounds; let the Palate not Taste, nor the Nose Smell, and all Colours, Tastes, Odors, and Sounds, as they are such particular *Ideas*, vanish and cease, and are reduced to their Causes, i.e., Bulk, Figure, and Motion of Parts".[10] He might even have had Galileo in mind in saying that our ideas of colours and other such qualities "are in the mind no more the likeness of something existing without us, than the Names, that stand for them, are the likeness of our *Ideas*, which yet upon hearing, they are apt to excite in us".[11]

These are all expressions of what is fundamentally the same distinction and the same metaphysical picture of reality. A positive science of physical nature tells us what the world is like—what qualities objects in the world do, in fact, have. But that physical science alone does not establish the metaphysical theory. Physical scientists professionally restrict their attention to the physical aspects of the world that can be captured in their theoretical network. If there is more to the world than that, physical science says nothing about it. The metaphysical theory of atomism or physicalism goes one step further. It says that atoms or the physical qualities of things are all there is. It does not remain noncommittal about whatever there might be beyond the purely physical aspects of things. It says that there is nothing beyond that, or that whatever is thought to go beyond the physical is nothing, or is not real. The natural or commonsense belief that objects have many qualities beyond the "primary" qualities mentioned in a purely physical account is thereby exposed as a mistake, illusion, confusion, or expression of mere "appearance".

This second, negative claim is the heart of the philosophical theory. Strictly speaking, it is independent of the particular details of positive

---

8. J. Locke, *An Essay concerning Human Understanding* (ed. P. H. Nidditch), Oxford, 1975, book II, chap. viii, 15 (p. 137).
9. Locke, *Human Understanding*, II, viii, 15 (p. 137).
10. Locke, *Human Understanding*, II, viii, 17 (p. 138).
11. Locke, *Human Understanding*, II, viii, 7 (p. 134).

physical science. Whatever that science happens to be like—whether it is Greek atomism, seventeenth-century Galilean physics, Newtonian mechanics, or late-twentieth-century quantum theory—the metaphysical part of the project says not just that science gives the truth about the world but that it gives the whole truth. The idea is that what is really so is *only* what that science says is so, and that everything else can be understood, if at all, only by being fitted into that austere physical story. That is perhaps why this grand metaphysical idea can survive radical change in the details of physical theory and so remain popular, even to many self-evident, today.

David Hume was not an atomist, or even much concerned with the details of physical science, but he endorsed what he saw as one major consequence of the scientific picture of the world—the idea that colours, sounds, and so on are nothing but "internal existences" which "arise from causes, which in no way resemble them".[12] But he went much further; colours, sounds, and heat and cold were not the only things he excluded from the world as it is in itself. He thought the same was true of causality, or the necessity with which one event is thought to succeed another. "Necessity is something, that exists in the mind, not in objects",[13] he declared. All that ever happens in the world independently of minds is that one thing succeeds another and resembles other instances that followed similar antecedents. We naturally believe that some things are causally connected with others, that one thing happens because another does; we even think we can see one thing cause another. But for Hume there is nothing in reality that answers to that idea of necessity. It is nothing but a "determination of the mind".[14]

Morality, too, was for Hume no part of reality, and in just the same way. "Vice and virtue", he said, "may be compar'd to sounds, colours, heat and cold, which according to modern philosophy, are not qualities in objects, but perceptions in the mind".[15] Nothing as it is in the world is either good or bad, virtuous or vicious. Only when we look into ourselves and find certain feelings towards the actions or characters around us do we find the source of whatever vice or virtue we attribute to them. This is perhaps the best known and most widely accepted application of a philosophical quest for reality. It arrives at a value-free world, and so at the unreality or "subjectivity" of all value.

---

12. D. Hume, *A Treatise of Human Nature* (ed. L. A. Selby-Bigge), Oxford, 1958, p. 227.

13. Hume, *Treatise*, p. 165.

14. Hume, *Treatise*, p. 166.

15. Hume, *Treatise*, p. 469.

In all these theories, there is a conception of the world or reality as being a certain way independently of the responses of any sentient beings; it would have been that way whether there had been such responses or not. There is also an acknowledgement of a rich variety of human responses to that world or beliefs about it. But the idea is that, given what the theories say that world is really like, not all of those responses or beliefs represent the world as it is. Beliefs about the existence of atoms do, for example; beliefs about the colours of things do not. Beliefs about the succession of events do; beliefs about causal connections between them do not. Beliefs about what happens do; beliefs about the goodness or badness of what happens do not. The philosophical conception of reality is a conception of some such independent world. The quest for reality is the process of reflection by which we arrive at a determinate view of such an independent world and see it as adequately represented by many but not all of our beliefs and experiences. The rest are assigned to a "subjective" domain of "appearance" with a wholly or partly human source.

Although this conception of reality and of the project of separating the "subjective" from the "objective" is a very old idea, it is by no means a thing of the past. It is to be found, for example, in any philosophy which would distinguish in general between the "given" that we receive from the world and the "interpretation" we put upon it, or between the "flux of experience" and the "conceptual scheme" we impose upon it to make sense of our experience and learn from it. Virtually every general philosophical theory of this century has relied on this distinction in one form or another. W. V. Quine in *Word and Object* puts the philosophical task almost mathematically in these terms:

> we can investigate the world, and man as part of it, and thus find out what cues he could have of what goes on around him. Subtracting his cues from his world view, we get man's net contribution as the difference. This difference marks the extent of man's conceptual sovereignty—the domain within which he can revise theory while saving the data.[16]

The idea is that if human beings come to think or act or experience in certain ways only because of their interaction with the world around them, there must be something about what human beings are like, and something about what the world is like, which combine to produce those ways of thinking or acting or experiencing. It therefore seems legitimate to ask how much of what we think and feel is due to the way

16. W. V. Quine, *Word and Object*, Cambridge, Mass., 1960, p. 5.

the world is—the "objective" factor—and how much is due to features of us, the "subjective" factor. If the contribution of the world is meagre in relation to our elaborate conception of the world, our own minds or sensibilities must be playing a large role. If certain ways of thinking or experiencing could be fully explained by "subjective" factors alone, those ways of thinking would be seen to have a purely "subjective" source. The world would not have to contain anything corresponding to them for us quite naturally to think that it does. But those ways of thinking would give us, at best, "appearance", not reality.

The fundamental idea is of two separate ingredients in our conception of the world, or two separate sources of our conception. Whatever one thinks the "objective" data contributed by the world and the "subjective" contribution of human beings separately happen to be, a bipartite picture of the source of our conception of the world is at work.

The same general idea is present in controversies about the "objectivity" of certain other domains of alleged fact—scientific laws, for example, or mathematics, or necessary truth. Do laws of nature express "natural necessities" that somehow hold in the world, or are they purely extensional generalizations which differ from "accidental" general truths only in being treated by us in certain ways or playing an epistemically special role in our theories? Is their "lawlike" status due to something in the world, or only to something about us? The question derives from a bifurcated conception of the world or reality on one side and the "subjective" contribution of human beings on the other.

The same is true of the question of whether mathematics discovers a domain of fact existing independently of us or somehow invents or constructs the truth of the theorems it proves. The question arises for logical or necessary truths in general. Are they all in some sense "analytic", or "true by virtue of meaning" or "convention" alone? That widely shared idea was part of a metaphysical theory according to which there are no such things in reality as the things mathematics appears to be about, and no such necessities. Necessary or mathematical truths are somehow due only to "us", to our conventions or decisions to speak or think in certain ways—something only on the "subjective" side. The philosophical idea of reality that I am interested in is essential to the very formulation of the question, not only to particular answers to it.

It is present as well in that philosophical inquiry known as "ontology". "Are there numbers?" "Are there qualities and relations, as well as objects?" "Are there events?" We apparently speak about all those things from time to time in everyday discourse, and sometimes we even seem to assert that there are such things. But the philosophical question in each case is whether objects of the appropriate kinds really exist in the world that makes the things we say true or false. The question, even the whole enterprise, makes sense only if the philosophical quest for reality makes sense. Searching for the objects that exist in reality is part of the question of what reality is like.

Any metaphysical theory about the nature of reality would seem to make essential use of the same idea. Physicalism, for example, or materialism is a philosophical doctrine about reality. It says that reality is purely physical. Anything that we think of as nonphysical, or any apparently nonphysical fact that we think holds, is either reducible to a physical thing or fact, or it is a fiction, illusion, or mere manner of speaking. That is true of any apparently mental items or facts if physicalism is true. But physicalism is not the only view of the world that expresses the philosophical quest for reality. Mind-body dualism and idealism are different answers to the same philosophical question. The idea behind that shared question is what I am interested in. I want to understand the sense, and the source, of a question about reality to which the physicalist answers, "It is physical" and the dualist answers, "It is both physical and mental". It is a philosophical question about reality.

The quest for reality remains at the heart of some of the best work on the most pressing philosophical issues of today, just as it always has. It is an old philosophical idea. But being old and being well understood are not the same thing—as we learn as we get older.

One thing that makes it difficult to understand is the ease with which we shift back and forth between philosophical and more mundane questions about reality without noticing the differences between them. We ask on a particular occasion, "Is this paper really yellow or does it only look that way because of the glasses through which I am now seeing it?" The philosopher asks, "Is anything really coloured at all, or do things only look that way because of the means by which we see them?" The point of the second question is difficult to distinguish from that of the first. And even if the questions do differ in some way, it seems that if the answer to the more general second question is that nothing is really coloured, that settles the more specific question as well.

We sometimes find that events we took to be causally connected were, in fact, pure coincidence, with no connection between them. More often, we find that one thing is the effect of another. Philosophers have asked whether there are any causal connections between events in the world at all: whether causality is real. If it is not, it is hard to see how we could be right in thinking, as we do, that a paticular billiard ball colliding with another causes the second ball to move.

We know that sometimes a person regards something as good only because it touches his own personal interest in some way, and that there really is nothing good about it independently of that. Philosophers have asked whether anything at all is ever really good, independently of our regarding it so. It is hard to see a difference between what those philosophers ask about and what we ordinarily believe. It is also difficult to see how philosophical questions about whether there really are such things as numbers, qualities, or events differ from the more familiar questions we ask every day about what is real or what is really so. "Is there really a man in a uniform standing by the door?" "Is that a real man?" "Is there really a lake over there in the desert?"

I say it is difficult to see or describe the difference between the two kinds of question; I do not say there is no difference. The problem is to understand what the difference amounts to. One suggestion that does not take us very far is that the philosophical or metaphysical questions are simply more general than scientific or everyday questions; they are perhaps the most general questions there can be. There is perhaps something in this suggestion, but as it stands it does not seem to be correct. I do not believe in ghosts, for example. I regard my view on that matter as a perfectly ordinary or perhaps semiscientific denial of the reality of such things. It is not any philosophical thesis. But what I believe is that there are no ghosts anywhere. That is a completely general proposition; it seems that nothing could be more general. And surely nothing could be more general or more universal (if that made any sense) than the laws sought by a physicist or chemist or mathematician. How could philosophical questions or theses differ in being even more general than that?

It also seems that philosophical or metaphysical questions can equally be raised about particular things. For example, "Is the colour of that wall right before me something real or not? Is that part of the wall really coloured?" Philosophers who deny the reality of colour will say "No". To the question "Is there really such a thing as the number two?" some philosophers will say "No"; others, after perhaps years of reflection, will say "Yes". It is not generality or particularity alone that distinguishes a philosophical or metaphysical question from scientific or everyday questions. It is not simply the range or scope or size of the question; it is not what it asks about, but rather how it asks it.

The philosophical quest for reality asks about the relation between the world and our conception or beliefs about it. It asks that question with the prospect of eliminating from our conception of the world certain features which most or all people appear to believe in. But eliminating something from our conception of the world is often a perfectly ordinary procedure. We do it every time we find out that something we believed is not so. This happens frequently in small matters: I find that the flight I am interested in leaves at 11:00 A.M., and so eliminate from my view of the world my earlier belief that it leaves at 10:00. It can also happen with respect to large general features of the world. Scientific breakthroughs eliminate much that was accepted in the past and can eventually transform our conception of the whole universe. Smaller changes require less disruption. But in each case something is exposed and eliminated. It is perhaps easy to think that the elimination sought for in the philosophical quest is only a more systematic and more sweeping version of what we are already familiar with. But that is not so. The philosophical question about the reality of colours or numbers or goodness or whatever it might be is asked in a special way.

In trying to understand that special quest, we know that the philosophical question about the reality of the colour of the wall will not be answered simply by taking off our sunglasses or turning up the lights or taking a piece of the wall out into the sunlight. It is not a question that can be settled by the kind of further investigation that settles everyday or scientific questions about what is so. The metaphysical question about the number two is not settled by arithmetic. If that is all it took, it would already be answered. And where further investigation of a mathematical question is still needed, the question, the procedures, and the answer are all mathematical, not metaphysical. Philosophical questions about reality remain strangely unanswered, even when we have done our best scientifically, mathematically, morally, and in every other ordinary way to find out how things really are.

The philosophical quest must start somewhere. It needs a set of beliefs about what the world is like. Without some attitudes, perceptions, beliefs, or theories to start with, it would have nothing to reflect on. So it relies from the outset on the results of our best efforts to find out what is so, and it begins by accepting the deliverances of the sciences and everyday experience and everything else we think we know. But the project also involves standing back in a way from all those perceptions, beliefs, and theories. It asks how they are related to the independent world they are meant to be about. But even this does not identify the metaphysical quest uniquely. Not every kind of reflection on the relation between our beliefs and an independent reality helps answer the philosophical question. The detached scrutiny of our beliefs must be understood in a special way if it is to amount to the philosophical quest for reality.

I can reflect in different ways on some or all of my beliefs and ask about their relation to reality. I might simply ask whether my beliefs are true—or more realistically, which of them are true. I would be asking whether I have got things more or less right so far and, if not, where

I have gone wrong. Of course, I do *believe* everything I believe or take to be true at the moment, but I can ask in a critical or reflective spirit how much of what I believe really is true.

Such a question makes sense, even if we do not always have good reason to ask it or any reason to doubt the beliefs we already have. Even if we have little or no conception of what a plausible set of alternative beliefs would look like, the question whether our current beliefs are true is always at least intelligible. That is because our believing something and its being true are not the same thing; the truth of something does not follow from our believing it. And there is certainly no general guarantee that we have reached the truth, no unimpeachable assurance that what we have believed up till now for the best reasons will never be overthrown. That in itself is no reason for doubt or even discomfort. It is reason to keep trying to do the best we can: to continue to reject what we find to be less satisfactory in favour of more satisfactory and better supported beliefs.

Subjecting our beliefs to scrutiny would amount to checking or re-confirming them. Where we find reason for doubt or hesitation, we can investigate matters further, look again, try additional experiments, re-calculate, or carry out whatever further examination is most appropriate to the case. We can always ask whether we, either individually or as a community or a culture, are getting things more or less right on certain matters, whether our best views are on the right track so far, or at least are closer to the truth than previous efforts had been.

When we do that, we will not always be led to change our beliefs. If I believe that the ripe tomato before me in bright sunlight is red, for example, it is overwhelmingly likely that if I look again in ideal circumstances and conscientiously reconsider the matter, I will find nothing to alter my original belief. My belief that there is a number two between one and three seems simply unimprovable; any re-examination I can imagine would leave me with the same belief. My expectation that a billiard ball about be struck cannot fail to move has all past experience and physical theory behind it; I can find no reason to alter my conviction. I think it goes without saying that in general it is better to comfort someone than to kill him; I can find nothing on reflection that casts the slightest doubt on that. When I ask myself whether all these beliefs I hold are really true, I answer "Yes". But still the metaphysical questions about colours, numbers, necessity, and value presumably remain unsettled. They are not answered one way or the other by my having said what I have said, and they would not be answered by further or more informed investigation of the same kind, if that were possible. This could be put by saying that the philosophical question is not merely a question of the truth or acceptability of our beliefs. It is not simply a question of what to believe.

The point is not that no ordinary enquiry into the truth of our beliefs could ever lead us to alter our beliefs. It could. We might find that although many of the things we now accept stand up to further scrutiny, others do not and so can no longer be accepted. But if that happened through further, if more careful, investigation, it would not be the philosophical discovery that our beliefs do not stand in the appropriate relation to reality. It would be the all-too-familiar discovery that some of the things we used to believe are not true, that things are not as we previously supposed. And we would have reached that conclusion by further investigation of the appropriate kind in the area in question.

One way of taking a question about the relation between the world and some or all of our beliefs about it is therefore just the question of whether our beliefs, or which of our beliefs, are true. And that is just the question of what is true, or how things are. We answer that question, if we can, by putting ourselves in the best position for getting the most accurate and reliable beliefs about whatever is in question. This is platitude. But it does not tell us what is needed to answer the philosophical question about the relation between our beliefs and the world.

Another way to describe the philosophical question is to say that it asks which of our beliefs *represent* reality as it is in itself, or which of them *correspond to* the way the world really is. This is a perfectly natural way of putting it, but it encourages a certain facile dismissal of the question. It can then be asked what this relation of "correspondence" or "representing" is, and what sorts of things stand as the terms of that relation. There are presumably beliefs or statements or even sentences on the one hand, but what sorts of things are they supposed to correspond to on the other? And whatever those things are, how are we to investigate the relation between them and the beliefs or statements we are interested in? Can we study it empirically, by observation? And if not, does the idea of corresponding to or representing the world really make sense?

These and similar questions lie behind objections to what its critics call "the correspondence theory of truth". Those objections seem to me to be a rich mixture of justified puzzlement, good sense, valid argument, confusion, and overreaction. Much of the trouble comes from unclarity about what a "theory of truth" is supposed to be, or do. If it is meant to define the notion of truth in terms which make no use of 'true' or any equivalent notion, its prospects do not seem bright. But I do not think we presuppose any such definition in asking about the correspondence between our beliefs and the world. Talk of correspondence in that connection is not all bad.

Saying that someone's belief does not correspond to reality or does not represent things as they really are can be a way of saying that his belief is not true. "He believes he has $2,000 in his account, but there is no correspondence between his belief and reality." In believing or asserting things, we believe or assert them as true. Talk of corresponding to the world or representing things as they are can therefore make as much sense as talk of truth does.[17] We can ask whether the things we believe are true, and there is nothing wrong with asking in that same way whether our beliefs correspond to reality or represent the way things really are. The so-called correspondence theory of truth is unsatisfying as an explanation of truth precisely because talk of correspondence seems to mean nothing more than talk of truth. But if that is so, we cannot object that talk of correspondence makes no sense. We talk sensibly of the truth or falsity of our beliefs.

We need the notion of truth in speaking in general about beliefs without identifying particular specimens. We can ask whether any beliefs of a certain kind are true. "Is anything he said true?" When a belief is specifically identified—the belief that the wall is brown or the belief that there is a lake in this desert—the question of its truth can be put directly, with no explicit mention of truth. "Is the wall brown?", "Is there a lake in this desert?", or even "Is there really a lake in this desert?". If we ask such questions about something we already believe, we ask whether the belief is true, but we do not mention truth. We simply ask what is so. And the question which of our beliefs correspond to the way things are can be understood in the same innocuous way. The notion of the world as something our beliefs can correspond to can be used in speaking in general about beliefs without mentioning particular specimens, just as the notion of truth is used. But to ask whether my belief that the wall is brown corresponds to the way things are is just a way of asking whether, as I believe, the wall is brown.

Even if innocuous talk of correspondence or representing does make sense in this way, that does not explain the philosophical question about the correspondence between our beliefs and reality. We have seen that

---

17. J. L. Austin says that 'corresponds to the facts' is "a wholesome English expression" and that claiming that it is mistaken to look for something in the world to which a statement corresponds when it is true is to treat it "as though it were a philosopher's invented expression" meant to answer a "bogus demand". But it is not. See "Unfair to Facts" in his *Philosophical Papers*, Oxford, 1961, p. 107.

the philosophical project cannot be understood as the straightforward investigation of how things are. It does not ask simply which of our beliefs are true or worthy of acceptance. To find in the special philosophical way that there is nothing in reality corresponding to a particular belief is not simply to find the belief false or epistemically wanting, as we might ordinarily discover we were wrong about something or that our reasons are not as good as we thought they were. The philosophical project aims to reveal a different kind of deficiency or lack of correspondence in a belief.

This is where doubts about the correspondence theory are more to the point. The difficulty is not so much with the notion of correspondence as with the idea of an independent "reality" or "world" to which some but not all of our beliefs correspond. What is that "world"? What conception of "reality" is involved in asking which of the beliefs we hold for the best reasons correspond to reality and which do not? We need some conception of an independent reality to ask the question. And we must arrive at that conception from things we believe for good reasons. The question is how we arrive at a determinate conception of an independent reality out of everything we believe to be so before any philosophical reflection begins.

2

The Philosophical Conception
of an Independent Reality

The philosophical project relies on a conception of a "reality" or a "world" that is independent of the thoughts, experiences, and responses of human and other animals who think about or respond to it. We do have some such conception. We think of the world as independent of ourselves and our responses in a perfectly ordinary way. Many things are as they are whether we have any response to them or not; the world was here long before we were, and will remain in some form after we are all gone. But that mundane conception of an independent world is not the conception that is needed to give the philosophical question about reality its proper sense or point.

We have seen that we can always ask in a critical or reflective spirit which of our beliefs are true. Even if we end up giving a reassuring positive answer in each case, we show by understanding the question and trying to answer it as we do that the question of the truth of a belief is different from the question of whether we have that belief. We acknowledge that, in general, from the fact that we believe a certain thing it does not follow that it is true. Something could fail to be true even if I, or many people, or even everyone, believed it.

There are exceptions which prevent this from holding universally. If someone believes something, whatever it might be, then that person exists and believes something. So anyone who cautiously believes no more than 'Something exists' or 'Somebody believes something' could not possibly be wrong. For such beliefs, falsity is impossible. But for almost everything else that anyone might believe, it is possible for it to be believed without its being true. Whether something is believed is one thing; whether it is true is another.

Nor is there any implication in the other direction. From something's being true, it obviously does not follow that it is believed. This is clear enough from everything that was true before there were any people, and so any believers or beliefs, at all. It holds equally for all those things which are or will be true but will never be believed by anyone. But even among truths that have been or will be believed, their being believed does not follow from their being true. Whatever is so, it is always a separate question whether anyone believes that it is so.

We could put this by saying that something's being so is independent of its being believed to be so. This is no more than logical independence; it does not imply any barrier or obstacle to getting true beliefs. It is simply the fact that from someone's believing that p, it does not follow that p, and from the fact that p, it does not follow that someone believes that p. We aspire to believe the truth, and there is nothing in this idea of independence which suggests that we cannot get it. When we believe something, we want what we believe not to differ from what is true; and when we seek the truth about something, we want what is true not to differ from what we come to believe about it. We often succeed in these aims. But still our beliefs remain independent of their truth in the ways just explained. It is precisely because the truth of something is in that sense independent of its being believed by anyone that coming to believe the truth on some particular question can be an achievement. The truth of the matter could have gone unrecognized by everyone, and what we came to believe about the matter could have failed to be the truth. In getting things right, then, both those possibilities have been eliminated, so we have made a real advance. It is a task in which we might not have succeeded. If the truth of something implied that it is believed, or if something's being believed implied that it is true, we could not possibly fail.

What we believe to be so is how we think things are. So how things are is also in this sense independent of their being believed to be one way rather than another. It is in this sense that we all have a conception of things' being a certain way independently of their being believed to be that way. If we can think in general of everything we believe, and take all of it together as giving our whole conception of the world, we can acknowledge that in understanding beliefs as we do we have a conception of the world as independent of its being believed by us to be one way rather than another.

Even if we regard our conception of what is so as something we *know* and not merely believe, we must acknowledge that what is so is also independent of its being regarded as known by us or by anyone. What is known cannot be false. But what we seek knowledge of is what is so, whether it is known or not. This engagement with an independent world is basic to the very notion of knowledge, something without which it would be of no interest. C. I. Lewis put it this way:

> Unless the content of knowledge is recognized to have a condition independent of the mind, the peculiar significance of knowledge is likely to be lost. For the purpose of knowledge is to be true to something which is beyond it. Its intent is to be governed and dictated to in certain respects. It is a real act with a real purpose because it seeks something which it knows it may miss. If knowledge had no condition independent of the knowing act, would this be so?[1]

What is essentially the same idea has been expressed more recently by Bernard Williams in his explanation of the required notion of independence:

> a very basic thought, that if knowledge is what it claims to be, then knowledge is of a reality which exists independently of that knowledge, and indeed (except for the special case where the reality known happens itself to be some psychological item) independently of any thought or experience. Knowledge is of what is there *anyway*.[2]

The central thought here is not really a thought about knowledge in particular. The independence in question is equally present for belief. Belief is belief in a reality which exists independently of that belief; it is belief that what is so is so *anyway*. Of course, what you believe to be there *anyway* might not be there. Belief differs in that way from knowledge. But even when what you believe is (unknown to you) not so, you do believe it to be so, and to be so *anyway*. That is, you believe it, and its being so or not is independent of your believing it. That does not hold for knowledge; what you know must be true if you know it. But even then there is no implication in the other direction. From something's being true, it does not follow that it is known. That is why gaining knowledge can be an achievement.

This independence of what is so from its being believed or known to be so holds in general, with some special exceptions, even when what

---

1. C. I. Lewis, *Mind and the World-Order*, New York, 1956, p. 192.
2. B. Williams, *Descartes: The Project of Pure Enquiry*, Harmondsworth, 1978, p. 64.

is so is something about human belief or experience or responses themselves. That human beings behave in certain ways, for example, or that they believe or experience this or that is just as much something that is there *anyway* as is the fact that there are mountains on earth or fish in the sea. From the fact that human beings believe or experience or behave in certain ways, it does not follow that someone believes or knows that human beings believe or experience or behave in those ways, and there is, in general, no implication in the other direction. Of course, the existence of mountains and fish and such things is also independent of human thought or experience in a way that humans' experiencing, believing, and behaving as they do are not. Mountains and fish could have existed and could have been just as they are now even if human beings had never come along. But human thoughts, experiences, and responses could not. Still, there remains a sense in which psychological facts involving human beings are independent of their being known or believed by human beings.

The thought of things' being a certain way independently of their being known or believed to be that way is so far a very general and indeterminate idea. It is only the idea of whatever is so being so independently of its being known or believed to be so. A conception of a whole world that is independent of us in that sense is equally indeterminate. It is nothing more than a conception of whatever is so, what is said to be so by whatever is true. But we also have a determinate, filled-in conception of how things are; we have a great many beliefs as to what is so. We believe that there are mountains on earth, that there are fish in the sea, that human beings believe that there are mountains on earth and fish in the sea, that human beings have many different experiences, and so on. And for virtually everything we believe, we see that its truth or falsity is independent of our believing it. In that sense, we have a rich, determinate conception of an independent reality: a specific view of the world that is there *anyway*.

Of course, I do not mean that because we have such a conception we are therefore right in what we believe—that the world is the way we think it is. I mean only that we understand most of the things we believe—that there are mountains on earth, that human beings have many different experiences, and so on—to be so, or not, independently of our believing them to be so. A conception of the world embodied in everything we believe is a conception of a world that is as those beliefs specifically say it is, and it is a conception of its being that way *anyway*. It is a richly detailed, determinate conception of how things are independently of anyone's having that or any other conception of their being that way.

We can and do think of an independent world in these ways. But neither a purely abstract, indeterminate conception of whatever is so nor a fully determinate, filled-in conception expressed in everything we believe can serve as the conception needed to ask the special philosophical question about the relation between our beliefs and reality. They do not give us a way of formulating the philosophical quest.

If we start with nothing more than the indeterminate idea of reality as whatever is so, and we ask which of the things we believe correspond to or represent that reality, we will be asking which of the things we believe are true. We will be asking whether what we believe to be so *is* so. That is always a meaningful question. But we saw that the way to answer that question is to investigate, or reinvestigate, the way things are—to put ourselves into the best position for getting reliable beliefs about the matter in question, and see what we find. There is, of course, no guarantee that what we come up with will be true, just as there was no guarantee when we first acquired the beliefs we've got. The most we can do is to continue to do our best. The way to do that is to engage in further investigation of the appropriate kind in the domain in question. But we have seen that that is not what is at stake in the philosophical question.

The quest for reality therefore requires something more than a completely open conception of reality as whatever is so. It must employ a conception filled with specific, determinate content to have something against which the correspondence of our beliefs could be appropriately assessed. For example, suppose you knew what furniture there is in a certain room: there is a table, three chairs, a rug, and nothing else. You could then ask and answer questions about the extent to which certain beliefs about the contents of that room correspond to reality. A set of beliefs which made no mention of the rug would fail to capture everything that is there, and a belief that there is a table, three chairs, a rug, and a sofa would go beyond what is there. You could assess the degree of correspondence in each case because you would know what the beliefs in question are, and you would have a specific, determinate conception of what is in the room.

When you assess the beliefs of other people, you can sometimes find that they do and sometimes find that they do not correspond to what is so. But if you ask yourself whether your own beliefs correspond to what is actually so in the room, and you do not come to reject the beliefs you started with, you will find the same answer for each belief—"Yes". That is the kind of position all of us are in with the question about our own beliefs and their relation to reality. Our determinate conception of what reality or the world is like is embodied in all our beliefs; what we think the world is like is what we believe to be so. But if our conception of the world is *everything* we believe, we could not arrive at the conclusion that some of our beliefs do not represent or correspond to that reality as we conceive of it. There would be no possibility of finding a gap or mismatch, and so no prospect of eliminating some well-supported beliefs for their failure to correspond to an independent reality.

If we believe, for example, that the ripe tomato before us is red, that there is a number two between one and three, that the struck billiard ball must move, and that it is better to comfort than to kill, then our conception of reality, if it includes everything we believe, will be a conception of a world in which those things are true. That is what reality will be like for us. If we then ask which of our beliefs correspond to reality so understood, we could not discover that in reality nothing is coloured, there are no numbers, nothing must be so, or nothing is better than anything else.

In saying that that is what reality would be like for us, I mean only that that is what we would take reality to be—what we take to be true. I do not mean that the world or reality would be that way simply because we take it to be that way. What we take to be true might not be true; that logical independence cannot be denied. Nor am I saying that we could never discover a failure of correspondence between our beliefs and what is so. We can and often do discover that what we have believed up till now is not really true, that our conception of the world is not correct in this or that respect. But the conception of reality we use in making that mundane discovery is the indeterminate conception of reality as whatever is so. We find that what we believed is not so.

To find that some of our beliefs are not true is to eliminate them from our conception of the world. To replace them with others, which then become part of what we take to be the way things are, is to change our conception of the world—to (as we see it) improve it. Having done that, we will once again be unable to find a gap between our new set of beliefs and what the world is like. A determinate conception of reality filled with *everything* we believe therefore provides no way of asking the special philosophical question about the correspondence between our beliefs and an independent reality. That question must leave room for a negative verdict in some cases. With a fully determinate conception of reality, the answer we found would be "Yes" for everything we believe.

The conception of reality needed for the philosophical reflection must be a determinate conception with specific content. But to allow for the possibility of a negative answer in some cases, it cannot simply be identified with everything we believe. We therefore need a conception expressed in terms of only some, but not necessarily all, of our current beliefs. Those to which reality does not correspond are to be eliminated. But it must contain *some* of our beliefs, since to have a conception of the world's being a certain way is to have certain beliefs about it.

The reality we ask about in the philosophical question is obviously not something we could hope to consult independently of believing or knowing the world to be a certain way. We can directly compare one picture with another, for example, to see how closely they correspond, and perhaps we can even assess the degree of correspondence between a picture and its subject. But we cannot hold all our current beliefs about the world up against the world and somehow measure the degree of correspondence between the two. If we can arrive at the philosophical conception of reality at all, then, it will have to be by starting out with all our beliefs about everything and somehow carving out of that immense totality a conception which, after philosophical scrutiny, will have been reduced to only a portion of the original total. What we end up with will be what we then take reality to be: what we think is "really" so. The rest will be declared not part of reality, or as not representing the world as it "really" is. It will perhaps be consigned to mere belief, or "appearance", or some other purely "subjective" status.

When I say we must somehow carve such a conception of reality out of all the things we currently believe to be true, I mean there is simply no other way of getting it. We cannot have a conception of the world that is somehow completely separate from the way we take things to be. Nor could it be a matter of building up a justified picture of the world from experience, or from anywhere else. The task is not epistemic; it is not a question of getting support for a set of beliefs. It is the task of distinguishing, within everything we now accept, between the part that corresponds to or represents an independent "reality" and all the rest that we conclude does not, and so is in one way or another only "appearance" or "subjective". It is therefore a matter of working from within what we already think we know or take to be true. Only in that way can we retain a determinate conception of reality in contrast with which the rest of what we accept can be seen to fall short.

There are good independent reasons to be encouraged by the inevitability of this engagement or immersion in our current beliefs and ways of thinking. For one thing, it excuses us from the unintelligible task of trying to peel our perceptions and beliefs off the world, as it were, and compare them in some direct way with what they are about. For another thing, engagement with the world as we find it is nothing less than the only alternative available to us. If we want to find out what is really so, we have no choice but to start where we are, with what we already believe or think we know, and go on from there. We have to keep some beliefs or other, or get new ones which win out over those we used to have.

But the philosophical project also requires a certain withdrawal or detachment from the things we believe. We have to be able to examine and assess them independently of our believing them or having very good reasons to believe them. The question is not simply whether they are true or whether we should continue to accept them. Even if all the beliefs we examine are the outcome of careful investigation and are as strongly supported as they can be, the question is not their epistemic credentials but the further metaphysical question of their relation to an independent reality. It is perhaps not surprising that a metaphysical enquiry into the relation between our beliefs and reality should require both engagement with and detachment from our beliefs about the world. The question is whether we can take those opposing attitudes towards the same set of beliefs. And there is the further question whether the project requires that we do so at the same time.

The best recent attempt to describe a conception of this kind, and so to identify the goal of the philosophical quest, is Bernard Williams' account of what he calls the "absolute conception of reality". We saw that a conception of a world that in his words is "there *anyway*", independently of its being believed to be that way, is involved in our understanding of the very idea of knowledge of, or belief about, the world. Williams thinks that is an idea that contains very rich commitments.

If we can think of two people as each having knowledge of the world but each knowing something different from what the other knows, there must be some coherent way in which the two different knowledge claims are related to each other and to the world they are about. For example, if one person knows that it is raining and another knows that it is not, it must be because their knowledge is of different places or of the same place at different times. If one person knows that there is an apple to the left of the bowl on the table and another knows that there is an apple to the right of the bowl on that table, either there is more than one apple or bowl or the two claims are made from different sides of the table. For us to think of them both as cases of knowledge, it must somehow be possible for us to think of them as claims about or perspectives on the same reality. And for us to have that thought, we must possess a larger conception of the world that contains the thoughts and beliefs of the knowers in question, along with those parts of the world that they amount to knowledge of. To see that enlarged conception, in turn, as expressing something we know, it must be possible to carry the process further. For every conception of the world which we can think of as a piece of knowledge, we must be able to see that conception as related to other conceptions which equally amount to knowledge, and all of them as related in the right way to the world they represent. If we cannot, we will have abandoned the idea that the notion of knowledge requires a conception of a world that is "there *anyway*".

Williams sometimes calls the conception of a world that is involved in this way in the very idea of knowledge "the absolute conception of reality". It accommodates different agents' different perspectives on or positions in a single world in a way that makes sense of their relations to it and to each other. He concludes from his observations on knowledge that "if knowledge is possible at all, . . . the absolute conception must be possible too."[3] I think that in this sense we do have an "absolute conception", or a conception of a world that is "there *anyway*". We have a conception of a world that is the way it is independently of its being known or believed to be that way. Such a conception is involved in our understanding of the possibility of knowledge.

But to say that we all have a conception of the world's being "there anyway", and that that conception is embodied in everything we believe, is not to say that we all have the conception of a world independent of us that is needed for the philosophical question about reality. That requires a conception that is "absolute" or a reality that is "independent" in a different and richer sense. A conception of reality that is "absolute" in this richer sense does not necessarily contain everything we believe before we begin philosophical reflection. Williams thinks the philosophical conception we end up with will be "a long way from a naïve and unreflective conception of the world".[4] It will even be a long way from everything we accept after sophisticated, reflective investigation. Even if we have settled to our (temporary) satisfaction the question of what to believe, we would still not have settled what he calls "the highly general and philosophical issues of what the world is fundamentally like".[5] An "absolute" or philosophical conception of an independent reality is not simply a conception of what the world is like; it is a conception of "what the world is fundamentally like". That is what the philosophical quest for reality seeks.

What is an "absolute conception of reality" in this richer sense? Why is it thought to be needed? And what can we do to arrive at it? These

3. Williams, *Descartes*, p. 65.
4. Williams, *Descartes*, p. 235.
5. Williams, *Descartes*, p. 235.

questions are difficult to answer in abstract, general terms. One thing that can lead to the idea that we need such an "absolute" conception is the undeniable thought that any conception of the world we can form is, after all, *our* conception of the world. We arrive at it in our own ways and from our own particular position in the world. It might for that reason be thought likely to show certain signs of being *only* our conception. This is where the idea of two separate ingredients in the formation of our conception of the world comes into play. Whatever is due only to us and to our own ways of responding to and interacting with the world does not reflect or correspond to anything present in the world as it is independently of us. The aim of an "absolute" conception, then, is to form a description of the way the world is, not just independently of its being believed to be that way, but independently, too, of all the ways in which it happens to present itself to us human beings from our particular standpoint within it. An "absolute" conception would be a conception from which all such traces of ourselves have been removed. Nothing would remain that would indicate whose conception it is, how those who form or possess that conception experience the world, or when or where they find themselves in it. It would be as impersonal, impartial, and objective a picture of the world as we can achieve.

We know that partiality, self-interest, peculiar perspective, and limited experience are all potential sources of error or distortion in our beliefs. Anyone who tries to get the best supported beliefs possible will be alert to their presence and will do what can be done to avoid them. If you look at things through yellow sunglasses, especially if you don't know that you are wearing them, you might develop a distorted view of how things are. We therefore can try to arrive at "a conception of reality corrected for the special situation or other peculiarity of various observers".[6]

But the philosophical task is not simply a matter of acquiring our beliefs in the most impartial, objective way. That might leave us with a huge set of well-supported beliefs, but that is where the philosophical project begins, not where it ends. It requires further assessment of those well-supported beliefs:

> It is a matter not just of overcoming limitations on enquiry and hence of occasional error, as understood within the framework of our outlook, but of overcoming any systematic bias or distortion or partiality in our outlook as a whole, in our representation of the world: over-

---

6. Williams, *Descartes*, p. 241.

coming it, that is to say, in the sense of gaining a standpoint (the absolute standpoint) from which it can be understood in relation to reality, and comprehensively related to other conceivable representations.[7]

In the philosophical project we must generalize and eliminate from our conception of the world all those features that are due to uniquely human characteristics, position, or perspective. Williams thinks the effort to identify everything that is peculiarly human in this way "leads eventually to a conception of the world as it is independently of the peculiarities of any observers".[8]

When we move beyond individual or even group partiality or perspective to this level of cosmic generality, the goal of a "corrected" and therefore "absolute" conception of the world is not easy to understand. How do we tell what features of our conception are peculiarly human? We must begin with everything we believe to be true, and we must examine that conception of the world and somehow assess it in relation to a reality we conceive of as being fully independent of us and of that conception. That requires that we have or form some conception of that independent reality and come to understand parts or aspects of our original conception of the world as not representing it as it is. If we see them as products or reflections of something peculiar to human experience or to the human perspective on the universe, we assign them a merely "subjective" or dependent status and eliminate them from our conception of the world as it is independently of us.

Williams describes this as a process of "correction" by which the original body of beliefs is transformed into a conception that is as free as possible of its uniquely human sources:

> In reflecting on the world that is there *anyway*, independent of our experience, we must concentrate not in the first instance on what our beliefs are about, but on how they represent what they are about. We can select among our beliefs and features of our world picture some that we can reasonably claim to represent the world in a way to the maximum degree independent of our perspective and its peculiarities. The resultant picture of things, if we can carry through this task, can be called the "absolute conception" of the world.[9]

It is our ways of "representing" the world that are to be freed as much as possible from "our perspective and its peculiarities". An "absolute"

---

7. Williams, *Descartes*, p. 66.
8. Williams, *Descartes*, p. 241.
9. B. Williams, *Ethics and the Limits of Philosophy*, Cambridge, Mass., 1985, pp. 138–139.

conception of the world is a conception that "represents" the world only in certain ways and not others.

What shows that a certain way of thinking is less than "absolute" in this sense? How is our "peculiarly human perspective" revealed in our thought about the world? Anyone who thinks about the world at all must think about it in some terms or other. Might some of the very terms or concepts in which we think betray a certain human peculiarity or perspective? Williams sometimes suggests this. He thinks there might be certain concepts that are "peculiarly ours" or "peculiarly relative to our experience", and that they must be left behind if we wish to describe the world "absolutely", as it really is. The resulting conception of the world would not have "among its concepts any which reflect merely a local interest, taste or sensory peculiarity".[10]

This same idea that certain concepts are what we must be on the lookout for is present also in J. J. C. Smart's defence of a similar conception of objectivity or independence. He cites the familiar example of coloured spectacles distorting one's conception of the world, and draws a general parallel:

> In the same sort of way our ordinary manner of talking about the world is suffused with concepts which relate the things in the world to our human concerns and interests, and which depend, in often unnoticed ways, on our human physiology and our particular station in space-time.[11]

He thinks there is an "anthropocentricity" inherent in many of our concepts. To understand the world "truly as it is", to see it in "a truly objective way", we must eliminate such concepts and so come to see the world "impartially or *sub specie aeternitatis*".[12]

This is more than the claim that in moving from a naive and unreflective to a sophisticated and more carefully considered set of beliefs about the world we should try to eliminate partiality, special interest, or even general human peculiarity as possible sources of ignorance or error. Smart says we should eliminate certain *concepts* from our considered conception of the world. It is the "anthropocentricity" said to be inherent in some of our concepts that can mislead us into a less than fully objective or "absolute" picture of the world. "Concepts which depend on the idiosyncrasies of the neurophysiology of *homo sapiens* can easily be thought to have a cosmic significance"[13] when they do not.

---

10. Williams, *Descartes*, p. 245.
11. J. J. C. Smart, *Philosophy and Scientific Realism*, London, 1963, p. 149.
12. Smart, *Philosophy and Scientific Realism*, p. 151.
13. Smart, *Philosophy and Scientific Realism*, p. 149.

Smart warns that this can happen with our conception of the world in general, "much as the Hebrews looked up at the dome of the sky and thought that this was a solid half-spherical shell, or *firmament*, and did not realise that this apparently solid object was an illusion of their own perspective".[14]

Now if those Hebrews Smart has in mind believed that the sky is a solid shell or dome, they were wrong. They might well have been insufficiently impartial or disinterested in their efforts to find out what is so, and there were many things they did not know. They might have reached that false belief because of the way what happens in the sky looked to them from their position on earth. Perhaps the belief even served their interests or soothed their fears. But Smart claims in addition that it was the "anthropocentricity" inherent in some of their *concepts* that led them to their false belief. We might ask which concepts in particular were at fault. Was it the concept 'shell', or 'dome', or 'solid'? We still have all those concepts today, but we do not believe that the sky above us is a solid shell or dome. And when we fall into error from wearing coloured spectacles, it is surely not because we are using concepts "which relate the things in the world to our human concerns and interests".

How plausible is it to say, then, that the "anthropocentricity" to be avoided in a fully "absolute" conception of the world resides in some of our concepts? Which concepts, and what shows that they are anthropocentric? We must ask what it is for a concept to "reflect" a "local interest, taste or sensory peculiarity", to be "peculiarly relative" to human experience, or to "depend on" idiosyncrasies of *homo sapiens*. It cannot mean only that the concept is peculiarly or uniquely ours. We humans are perhaps the only beings who have any concepts at all, so all concepts are peculiarly or uniquely ours. That would mean that all concepts should be eliminated from the description we give of the world, and that would leave us with no concepts and no beliefs and no conception of a world at all.

Can we say that the concepts to be eliminated are all those we possess or employ because of certain peculiarities or interests unique to human beings? That again seems to be true of most if not all of our concepts. We would have few if any concepts if we could not speak a language. We are perhaps the only inhabitants of the universe who can do that. But if that meant that all the concepts we unique human beings employ must be eliminated from a fully objective or "absolute" conception of the world, we would again be left with no conception at all.

---

14. Smart, *Philosophy and Scientific Realism*, p. 149.

The same is true of human interests. Even the most austere mathematical and physical concepts we have are employed because human beings have certain uniquely human interests and concerns. The development of a scientific understanding of the universe appears to be something that only human beings have come to be interested in, and for reasons that are unique to human beings. But presumably that does not show that all scientific concepts "reflect" that unique human "peculiarity", or are "peculiarly relative" to it, in a way that disqualifies them from being used in a description of how the world is *anyway*.

It is perhaps tempting to think that there are some concepts we possess only because of certain "peculiarly" human "idiosyncrasies", but there are others which would have to be employed by any beings who could form an adequate conception of the world at all. Thus Smart imagines the possibility of a "cosmic language" in which we might communicate with "rational beings" anywhere in the universe.[15] We might try to avoid concepts with built-in "anthropocentricity" by accepting as our conception of the world only what could be expressed in such a cosmic language. Williams, too, speaks of "nonperspectival materials available to any adequate investigator, of whatever constitution",[16] "even if . . . very different from us".[17] He appears to think of an "absolute conception" as something expressible exclusively in terms available to all, or even all possible, investigators.

I do not think this idea can take us far towards understanding the idea of a determinate "absolute" conception of the world. Trying to conceive of nonhuman investigators elsewhere in the universe does not provide an effective test for disqualifying certain concepts from use in describing a world that is there *anyway*. For one thing, it is simply too speculative. When we try to think about such possible beings, we do not always know whether what we are imagining is really possible. But more important, it is not simply a matter of conceiving other beings, even if we know that the beings we imagine are really possible. The main difficulty is that what conclusions we draw about our conception of the world from conceiving of such beings will depend on what we already believe the world to be like.

For example, we human beings can smell things, and we can see the colours of things. It seems possible to conceive of beings who know a great deal about the world but lack those human senses, so we might be tempted to conclude that whatever we think we find out by means

15. Smart, *Philosophy and Scientific Realism*, pp. 149–150.
16. Williams, *Ethics and the Limits of Philosophy*, p. 140.
17. Williams, *Ethics and the Limits of Philosophy*, p. 139.

of those "sensory peculiarities" are not really part of the world as it is independently of us. That would disqualify concepts of smell and of colour from an "absolute" conception because of the possibility of beings who form a conception of the world which does not contain them. But we humans also can touch things and feel their shape and solidity, and it seems possible to conceive of beings who lack a sense of touch. Could we conclude that concepts of shape and solidity should be disqualified from a conception of a world that is there *anyway*? That would mean that it could not be part of our "absolute" conception of the world that objects have shapes. Perhaps shape could be said to remain because it can be seen as well as felt. But we also imagined that there could be beings without sight. They could not see the colours of things, but they could not see the shapes of things either. They might still know things about the world. To try to conceive of beings who lack both sight and touch perhaps approaches the limits of what a possible investigator of the world can be like. But if we do grant that such beings are even as much as possible, surely we do not commit ourselves to the conclusion that all concepts of shape must be eliminated from any conception of the way things are independently of us.

Human beings also count objects and determine how many things of a certain kind are in a particular place, and they use mathematical concepts to state many of the things they believe about the world. But it seems possible to conceive of beings who know many things about the world without counting anything, or without possessing the mathematics we do. Admitting the possibility of such "investigators", if, indeed, they are possible, should not lead us to conclude that in counting objects as we do we are not determining how many such objects there really are in that place in the world as it is independently of us. Nor should the possibility of "investigators" who lack the differential calculus lead us to think that when we express what we take to be facts of the world in terms of the calculus we reveal merely a "local" or human "peculiarity" which should be expunged from any account of how things are "absolutely". Many highly competent actual, and not merely possible, investigators of the world lacked much of the mathematical knowledge we now possess. We should not conclude that at most only what we share with them is part of reality as it is independently of us.

I think the most we would conclude about beings who differ from human beings in those numerical or mathematical ways is that they are simply not equipped to find out certain things that are independently true of the world. Those who cannot count could not find out how many chairs there are in a certain room, for example. The same is true of imagined beings who differ from us in other ways. Those without smell would get no views about the smells of things, those without sight would get no views about the colours of things, and those without both sight and touch would perhaps have no conception of the shapes or solidity of things. But why should we not conclude in each case that those possible "investigators" would simply be missing something that is there? Our being able to conceive of such beings does not in itself give us reason to exclude concepts of smell, colour, or shape from an "absolute" conception of how things are, any more than the possibility of innumerate or mathematically impoverished "investigators" gives us reason to exclude mathematical concepts.

I think our conception of what the world is actually like—how we believe the world to be—is what determines in each case whether conceiving of other possible beings is taken to reveal a special human "peculiarity" or only to show that those other beings would be missing something that is independently there. If we had already arrived at a conception of a world that contains no smells or colours, we might take our ability to conceive of investigators who lack smell and sight to reveal the merely human "peculiarity" of smell and colour. But the possibility of such beings could not be what leads us to that odour-free and colour-free "absolute" conception in the first place. If we thought (as we do) that things do have smell and colour, the possibility of (as we would see them) sensorily deprived beings would not lead us to alter those views. It is because we already think of the world as containing a definite number of objects of a certain kind in a particular place, for example, that we regard the possibility of (as we see them) mathematically deprived beings as irrelevant to the legitimacy of mathematical concepts in our conception of the world. Merely conceiving of such possible beings therefore does not enable us to distinguish concepts that are "peculiarly ours", and so do not apply to the world as it is in itself, from those that apply to that world because they are "available to any adequate investigator, of whatever constitution".

There remains a question, then, of what the "anthropocentricity" or human peculiarity to be avoided in any "absolute" conception of the world amounts to and where it is to be found in our ordinary, unphilosophical conception of the world. Is it present in some of our concepts? If so, in which, and how does it manifest itself there?

Our concepts might be said to "reflect" human interests, aims, and tastes in the fairly straightforward sense that without those interests and aims we would have had, or there would have been, no such concepts. But then it is our *possession* of those concepts that "reflects" those interests, aims, and tastes. That we single out such things as trees and mountains and fish in the ways we do is undoubtedly the result of our having certain interests in, and designs on, parts of the world around us. Without those interests, we might never have had concepts of those things at all. But does that reveal a certain "anthropocentricity" or human relativity in the concepts themselves? Surely not. There would have been trees and mountains and fish, just as we now think of them, whether or not human beings existed or had different interests and aims. The concepts we have of such things are true of them independently of human interests and aims. Because our possession of concepts reflects our interests and aims in this way, there are probably a great many things in the world for which we do not have concepts, or at least very determinate concepts, since we lack the relevantly specific interests in those aspects of the world. I hope I will be excused from giving examples.

Our interests and aims are responsible not just for our having some of the concepts we do but even for there being some things in the world for some of those concepts to apply to. Terms like 'knife', 'wheel', and 'sofa', for example, apply only to objects which have a certain function or use for human beings. If we had not wanted to cut or move or sit on things in the ways we do, we probably would never have acquired such concepts. Those objects are all manufactured objects, so their existence equally depends on or reflects certain interests. But that does not make the concept of a knife or a wheel or a sofa in any way suspiciously "anthropocentric". A knife is a sharp object used by human beings for cutting, but the concept 'used by human beings for cutting' does not appear to reflect some human interest or peculiarity. It applies to things in the world only because human beings have certain interests or aims.

There are many concepts that apply to human beings and what they do; the concept 'human being' is one of them. There would be nothing for such concepts to be true of if there were no human beings, but that again does not seem to render those concepts "peculiarly relative" to human beings or their interests or experiences. There are even concepts which apply uniquely to human experiences or to the experiences of conscious beings in general, but that does not make them "anthropocentric" concepts in any sense which need lead us into cosmic illusion. The concepts 'feels pain', 'is thinking of her mother', and 'hopes for rain' would not be true of anything if there were no experiencing, thinking subjects in the world. Pains and thoughts and hopes are in that sense "subjective", but a concept of something subjective is not necessarily a concept which is itself "peculiarly relative to our experience".

If human beings and their thoughts and experiences are to be accorded a place in an independent world at all, the concepts we use to think about them must be acceptable for use in even our most reflective conception of that world. To reach an "absolute" conception that is "to the maximum degree independent of our perspective and its peculiarities", we must eliminate from our thought about the world all "peculiarly human" relativity. But to *say* that human beings have certain experiences, or that they have a unique or peculiar perspective on the world, is presumably not to say something that is itself misleadingly "relative" to or "dependent" on that peculiar perspective. If we are careful in applying the concepts we have, even those that apply to human beings and their interests in and perspective on the world, are they not adequate to describe "absolutely" without distortion both those parts of the world that are dependent on human beings and their experiences and those parts that are not?

Some of the ways human beings think about or express what they believe about the world do depend on or reveal a particular perspective or position from which the thought is held or expressed. Someone who believes and says, "There are three trees here now", for example, says something about what is so at a particular place and time. The expressions 'here' and 'now' pick out the particular place and time that they do only because they are uttered at a particular place and time. Use of those same words on another occasion would say something different about the world. In that sense, what a person who utters the sentence has said to be so depends on the place and time at which the assertion is made or the belief is held. We who are interested in what the person says or believes cannot understand him or know what would make his assertion or belief true unless we know what his words 'here' and 'now' refer to on that occasion. What he says or believes depends in that way on where and when he says or believes it.

We might then try to "correct for" the "special situation" of a person's assertions or beliefs expressed in that form by eliminating indexical or demonstrative terms from our description of his conception of the world. If we know where and when he said, "There are three trees here now", our description of his conception of the world could be "corrected for" its "reflection" of its particular perspective. We might then ascribe to him the belief that there are three trees in New York's Central Park at noon on 1 January 1995. That might still fail to capture what he believes, since he might not know or believe that he is at that place at that time, although he does believe what he says using 'here' and 'now'. We could do better by saying that he believes, of that place and time, that there are three trees there then. A human conception of the world that represents it "in a way to the maximum degree independent of our perspective and its peculiarities" might then be thought of as a generalized version of what we get by making such "corrections" in individual cases. It would be a conception of the world held by human beings, but it would contain no indexical or demonstrative terms, so it would not in that way exhibit or reflect the fact that it is held from a particular position in the world.

Even such an indexical-free conception of the world, if "corrected" in the ways I have suggested, will nevertheless contain names and other singular terms like 'New York' and 'noon EST 1 January 1995'. Such terms do not exhibit or reflect a particular perspective or position in the way indexicals or demonstratives do. They serve to refer to unique particulars, but without carrying on the face of them any indication that the reference is made "from" any particular perspective or position. But for us to *understand* such terms and to pick out the unique objects they refer to, we must at some point make use of some devices of demonstration or ostension to "fix" our conception of the world onto the particular objects we believe to be in it. Anyone who achieves a conception of the world containing singular references to objects must be part of, or connected with, the world her conception is about. But the fact that such a conception is *held* by someone with a particular position in or perspective on the world presumably does not disqualify it from being an "absolute" conception in the relevant sense. It is supposed to be the *way* the world is conceived of that must be purged of human or other "local peculiarities". Everyone must occupy some position or perspective in order to possess a conception of the world at all, but the conception itself (what the person believes) need not reveal or reflect that fact.

How then are we to understand the "anthropocentricity" or "peculiarly human perspective" which the philosophical project seeks to eliminate from our most reflective conception of the world? If it is not explicitly reflected in the terms or concepts in which that conception is expressed, what shows that it is present? The "peculiarities" of one group of believers might lead them to form a conception of the world which other believers who lack those "peculiarities" could not come to understand and share. The two conceptions of the world might differ because of the different characteristics of those who hold them. If the second conception is included in the first but is more restricted, the most plausible conclusion for both groups to draw would be that the more restricted believers are simply missing part of what is there. Their "peculiarities" limit them to only part of what believers with additional "peculiarities" can find out. If the two conceptions are different and do not overlap, it would be equally plausible for each group to conclude that, because of its own "peculiarities", it is finding out about a different part, or different aspects, of the world from the other group.

I suspect that what encourages the worry that a conception that bears no obvious "peculiarity" or "relativity" on its face might nonetheless remain a conception only of the world as it appears and not as it is "absolutely" is the thought that our conception of the world is *our* conception of the world, and that there might be different and possibly conflicting conceptions. But how far can such thoughts take us? Just as we can think that investigators with limited capacities might miss part of what others with greater capacities know about the world, so we can acknowledge the possibility that our own conception of the world does not capture everything. Those with greater capacities might know and understand more. We can even think that perhaps we believe more than is actually true of the world. We can concede that there might be more dreamt of in our conception than there is in heaven and earth, just as there might be more in heaven and earth than is dreamt of in our conception. But these concessions leave us with at most an unfocussed worry about the adequacy of our conception of the world, not a coherent test of "absoluteness" or "nonanthropocentricity".

We can certainly have the coherent thought that part of what we believe about the world might not be true, and that for peculiarly human reasons we easily fall into error or illusion in certain characteristic ways. But the thing to do when that possibility is raised is to re-examine our beliefs and to be especially vigilant in looking for partiality, self-interest, peculiar perspective, limited experience, or the influence of other "human peculiarities" in our reasons for holding them. There is no end to the task of getting the best supported set of beliefs we can; at every point we must admit that error or illusion might still remain undetected. But the search for an "absolute" conception of the world is supposed to begin only after all such epistemic questions have been answered as well as they can be for the moment. It is not simply an epistemic search for what to believe.

The thought that some of our best supported beliefs might "go beyond" what is so independently of us is meant to present us with a different kind of problem or task. The question of the "absoluteness" of our conception concerns the *way* in which we think of the world, not simply the truth or falsity of what we believe. But we still have not identified that nonepistemic question. We have yet to give coherent sense to the idea of the "anthropocentricity" or "human relativity" that is said to be present in some of our *ways* of thinking of the world. It is not a matter of biassed or partial or otherwise inadequate support for our beliefs. It is *how* we think of the world that is said to be stained with our own human "peculiarities", but we have found no general test for exposing the presence of such "relativity" in a conception of the world that shows no evident signs of it.

This is probably about as far as we can get in trying to understand the general form of a metaphysical quest for reality while remaining at this purely abstract and completely general level. It is better now to investigate the project in one particular area, focussing on one specific issue, to see how the misleading "peculiarly human" material is to be identified and eliminated in that case. There is no reason to think that it must work the same way wherever the philosophical idea of reality is applied.

Democritus thought none of our beliefs about anything other than the movements of atoms in a void represents the world as it is independently of us. That is all that is true in the world, and the rest of what we believe holds only "by convention". Galileo thought that the shapes and motions of objects would remain, but the odours, tastes, and colours of objects would be "annihilated" if perceiving animals were removed from the world. Our beliefs about things' possessing such qualities therefore do not represent the world as it is independently of us. These are precursors of the distinction between the "primary" and "secondary" qualities of things, which by now appears to have achieved the status of scientifically enlightened common sense.

That is the issue I want to take up as an instance of the general metaphysical project. The task in this case is not simply to find some distinction or other between two kinds of qualities of objects. The idea is that "secondary" qualities like colours, sounds, and tastes are to be shown to be somehow dependent on perceivers or experiencing subjects in a way that the "primary" qualities of things are not, so our beliefs about the "secondary" qualities of things do not represent the world as it is fully independently of us. They are said to exhibit the kind of "anthropocentricity" or "human relativity" that I have been trying and failing to identify in purely general and schematic terms. By contrast, our beliefs about the "primary" qualities of things are said to be free of that "anthropocentricity".

The term 'secondary quality' has been used in different ways, several of which we will explore in more specific form in what follows. I will not try to define it at the outset. I want to narrow the focus even more. Tastes, odours, sounds, colours, and other qualities have all been classified as secondary qualities of things. I think we must be careful not to assume that these are all to be understood in the same way, or that our beliefs about them are all of the same form. I will not consider everything that has been called a "secondary quality". I take up only the question of the metaphysical status of the colours of things. The task is to describe and try to carry out the philosophical quest for reality in that particular case. I want to assess the prospects of arriving at the conclusion that colour is not part of the world as it is independently of us, or is "subjective" or dependent on us in a way that shape, size, motion, and other "primary" qualities of things are not.

The case of colour has been of great interest. It has served as a model of the metaphysical distinction between "reality" and "appearance", or the "objective" and the "subjective", in general, and has been freely applied to other areas and issues. Today it is through the proper understanding of the metaphysics of colour that we are encouraged to measure the "reality" or "objectivity" of moral and aesthetic values, numbers, minds, causal connections, necessity, and even meaning. If the claim of full "objectivity" stands so ill in the case of colours, it is thought, so much the worse for the rest. I will not enter into a full evaluation of that more general line of thinking. I concentrate only on the colours of things. If we can manage to make some progress in that case, perhaps some more general lessons can be learned.

Bernard Williams holds that there is every reason to think that a conception of the world that is "absolute" in his sense will leave out the colours of things. He concedes that the ordinary language in which we talk and think about colours does not clearly display their dependence on our "peculiarities" as a species, but what is there on the surface of the language, he finds, does not go very deep. He compares colour terms with the term 'amusing', which he thinks is clearly "relative, relating to human tastes and interests":

> Descriptions which embody it, though they may not explicitly mention or include a distinctively human perspective, recognizably and diagnosibly come from that perspective. One can in describing an unobserved scene properly describe it as amusing, but if one's attention were specifically directed to describing it as it was without observers, one would have good reason to leave that concept aside. It is much the same with 'green' or any other secondary quality term: they may not mention their human relativity, but they only too obviously display it to reflection.[18]

I want to see exactly what that reflection is, and how it works. It is meant to remove what Williams calls "such large-scale mistakes as that the world is in itself coloured".[19]

---

18. Williams, *Descartes*, p. 243.
19. Williams, *Descartes*, p. 249.

For J. J. C. Smart, "colour is an anthropocentric concept":

> If our philosophical task is, in part, to see the world *sub specie ae-*
> *ternitatis*, to see the world in such a way as to discount our idiosyn-
> cratic, human, terrestrial perspective, then we must eschew the con-
> cepts of colour and other secondary qualities.[20]

He thinks that "when all is said and done, . . . there is no reason to expect a close correspondence between these classifications and the way
things are in nature".[21] I want to see exactly what has to be "said and
done" to reach that conception of "the way things are in nature".

J. L. Mackie in *Problems from Locke* holds simply that "no colour as
we see colour . . . is literally in or on the things we call coloured".[22]
We must admit that things look to be coloured, and perhaps for that
reason we cannot help believing that they are. But that is only how the
world "appears" to us, not how it is. When we ascribe colours to things,
Mackie says, "this is all a mistake, a systematic error. All that is out
there in reality is the shape, size, position, number, motion-or-rest, and
solidity" of physical bodies.[23] What is "out there in reality" contains
no colours.

Colin McGinn in *The Subjective View* finds no error or mistake in
our beliefs about the colours of things. He thinks those beliefs can be
accounted for in a way that preserves the truth of many of them. But
the status of colour is questionable, since in reflecting on what the world
is really like he thinks "we inevitably arrive at the idea that objects in
themselves have only primary qualities".[24] Primary qualities, he holds,
are the only qualities that "correspond to how things are in themselves",
and for McGinn colour is not a "primary quality". I am interested in
the reflections that he thinks inevitably lead to that conclusion.

These and many other philosophers share a line of thinking that is
meant to lead in one way or another to a conception of a colourless
world or to a world in which the colours of things depend on how they
are perceived. As things are fully independent of us in such a world,
objects are not coloured. The view is not that everything is a uniform
shade of grey, or even clear and transparent, like a colourless crystal
bowl. The colourlessness in question is metaphysical. I want to try to
understand that conclusion, and how it is supposed to be reached. It is

---

20. Smart, *Philosophy and Scientific Realism*, p. 84.
21. Smart, *Philosophy and Scientific Realism*, p. 86.
22. J. L. Mackie, *Problems from Locke*, Oxford, 1976, p. 14.
23. Mackie, *Problems from Locke*, p. 11.
24. C. McGinn, *The Subjective View*, Oxford, 1983, p. 115.

a view according to which colours are, in Gilbert Ryle's phrase, a beholder's "rejected gift to the world"[25]—"gift" because they are given by us to a world that does not contain them, "rejected" because there is simply no place for colours in the world as it is "absolutely", independently of us.

---

25. G. Ryle, *Dilemmas*, Cambridge, 1956, p. 82. Ryle does not hold the view he expresses with that phrase.

3

The Idea of Physical Reality

When we ask whether colour really belongs to the world as it is independently of us, or is really only something "subjective" and dependent upon perceivers, we need a conception of "the world" or "reality" in order to ask the question. It cannot be simply an indeterminate conception of the world or reality as whatever is so. Only with a determinate, filled-in conception can we ask how what we think and experience with respect to colour is related to the way things are thought to be in the rest of that conception. Any determinate conception we could arrive at for that purpose would have to be derived from the huge conglomerate of things we believe before the philosophical reflection begins. The conception that is needed for the philosophical question must somehow be carved out of everything we start off unreflectively taking to be true.

I began to explore the idea that the conception we need must be "absolute" in the sense of bearing no signs of whose conception it is or of any special peculiarities of those who employ it. The question is whether our beliefs about the colours of things have a place in such a conception or not. But we found difficulty in arriving at any general criterion of "absoluteness" that could be applied to a conception of the world to eliminate those features that are peculiarly due to us and so not indicative of reality. I therefore propose to abandon the attempt to proceed from the top down in that way and to work rather from the bottom up. I want to start with a minimal conception of the world that seems about as "absolute" as any human conception could be, and see what must be added to it to eventually arrive at as full and adequate a conception as we need. The question will then be whether the colours of things must be part of that world as eventually conceived and, if they are, whether they must be thought of as dependent on perceivers or perceptions in some way.

Let us begin by trying to form a purely physical conception of the world. I think there is little doubt that, in the past, that is the idea from which the unreality or the "subjectivity" of colour has derived its greatest support. The thought is that the world as it is independently of us is fundamentally a physical world, a world of purely physical goings-on. That was the basic idea of Democritus. He started with a conception of a world of nothing but atoms moving in a void, and everything else we believe in was therefore said to have only a human or "conventional" source. Galileo shared that same general idea of the physical world, but what added enormously to its richness and power in the sixteenth and seventeenth centuries was the new idea of a mathematical science which ideally would explain why everything happens in the physical world as it does. That is what posed the question of the metaphysical status of colour in its most challenging form. How could colour (or anything else that is not included in that austere physical conception) be fitted into a world that in itself is purely physical? Whatever is not capturable in that basic science must be at best dependent on perceiving animals and would be nothing at all if they were taken away. Colour then seemed inevitably to find a place in the world only as something "subjective", as dependent in some way on perceivers and their experiences.

Descartes endorsed and advanced the idea of a purely physical science but without believing that the world is exclusively physical. The world for him contained not one but two distinct kinds of thing. One of them was body, whose essence was extension, or taking up space. Every property a body could have therefore had to be a "mode" of extension—a way of being extended in space. And colour was said to be no such "mode" of physical things. It was not referred to by any of the terms needed for a clear and distinct conception of body. It could be understood only as something dependent on happenings in the other world of purely mental things, whose sole essence it is to think. Colour could be put together with a purely physical world only in the way (whatever that might be) in which the mental world and the physical world could be put together.

J. L. Mackie in our own day regards our ascription of colours to things as "a mistake, a systematic error". That is because he thinks that when we make such ascriptions, "all that is out there in reality" are certain material bodies which in themselves have only such qualities as shape, size, position, number, motion-or-rest, and solidity. Colour is excluded from objective reality because the world is exclusively physical, and colour has no place in that purely physical world.

When J. J. C. Smart says that colours are not part of the world as it is in itself, he means that they "are not part of the world as described in the physical sciences".[1] "The scientific description of the world", he says, "makes no use of words for colour".[2] What it is in an object that gives rise to a perception of colour is "the state of its minute parts", and he means the physical state of those parts. "The physicist does not need the word 'red': he can do what he wants simply by talking about wavelengths of light".[3] And the world as described by the physicist (if what he says is true) is the world as it is in itself, non-"anthropocentrically" described.

Bernard Williams above all stresses the essential connection between the idea of "the material world as it is understood by natural science" and the idea of the world "as it really is".[4] The scientific conception is arrived at by "correcting for" the peculiarities of various observers, so it ideally bears no signs of whose conception it is. That is, in part, why the scientific conception above all others can be taken to represent the world as it really is independently of all observers; it is not just how the world appears to us. Williams thinks colours will be left out of any "absolute" conception of an independent world because the natural science of the material world is "a conception in which colour does not figure at all as a quality of the things" in that world.[5]

Common to all these views of the world as it is independently of us is the idea that, in Mackie's phrase, "all that is out there in reality" are certain physical things interacting in accordance with certain physical laws. That is, in Smart's phrase, "the way things are in nature". For Williams, it is the way the world "really" or "fundamentally" is.

Physical science tries to discover the laws of the world and so explain everything that happens. It is a mathematical science of the quantifiable dimensions of bodies, motions, and forces. It speaks of light and its transmission from one region to another, for example, but not of the colours of any things in those regions. That is not to say that physical science cannot express differences among things which we think differ

1. J. J. C. Smart, *Philosophy and Scientific Realism*, London, 1963, p. 65.

2. Smart, *Philosophy and Scientific Realism*, p. 65.

3. Smart, *Philosophy and Scientific Realism*, p. 65.

4. Williams, *Descartes. The Project of Pure Enquiry*, Harmondsworth, 1978, p. 241.

5. Williams, *Descartes*, p. 242.

in colour. A ripe tomato and a ripe lemon are different. But the descriptions physical science gives of those differently coloured things are in terms of measurable physical magnitudes. The differences are physically described. And if "all that is out there in reality" or "in nature" are the physical things with their physical properties, those are the only differences there can be in reality between the tomato and the lemon. We humans naturally speak and think of the one as red and the other as yellow, but the features which physical science describes in those objects are something else, not colours. They are said to be the "real" differences between those objects—the only differences there are that are fully independent of all perceivers and their responses.

There is no question that the metaphysical idea of the unreality or "subjectivity" of colour is given great impetus by this compelling picture of a physical world. But impetus is not the same thing as justified support. The basic idea is that the physical world contains no colour. But that idea is more complex than it looks. It contains two distinct thoughts: that the world as it is independently of us is the physical world, and that the physical world contains no colour. What do these two claims really amount to? Even if each can be understood in a way that shows it is true, can they be put together to yield the conclusion that the world as it is independently of us contains no colour? The question is complicated.

Let us start with what is meant by 'the physical world'. I have said that the metaphysical reflection needs a determinate, filled-in conception of the world against which to measure the reality of this or that problematic feature. What is being said about a world described in such a conception when it is said to be a physical world?

For Descartes, the physical world was the world of all the physical things: bodies. There was another world of minds or thinking things. The whole world was exhausted by both. That is dualism of "substances"; there are two different kinds of things in the world. There is accordingly a species of materialism or physicalism that denies half of that dualistic picture. It is monism of "substances"; there is only one kind of thing in the world: every object is a body. What Descartes meant by 'body' was any object which occupies space (and perhaps also excludes other physical objects from that space—but this idea of solidity or impenetrability caused difficulties for Descartes). The corresponding materialism would say that the only objects there are in the world are objects which occupy space (and perhaps are impenetrable).

I will not pause to assess the plausibility of this thesis. As it stands, it seems to imply not only that there are no such things as minds or spirits, as it was no doubt meant to, but also that there are no such things as numbers or classes, or particular places or times, or hopes, fears, wishes, experiences, or any other things which do not themselves have spatial dimensions (and perhaps solidity). No such things are bodies, but we appear to think and speak about them all the time. To deny that what we think or say really does imply the existence of such things would require some way of telling what kinds of things are said to exist by a certain thought or stretch of discourse, and what are not. In addition to such a criterion of "ontological commitment", we would need a convincing demonstration that objects that occupy space are the only objects said or implied to exist by everything we hold to be true.

We can leave the details of any such ontological program aside. Ontology alone—what objects there are in the world—can never settle completely the question of what the world is like, or what is true of those objects. Given the very same objects, the world they existed in could be quite different, depending on what those objects were like, how they were related to one another, and how they interacted. The idea that every object is a physical object that occupies space puts few constraints on what a world containing only physical objects would be like. Tomatoes and lemons, for example, are physical objects that occupy space. But tomatoes are red and lemons are yellow, so the ontological view that says there are only physical objects would not in itself exclude colour from the world. For all it says or implies, some of the physical objects which exist could be red, and others yellow. That same ontology would not be enough to show that nothing in the world is beautiful either, or that nothing is virtuous, or that nothing is of value. Paintings are physical objects, and some of them are beautiful; and human beings are physical objects, and some of them are virtuous. Many other physical objects are of great value in a number of other ways. The world's containing only physical objects does not alone exclude such facts from being part of an independent reality.

Obviously, what is wanted is a physical world understood not just as a collection of physical objects but as a world in which those physical objects have only physical properties, stand only in physical relations to one another, and interact in only physical ways. Colour, beauty, virtue, and other forms of value could then be excluded from such a world on the grounds that they are not purely *physical* features of things. That is what creates the metaphysical problem: if the world is exclusively physical, how can colour or beauty or any other nonphysical feature be fitted into the world as it is independently of us?

What, then, is a *physical* property or relation? It will not do to say that it is any property or relation that belongs to or holds between physical objects. That would leave colour, beauty, virtue, market value, and

so on as physical properties after all. But we cannot say that a physical property is a property that is physical in the sense in which an object can be said to be physical. For Descartes, an object is a physical
object if and only if it occupies space (and perhaps is impenetrable).
But we cannot say that a property is a physical property if and only if
it occupies space (and perhaps is impenetrable), since properties and
relations do not occupy space. They have no spatial dimensions or location. They are instantiated at various points or regions in space, perhaps, but they do not literally occupy those regions, as physical objects
do. The property of being three feet long does not itself have a length,
and the relation that holds between two things when one of them is
three feet away from the other does not occupy the space between them.
If it did, it would be three feet long. Properties and relations must count
as "physical" in some way other than sharing with objects that are physical the property of occupying space.

Physical properties and relations are presumably what figure in
purely physical accounts of what goes on. They are the terms in which
purely physical descriptions and laws and explanations are given. But
again, what is a purely physical description or law or explanation? What
is needed is some notion of a physical state of affairs or a physical fact
or a physical truth. With a notion of "physical fact", the physical world
could be thought of, not as a collection of all the physical objects, but
as the totality of physical facts. Physical properties and relations could
then be thought of as those properties and relations which occur essentially in the physical facts. That a particular lemon is yellow, or that
a particular painting is beautiful, might then be held not to be physical
facts, even if it is granted that the objects in question are physical in
the sense of occupying space. The properties ascribed to an object in
thoughts about its colour or beauty or value could then be said not to
be physical properties. Even if it were true that an object is yellow, or
beautiful, it would not be a physical fact that it has those properties.
The metaphysical problem would then be how, if at all, there could be
such nonphysical facts, and how they are related to the facts acknowledged by physicalism. How could nonphysical properties like colour
and beauty and value belong to physical objects?

It certainly seems that we need some notion of physical fact even to
state the thesis of physicalism, or the idea of an exclusively physical
world. We have seen that to have any conception of a world we need
to be able to think about what is true of whatever objects there are. For
that, we need more than a set of objects. We need the quite different
notion of a fact, or of something's being so. But what is a physical fact?

As with properties and relations, there is no hope of identifying a physical fact as a fact that occupies space (and perhaps is impenetrable). Facts have no dimensions or location. They are not to be thought of as objects in the world alongside other objects like billiard balls, lemons, and paintings.

To think that something is so or that the world is a certain way, we must be able to think complete thoughts that can be true or false. To put it linguistically, we must be able not only to refer to objects with our words but also to understand and assert whole sentences; and sentences as so used are what are true or false. For our purposes here, it is perhaps enough to take a state of affairs as nothing more than what is said to be so by a sentence that is true or false. A fact would accordingly be what is said to be so by a sentence that is true. This is not meant as a definition of 'fact' or 'state of affairs', nor does it provide a principle of individuation of one fact from another. There are well-known difficulties in supplying such definitions or criteria, but I think we can put them to one side. We are only seeking some way of expressing the idea of a physical world which is more than the idea of a collection of physical objects.

Thinking of the world as made up of facts, or whatever is said to be so by sentences that are true, the claim that the world as it is independently of us is a physical world would be the claim that physical facts hold independently of us. If we had some way to pick out physical facts, and if all those facts together exhausted the way the world is independently of us, the world would be an exclusively physical world. And if objects' being coloured was not among the physical facts, colour would not be part of the world as it is independently of us.

Can we start from some such conception of a physical world and show in this way that objects are not really coloured? To do so, at least two questions must be answered first. Which facts are the physical facts? And what are we saying about those facts when we say that they are physical? An answer is needed to the second question to give some determinate content to the thesis that the world is a physical, or an exclusively physical, world. But first we need some way of picking out the facts we have in mind.

Thinking of facts as what is said to be so by sentences that are true, one way to identify facts as of one type rather than another would be in terms of the vocabulary in which they are expressed. On that criterion, physical facts would be facts stated only in physical vocabulary, or with physical concepts. Physical properties and relations would be those denoted by the predicates and relational expressions of the physical vocabulary. This raises the same two questions about a physical vocabulary. How do we pick it out? And what are we saying of it when we say it is a physical vocabulary?

We could answer the first question by picking out the vocabulary in question purely ostensively. Simply draw a line around all the terms or concepts employed in present-day physics, say, or in the physical sciences more generally, and focus on what is said to be so in those terms alone. This seems to be what Smart, for example, has in mind by "the physical world". He says that colour and other secondary qualities "are not part of the world as described in the physical sciences".[6] And for Williams, the world in which colour finds no place is "the material world as it is understood by natural science".[7] The statements of physical science, or of the natural science of the material world, as these philosophers speak of them, would give us something we could call a description of the physical world.

This would give us a way of answering the first of the two questions asked about physicalism. If we pick out by ostension the vocabulary we have in mind—the vocabulary of current physical science—this will determine a set of sentences. All the sentences of that kind that are taken to be true will express a conception of how things are, or of what the world is like. If we assert one or more of those sentences, or if we believe that all of them are true, we will be saying or thinking that the world is a certain way—just the way those sentences say it is. We will believe that the world is this way, that way, and the other way, and those different ways will all be expressed in sentences containing only the concepts we have specified. But we will not so far have said that the world we believe in is a *physical* world; we will not have applied a determinate concept of "physical" to all or any of those facts. We will have said things in a certain vocabulary about the world, but we will not have said anything about that vocabulary. We will not have said in particular that it is a physical vocabulary, so we will not be in a position to say that the world is physical, or a world of physical facts, let alone that it is purely physical, or only physical facts. For that additional claim, we need some determinate idea of the "physical".

We can, of course, say that what is true of the vocabulary we have picked out is that it is the vocabulary of the current physical sciences. That simply pushes the problem back one step. What is being said of a

---

6. Smart, *Philosophy and Scientific Realism*, p. 65.

7. Williams, *Descartes*, p. 241.

science when it is said to be a physical science? Do we have a fixed idea of what any physical science has to be like, or what it has to be about, or what its vocabulary has to be, in order to count as physical?

In the seventeenth century, the essence of the physical was thought to be known; it was said to be extension, or extension and mobility, or extension and mobility and impenetrability. Any science which met that conception of the physical would therefore have to be expressed in terms of the modes of extension and motion, whatever changes of detail it might undergo in trying to comprehend that fixed subject matter. But do we today have any such confidence about the essence of the physical? Do we know that any future physics, whatever it is like, will have to deal in extended, moving bodies? Presumably not; that is already a thing of the past. Do we have any fixed conception of what any future physical science will have to be about, or what it will have to be like, to count as a physical science? If not, there is a real question whether anything determinate is being said when it is said that the world is a physical world, or that the world as it is independently of us is exhausted by all the physical facts. If physicalism is not simply the view that the world contains only physical objects, but rather says that the world is exhausted by all the physical facts, what does that view say about the world? That is the second question about physicalism. It is a question that those who call themselves physicalists have never really answered.

There are sciences of our own day that we call physical sciences, but we cannot simply point to them and say that that exhausts our idea of what it is to be a physical science. Physical science changes. Physicists do not just change their minds as they learn more and more about the world; the very conception of what is to be included in physics changes. We have a different conception today from what they had in the seventeenth century; new kinds of phenomena are acknowledged and explained within physical science. When we think of our descendants in the future with a different conception of physical science from our own, just as ours is different from that of the seventeenth century, we do not think that they will simply attach the *words* 'physics' or 'physical science' to some enterprise of their own day. We can think of what they will be doing as physics, or physical science, even though it is different from what we do today under that name. Since physics can change its scope and its vocabulary and still remain physics, the idea of what is "physical" cannot be simply the idea of whatever is included in physical science as we currently think of its limits. The idea of the physical must be to some extent independent of the specific content of the sciences we give that name to at any particular time.

In fact, I think that, looking both backwards and forwards in time, we can think of something different from what we have today as nonetheless physical science because of what we can see to be the historical continuity of a single enterprise. What we now regard as physical sciences are so regarded because they are intelligible developments out of what was regarded as physical science in the past. And conceptions of future physical science can be acknowledged as such by us now if we think they will bear correspondingly continuous connections with the physical science of today. But that does not require or yield a single and fixed idea of the "physical", or a conception of the only proper subject matter or vocabulary of any possible physical science. It does not give us a determinate property or set of properties that is ascribed to the world in any thought to the effect that the world independent of us is a physical world.

But let us leave aside the question of what we are saying of a science or a vocabulary when we say it is physical and return to the task of singling out something we can think of as a physical world. Let us think only of everything that is taken to be true today in physics, or the physical sciences more generally. We can agree by ostension on what terms are included in those sciences as they are now, even though they might change in the future, just as they were different in the past. Let us try to do no better than to form a view of the world out of what is known, or thought to be known, in those sciences at the moment. We must start where we are.

Suppose we have picked out the vocabulary of the physical sciences, and so out of all the things we believe we could formulate a certain set of sentences that express all the things we regard as truths of the physical sciences. Let us grant that those truths are maximally "absolute" in the sense of showing no signs of who believes them or from what point of view they have been arrived at. Can we think that all the facts expressed in those sentences together exhaust the way we think the world is independently of us?

Whether we can depends in part on which terms we have picked out as exhausting the physical vocabulary. It seems too restrictive to limit ourselves to physics alone. If being expressed in the language of physics were a condition of a statement's being part of a description of the independent world, it would not be part of the independent world that there are such things as mountains on earth or fish in the sea. 'Mountain', 'earth', 'fish', and 'sea' are not terms of physics. On that criterion, it would not even be part of the physical world that there is a planet earth or that it is 93 million miles from the sun. 'Planet' and 'sun' are not terms of physics either. Obviously, we must think of the admissi-

ble vocabulary as extending beyond physics proper to include the physical sciences understood in some more general way. Perhaps 'planet',
'sun', and 'mountain' (and 'fish'?) could be accepted as falling within
the range of physical terms.

But even with the range of admissible general terms decided on, if
only by ostension, there is the question of what kinds of statements
those general terms can be used to make. If we can assert only general
statements of physical theory, we will have laws or generalizations
about what happens, or would happen, under certain kinds of circumstances, but no way of stating that something instantiates those laws,
or that the circumstances mentioned in them are, in fact, fulfilled. We
believe that there are physical bodies of such-and-such kinds, that the
forces mentioned in physical laws actually operate on things that exist
in the world, that physical events of certain kinds occur and are followed by events of other kinds, and so on. Laws or universally quanti-
fied conditional truths alone provide no means of asserting such things.
To get closer to expressing what we believe about the world as it is independently of us, we would have to expand our conception to include
not only what is said to be so by all the general laws of the physical
sciences, but also everything else that is true and is expressed in the
vocabulary of the physical sciences.

There remains the question of particular facts, objects, and events.
We believe that particular physical things exist and particular physical
events happen at particular places and times. We need proper names
or other singular terms to refer to such things. If the physical sciences,
even broadly construed with respect to vocabulary, contain only general truths, and if it is a condition of something's being part of the independent physical world that it be said to be so in the vocabulary of
the physical sciences alone, then it would not be part of the independent physical world that there is (or is not) a mountain at 40°N and
80°W on the earth on 1 January 2000 A.D. It would not even be part of
the physical world that the earth is 93 million miles from the sun. 'The
earth', '1 January 2000 A.D.', and 'the sun' are singular terms which
refer to unique particulars. They do not appear in any set of sentences
containing only general terms.

We believe that the earth is 93 million miles from the sun. That is
not something that can be expressed without reliance on singular or
demonstrative or indexical terms. There might be a truth in the physical sciences, broadly construed, to the effect that there is a planet of
such-and-such shape, size, and composition 93 million miles away from
a star of such-and-such different shape, size, and composition. But that
is a completely general truth. It states something to be true somewhere

in the universe. It is not equivalent to what we believe when we believe that the earth is 93 million miles from the sun. However richly the kinds of planet and star are specified in general terms, it is still possible for that general statement to be true while what we believe when we believe that the earth is 93 million miles from the sun is false. There could be a planet and star of the appropriate kinds related in just that way somewhere else, even if the earth did not exist at all or was not 93 million miles from the sun.

There is perhaps some temptation to think that physical facts themselves *are* in a sense all completely general in that way, even though some of our human thoughts about them are particular because they contain or rely on demonstrative or indexical connections with those facts. We human beings perforce express or think about physical facts in singular or demonstrative or indexical terms, but the physical facts themselves might be thought to be what they are independently of us and of the ways we typically express them. This would perhaps mean that there is a single physical fact or state of affairs expressed in our thought that the earth is 93 million miles from the sun, and also expressed in the physical sciences without using any singular terms. If we tried to state that fact, we might say that what is true in the physical world is that that thing we call "the earth" is 93 million miles from that thing we call "the sun", even though the purified general statements of the physical sciences do not express that fact in the idiosyncratic way we do. The idea would be that the physical fact is what it is quite independently of how it happens to get expressed by us, given our special position in the universe.

This line of thinking would amount to abandoning the idea of identifying physical facts as whatever is said to be so by true sentences in the vocabulary of the physical sciences. It appears to rely on a notion of a fact as something that can be picked out independently of the way in which it is expressed. If the sentence 'The earth is 93 million miles from the sun' is only a peculiarly human (or even an English-speaking human), way of stating a certain purely physical fact, what purely physical fact would that be? I tried to express it by saying, "That thing we happen to call 'the earth' is 93 million miles from that thing we happen to call 'the sun'". But that sentence is not a sentence of the physical sciences, even broadly construed. The physical sciences say nothing about what people call things. We might try to express the fact in question by saying simply, "*This* [pointing to the earth] is 93 million miles from *that* [pointing to the sun]". But that contains a demonstrative and so is presumably not a statement exclusively in the vocabulary of the physical sciences either.

If we insist that it is a physical fact that that thing we call "the earth" is 93 million miles from that thing we call "the sun", we must have in mind some conception of physical fact other than what I have been trying out so far. Perhaps we think there must be some such physical fact because the earth and the sun are physical objects, and the relation of being 93 million miles apart is a purely physical relation. That relation could be said to be physical in the sense of being denoted by a relational expression in the agreed-upon vocabulary of the physical sciences. But that does not solve the problem. Although there is a true sentence in the physical sciences which says that there is a planet of such-and-such kind and a star of such-and-such kind, and they are 93 million miles apart, there presumably is nothing in the physical sciences which says that *this* and *that* are the objects in question, or that *this* is the earth and *that* is the sun.

If we think that the general fact that there is at least one planet of a certain kind and one star of a certain kind which are 93 million miles apart is the same fact that we state when we say that the earth is 93 million miles from the sun, we must explain in some new way the notion of fact that is involved in that thought. It appears to allow for there being a single fact which two quite different sentences both manage to state, although the sentences are not equivalent. The general statement of the physical sciences, purged of all singular terms, could be true while 'The earth is 93 million miles from the sun' is false, or even if the earth and the sun did not exist.

This is a very obscure notion of a fact. It concedes that the statement expressed in the general terms of the physical sciences and the everyday statement stained with the human point of view by the presence of demonstrative or singular terms do not mean the same or say the same thing. But it holds that there is only one fact that "makes" both those sentences true or only one fact "in virtue of which" they are both true; that fact is a purely physical fact. Part of the obscurity lies in this idea of something's "making" a sentence true. It cannot be understood in the innocuous sense in which what "makes" a sentence true is that what it says to be so is so. In that sense, what "makes" the sentence 'The earth is 93 million miles from the sun' true is that the earth is 93 million miles from the sun. That innocuous notion of fact is all I have been relying on so far in an effort to identify the purely physical facts. A fact is simply what is said to be so by a sentence that is true.

Even in that sense, there is perhaps a way for one sentence to be said to be "made true" by the same fact that "makes" another nonequivalent sentence true. That will be so if the second sentence implies the first, but not vice versa. The first is "made" true by the second because it must be true if the second is. But 'There is a planet of a certain kind which is 93 million miles from a star of a certain kind' does not imply 'The earth is 93 million miles from the sun', so the general statement of physical science does not "make" our everyday judgement true in that sense. In fact, there is an implication in the other direction. If we insist on speaking of "making true" in this case, it will be the general scientific statement that is "made true" by what is said by the humanly stained sentence with singular terms.

There is another familiar sense in which one thing's being the case can be said to "make it true" that something else is the case, and so to "make" a certain sentence true. What can make it true that a certain billiard ball rolls into a certain pocket is that the ball is in a certain position on the table and is hit at a certain angle by another ball. The one event causes the other and so makes 'That ball is in that pocket' true. But there being a planet 93 million miles from a star somewhere in the universe is not what causes or brings it about that the earth is 93 million miles from the sun. The past course of events in the solar system is what brought that about.

I think this idea of a single fact "making" many different nonequivalent sentences true, or of being that "in virtue of which" they are true, is just another expression of the philosophical conception of "reality" or "the world" that we are trying to identify and understand and eventually reach. The philosophical project seeks an account of what there is "in reality" or in "the world as it is independently of us" that "makes" our beliefs true, something "in virtue of which" they are true, if they are. All these notions must be understood in a certain special way to express the goal of the philosophical project. To say only that 'The earth is 93 million miles from the sun' is true in virtue of the fact that the earth is 93 million miles from the sun, or that 'Lemons are yellow' is made true by the fact that lemons are yellow, would be felt to be metaphysically unsatisfying. The appeal to physical facts alone is an attempt to give a more satisfying answer. It is felt that the only thing there could be "in reality" to make our sentences or thoughts true is some purely physical fact or state of affairs. That is the assumption that physical reality or the physical world is the only independent world there is.

I have been asking first what that means. But once we understand it, the question is where that exclusionary assumption comes from, or whether there is any reason to believe it. Can we arrive at it, or support it, simply by starting from everything we believe and picking out a class of purely physical truths? That is the very enterprise we are now trying to describe and carry out.

There is one fairly clear way in which a single fact could make true both a general sentence of the physical sciences and a more familiar sentence of the kind we utter every day. That would be so if the two sentences were logically equivalent or had the same meaning. This was an idea briefly defended by Carnap and other physicalists in the 1930s.[8] It faced the problem I have raised about the scope of the physical vocabulary—which terms are to be included, and why. Those calling themselves physicalists at that time did not pin their hopes on the vocabulary of physics, or even of the physical sciences more generally. For their purposes, the physical was anything intersubjectively observable, public, in space, or in discoverable interactions with things in the observable, measurable world. Positivistic physicalists were mostly concerned to demystify the so-called inner or private psychological realm, so their physicalism concentrated on reducing mental or psychological phenomena to observable behaviour.[9]

That notion of the physical is too broad to be used here in raising metaphysical questions about the status of those parts of our conception of the world that allegedly bear signs of their idiosyncratically human source. Colour in particular was often cited as a publicly observable property of physical things, and thus to be contrasted with the "inner" or allegedly inaccessible. But even with that much broader notion of a physical vocabulary, the project failed. Purely physical truths equivalent in meaning or even just logically equivalent to each of the nonphysically expressed things we believe were simply not to be found. Physicalists therefore came to set their sights on something less than full translation or semantic reduction. We still await a clear statement of exactly what a newer and nonreductionist form of physicalism amounts to.

Despite its failure, the translational reductionist program had its merits. It did not need to rely on a conception of "fact" or "reality" or "the

8. See, e.g., R. Carnap, *The Unity of Science*, London, 1934; R. Carnap, "Psychology in Physical Language", and O. Neurath, "Sociology and Physicalism", both in A. J. Ayer (ed.), *Logical Positivism*, Glencoe, Ill., 1959.

9. In 1936, Carnap reports his having abandoned the thesis that "every statement can be translated into (every state of affairs can be expressed in)" the "physical language" in favour of "reduction" of one to the other in "reduction-sentences", and not by means of "definability of the terms and hence translatability of the sentences". "What we really had in mind as [the basis of the language of science] was rather the thing-language, or, even more narrowly, the observable predicates of the thing-language". The "thing-language" is identified as "that language which we use in everyday life in speaking about the perceptible things surrounding us" (R. Carnap, "Testability and Meaning", *Philosophy of Science*, vol. 3, 1936, p. 466).

world" that is obscure in the way we have just encountered. Given a satisfactory criterion of what it is to be a physical term, it would have yielded a perfectly coherent expression of the idea that the physical world is the only world there is, that it exhausts the way the world is independently of us. A conception of reality or the world would simply be a conception of everything that is so.

If the reductionist program had worked, everything that is true would have been expressible in purely physical terms. To say that the world as it is independently of us is an exclusively physical world would then have meant that everything that is true is translatable without remainder into purely physical truths. But since the program did not work, some other way must be found to give sense to the physicalist doctrine that the independent world is exclusively physical. With no straightforward reduction of all the apparently nonphysical things we believe to physical truths alone, the metaphysical problem is to explain how those apparently nonphysical facts are to be fitted in or accommodated to what is so in an exclusively physical world.

If the translational physicalist program had worked, it would not have left us with that metaphysical problem. There would then have been no metaphysical distinction, among all the things we believe, between those which represent the world as it is independently of us and those which do not. There would have been nothing left that had to be understood as at best in some way "subjective" or dependent upon us. If we started off with everything we believe and found a way of re-expressing all of it in terms of only part of itself—the physical part—there would be nothing left over to be seen as not representing the world as it is independently of us. All the nonphysical sentences we accept would be translated into sentences in purely physical terms, so all our beliefs about colours and minds and feelings and everything else we believe in would be truths about the independent world after all. They would be physical truths about that world.

That would leave no room for a denial of colour, or for "subjectivism" about the colours of things or about anything else. If expressibility in physical terms is a mark of "reality", or of being part of "the world as it is independently of us", and if every sentence about the colours of things could be expressed in equivalent physical terms, then colour could not be shown to be unreal or "subjective" and only dependent on us. There would be such a thing as colour in the independent world after all.

That is true of any semantic reduction. If statements of a certain kind mean the same as, or are strictly equivalent to, statements of another kind, it cannot be said that only statements of the second kind say how things really are. Being equivalent, both sorts of statements say the same thing, and so would be equally respectable, or equally expressive of reality. If all the nonphysical sentences we accept are equivalent to statements in purely physical terms, there is no distinction within everything we believe between a core that represents an independent world and all the rest that in one way or another does not.

This shows that to pursue a metaphysical project of the kind we are considering, we cannot hold that a statement in purely physical terms and a more familiar everyday statement allegedly stained with the human point of view mean the same, or say the very same thing. But physicalism does need the idea that the physical truths, or the world made up of all the physical facts, is all that could ever "make true" any other humanly stained sentences that seem to say something more than or different from the physical truth. A restricted physical core would be all there is in "reality" "in virtue of which" those other sentences would be true. Some such conception of "fact" or of "the world" appears to be needed to give the proper metaphysical sense to the question whether, or how, colour can be part of the world as it is independently of us.

What sense can we make of such a conception, and how are we to arrive at the conclusion that it is a conception of the *only* "world" there is? Let us suppose we have overcome the difficulty of what is to be included in the physical vocabulary, and of how we are to refer to particular things and express singular facts. Let us imagine that we have picked out all the physical statements, that we have identified a certain subclass of them which are all consistent and which we regard as true. We think of the physical world as everything that is said to be so by truths expressed exclusively in those terms. Let us concede, too, what Smart and Mackie and Williams and others would insist on, that nowhere in that purely physical vocabulary are there any colour words. Colour is not a property or force or phenomenon to be reckoned with in the physical sciences. We can now ask whether and how, if we have granted all this, we can reach the conclusion that the world as it is independently of us contains no colour. Have we even reached a conception of "the world" which presents a problem about the place or status of the colours of things?

If the physical world is understood as we are now understanding it—as everything that is said to be so by all the physical truths—we cannot move directly from the acknowledged fact that there is no colour in the physical world in that sense to the conclusion that there is no colour in the world as it is independently of us. Even on the assumption that the world as it is independently of us is a physical world, we cannot draw that conclusion. That is because the physical world as now understood is identified by means of the facts that constitute it, and those facts, in turn, are identified in terms of the vocabulary in which they are expressed. That is the way Smart identifies the world he says lacks all colour; it is "the world as described in the physical sciences". Williams says it is "the material world as it may be scientifically understood". But that is to speak of the world *as described in a certain way*. And to say that something (e.g., colour) is not part of the world as described in a certain way is to say that certain kinds of descriptions, or certain kinds of statements (e.g., statements about the colours of things), are not part of that way of describing the world. That does not imply that that feature is not part of the world at all. It does not imply that sentences describing the colours of things, for instance, are not true. It does not even imply that they are not true of the very same world that the more austere, purely physical statements are also true of.

For example, think of what we might call "the economic world", understood in that same way, or of "the psychological world". Those "worlds" will presumably be picked out by all the sentences in purely economic vocabulary, or purely psychological vocabulary, which we take to be true. There might be great uncertainty about just which expressions are to be included in those vocabularies and which not, but suppose we settle that question to our satisfaction. We then express a number of truths in purely economic, or purely psychological, terms. We might describe all the economic transactions that went on between individuals in the United States in the last week, for example. If they are described in exclusively economic or quantitative terms—cost, profit, and the like—we will find that nowhere among those economic statements are there any words for the height or the weight of the economic agents whose behaviour those sentences describe. Similarly, in all the purely psychological sentences we accept, there will be no mention of the atoms and electrons which the thinking, feeling subjects described in those sentences are made up of. If we say that an economic agent's height and weight are not part of the economic world, or that atoms and electrons are not part of the psychological world, we could not conclude that therefore the beings described in economics or psychology do not have any height or weight, or are not made up of atoms and electrons at all. The most we could say is that economic and psychological descriptions do not mention the height or weight or submicroscopic physical components of the beings they describe, not that those beings do not have such characteristics. Those characteristics do not get mentioned in those sciences, but their presence in the world is not threatened by that fact.

Could we not say the same of colour? We do believe that many sentences ascribing colours to things are true. When we notice that nowhere in purely physical descriptions of the world is there any mention of colour, why should we feel inclined to conclude that the things the physical sciences describe do not have any colour? Why should we draw more than the unremarkable conclusion that the physical sciences simply do not mention the colours of the things they describe? Colour is not alone in this respect. There are a great many other interesting features of the world that the physical sciences do not mention.

I think it is easy to feel that there is something special in an appeal to the physical world in particular. It is tempting to think that the world we live in is somehow a purely physical world in a way that it is not a purely economic or psychological world. Talk about "the economic world" or "the psychological world", if we engage in it at all, seems to be just a way of referring to what certain ways of describing the world say. But talk of physical reality or the physical world seems not to be talk only about a way of thinking or describing the world. It seems to be about something that is there, something obdurate and independent, something physical, that would be the way it is even if there were no economic or psychological or other nonphysical truths or "worlds" at all.

To get to the bottom of this feeling, we would have to say more about what it means to say that the world is physical. We have seen that it cannot be a matter of ascribing some determinate property to an object called "the world". But even if there were such a property, as Descartes thought, it would be a property of *objects* that are physical, not of a world that can be thought of as the physical world. A world, as we have seen, is made up of facts, not objects. What needs to be understood is what it means to say of the *world* that it is physical.

One thing it can mean, given our current understanding of the scope of the physical vocabulary, is that there are physical truths, that a great many statements expressed in purely physical terms are true. By asserting those truths, or saying of them that they are all true, we express our belief that the world is that way. But if that is what it means to say that the world is physical—that things are this way, that way, and the other way, physically speaking—then we must also agree that the world is economic, and psychological, and coloured, and so on. Many statements in purely economic or purely psychological terms are true. And many statements ascribing colours to things are true. At least, that is what we believe: that things are as the economic and psychological and colour statements that we accept say they are. That does not lead us to conclude that things are *only* as those economic or psychological truths say they are. How, then, could we conclude, from the fact that there are physical truths, that the world is *only* as the physical truths say it is, and therefore that nothing in the world has any colour?

So far, we have found nothing that looks as if it would support that inference. I have been conceding that we can pick out a set of statements in purely physical terms and separate them from all the other things we unreflectively believe. But that alone cannot establish the exclusiveness of "the physical world" as we have been understanding it, or put it in any special position. We can also pick out sets of statements in purely economic terms, or in psychological terms, or in terms which ascribe colours to things. But that does not establish the exclusiveness of those "worlds". It does not support the conclusion that statements we accept which are expressed in other terms are not true.

In thinking about how things are or what is so, we can abstract from certain features of the world and think only about certain other aspects of it. But from the fact that we can think truly in certain ways, we cannot conclude that we cannot think of the world equally truly in certain other ways. Whether we can depends only on what the world is like: on whether what we think in those ways is true. So if, as I am imagining, we start off with everything we believe, and we abstract out of it all the physical statements which we think of as saying how things are, we will have found no reason in that alone for abandoning or even questioning our beliefs about the colours of things. Even granting that those beliefs about colours are not true "in the physical world" understood as everything that is said to be so by the physical truths alone, something more is needed even to bring the metaphysical status of colours into question, let alone to deny that they are part of reality.

This might suggest that it was wrong to try to understand the notion of "the physical world" in the way we have been thinking of it. We saw that it cannot be understood as simply a collection of objects (the physical objects); we must identify it by means of facts or states of affairs, or by statements that say what is so in physical terms. This might seem to have left us no choice but to identify the physical world with the world *as described in a certain way*. And that way of understanding it is what now seems not to do justice to the idea of a self-sufficient, exclusively physical world which lacks all those features not mentioned in the physical sciences. It is not that understanding it as we have been means that the world is only a set of sentences or descriptions or thoughts. We have been taking it for granted that the sentences we assert or the thoughts we think in expressing our conception of the world are true. And we have been assuming further that those statements are true (or false) independently of our asserting them or believing them to be true. But that still left us at best with a notion of "the physical world" as whatever is said to be so by all the physical statements that are true. And those are only some of all the statements we accept. This way of identifying a "world" seems to leave us at best with only some but not all aspects of the world we take all our beliefs to describe or represent.

It is therefore tempting to try to understand the notion of "the physical world" in another way: to think of it not as "the world as described in the terms of the physical sciences", but rather as "the world that the physical sciences describe". This would give us a conception of a world that is not identified by means of the descriptions we use to say things about it. We would then seem to be getting right through the descriptions, as it were, to the world itself, which is what those descriptions are about. That is surely what we are interested in.

I think this suggestion has merits, but it offers no encouragement to the attempt to exclude colours or other nonphysical features from the world as it is independently of us. If the physical world is the world that the truths of the physical sciences describe, and the economic world is the world economic truths describe, and the coloured world is the world that all true colour statements describe, there is no reason for denying that all those worlds are one and the same world. If it is no longer essential to the physical world that it be described only in physical terms, there is so far no objection to describing that same world in economic terms or colour terms or any other terms in which true things can be said. The idea of "the world" here would be nothing other than "everything that is so". The world or reality would be an array of facts—what is said to be so by everything that is true. It would be as rich and varied as the richness of the variety of statements that are true. All true statements could be said to describe or to state what is so in *the same* world in the sense that the world is everything that is so, and each of those statements says something that is so. Each of them gives part of the world in that sense.

On this conception, to say that the world is an *exclusively* physical world, or that the physical world is the *only* world there is, would be to say that the physical truths are the only truths there are—that nothing else is true. But what could possibly be said in support of that conclusion? We take many more things to be true than statements expressed in physical terms alone. Granted, the exclusiveness of a physical world would be supported by a complete translation into physical terms of every other statement that is true. But that has been abandoned as an empty hope. How then is the conclusion of an exclusively physical world to be reached?

Materialist philosophers need some support for the apparent move from thinking of the world in exclusively physical terms to concluding that the world is an exclusively physical world. To regard the one as sufficient for the other is suspiciously similar to the very line of thinking that appears to have led Bishop Berkeley to deny materialism. He argued that it simply could not be true, as the materialist holds, that the only qualities objects have "in reality", on their own "without the mind", are the "primary qualities" recognized in purely physical science. He thought it was not possible for the world to be that way.

When he tried to "conceive the extension and motion of a body without all other sensible qualities", he found "that it is not in my power to frame an idea of a body extended and moved, but I must withal give it some colour or other sensible quality".[10] There is, in his word, a "repugnancy" in the conception of something extended and moved but not coloured; "extension, figure, and motion, abstracted from all other qualities, are inconceivable".[11] He concluded that what the materialists distinguished as two different kinds of qualities are "inseparably united"; "where the one exist, there necessarily the other exist likewise".[12] Combining this thesis of the inseparability of the two kinds of qualities with the materialists' concession that sensible qualities like colour depend on or exist only "in the mind", Berkeley drew the idealist conclusion that *all* the qualities of objects exist only "in the mind".

What is of interest here is not the idealist conclusion but the alleged inseparability of the two kinds of qualities and the inference Berkeley drew from it. His argument fails, but its failure offers no consolation to materialist defenders of the idea of an exclusively physical world. In fact, behind Berkeley's failed inference is the very assumption that some of his materialist opponents appear to share with him.

Berkeley says it is not possible to think of an object as having certain characteristics like extension and motion without thinking of it as having certain other characteristics like colour. But surely I can think of an object as having certain characteristics without having to think of *all* the other characteristics it does or might or even must have. If we had to think of *everything* that is true of a certain object in order to think of *anything* that is true of it, it would be impossible to think of an object at all. Just as I can think of something in the next room as

---

10. G. Berkeley, *A Treatise concerning the Principles of Human Knowledge*, Part I, Section 10, in *Berkeley: Philosophical Works* (ed. M. Ayers), London, 1975, p. 79.

11. Berkeley, *Treatise*, p. 80.

12. G. Berkeley, *Three Dialogues between Hylas and Philonous* in *Berkeley: Philosophical Works*, p. 153.

having a certain size and shape and weight, for example, without thinking of where or when it was made or of how much it costs, so, it seems, I do not have to think of its colour either. So thinking of an extended, moved object without thinking of it as coloured is easy. Just think of the thing as extended and moved, and don't think of it as coloured. This might prove difficult to do once these explicit instructions have been given, but it is something we do all the time, without instructions. So Berkeley's first step, freed from his restrictive assumption that thinking requires determinate items "present to the mind", cannot be right.

But even if that step had been right, the "inseparability" of "primary" qualities like extension and motion from qualities like colour would still not follow. That is the point relevant to the materialist's conception of an exclusively physical reality. Berkeley thought there is a "repugnancy" in the conception of something being extended and moved without being coloured, and that it is not possible that "that should exist in nature which implies a repugnancy in its conception".[13] But this uncontroversial principle says that a thing could not possibly exist in nature if there is an inconsistency or contradiction in the very conception of the thing—in what is said or thought about the thing. And that is not what Berkeley proves, or even says, about an object's being extended and moved but not coloured. He says only that it is not possible to think of something as extended and moved without also thinking of it as coloured; that it is not possible to think of a thing in a certain way without also thinking of it in another way. That says that you cannot do one sort of thing without doing another. But even if he were right about that—as I think he is not—he still would not have shown that there is a "repugnancy" or impossibility in an object's being extended and moved but not coloured.

Another feat you cannot perform is to say that you are not talking without talking. It is not possible for you to say that you are not speaking and thereby say something true. There is in that sense a "repugnancy" involved in saying truly that you are not speaking; it simply cannot be done. But there is no "repugnancy" or impossibility involved in what you are saying about yourself when you say that you are not speaking. It is not impossible for it to be true that you are not speaking. It is true of each of us much of the time.

Berkeley appears to have thought that if he had admitted that we *can* think of an object as extended and moved without having to think of it as coloured, he would have to grant that it is possible for an extended,

---

13. Berkeley, *Three Dialogues*, p. 153.

moved object to lack colour. That is the assumption shared by those who would infer directly from a true conception of the world expressed in physical terms to the conclusion that the world is an exclusively physical world and so lacks all colour. But that inference would be just as fallacious as the inference Berkeley actually drew from the opposite premiss.

Both inferences fail because we can think of objects as having certain characteristics and not think of them as having certain other characteristics, even though they, in fact, have both, or it is at least possible for them to have both. It can even be necessary for them to have both, even though someone can think of the one characteristic without thinking of the other. Someone can think of an object as a right-angled triangle without thinking of the square of its hypotenuse as equal to the sum of the squares of the other two sides. But it is not possible for a right-angled triangle to lack that property; it is a necessary truth that all right-angled triangles have it.

Berkeley spoke of conceiving or thinking of an object. The objection to his view is that to say or think only that an object has the qualities F, G, and H is not to say or think that the object has only the qualities F, G, and H. We have been trying to make sense of the idea of a whole "world". A purely physical world is a world described only in physical terms. Physical truths make no mention of the colours of things. But the conclusion that things in the independent world therefore have only the properties mentioned in those physical truths, and so have no colour, has no more to recommend it than the opposite conclusion that Berkeley drew.

If the conclusion that objects have no colour is going to be reached at all, then, it must be reached more indirectly, or on other grounds. The physical truths alone simply leave it open whether physical things are coloured, just as purely economic statements leave it open how tall economic agents are or how much they weigh. Something more is therefore needed to take us to the conclusion that the independent world lacks all those features not mentioned in the physical truths alone. Without some reason to believe that the facts stated in physical terms are the only facts there are, we cannot take the first step towards bringing the status of the colours of things into question.

4

Unmasking Explanation and the 'Unreality' of Colour

As late as the seventeenth-century—in Kepler, and possibly even to some extent in Galileo—there remained certain thoughts or attitudes that encouraged the idea that only what is quantifiable is real. They were part of a lingering neo-Platonist tradition, stemming from Pythagoras, according to which all reality is exclusively mathematical, or perhaps even numerical. That would seem to give some support to the idea that a comprehensive quantitative physical science can capture all there is to reality. And that, in turn, could take us from a conception of the world in exclusively quantifiable physical terms to the conclusion that the world is exclusively physical, and so the colours of things have no place in it.

But that Pythagorean idea was at best an article of faith, or a mystic vision. It gives us no reason to accept the view of reality that it leads to. Even without that vision it is possible to hold that quantification is essential to science, that any science worthy of the name must treat its subject matter mathematically. But that is a demand on science, or the best science, not a claim about reality. Even to accept that demand on science, and to insist in addition that all reality must be in principle knowable, would not restrict one's view of reality to what such a mathematically expressible science could in principle discover to be so. Reality might still contain much more than is capturable in that science alone.

I do think that certain features of the physical sciences appear to support the conclusion that reality is exhaustively physical, and so to support the view that colours and certain other apparent qualities of things must be unreal or dependent on the sense organs of perceiving animals. But it is not simply the quantitative character of the physical sciences or the special vocabulary they use that provides that encouragement. It is what the physical sciences can do. Even if everything they say is true and is expressed in "absolute" and fully "nonanthropocentric" terms, what is more significant is the *understanding* they can give us. They serve to *explain* why things are the way they are and why things happen in the world as they do. This potential explanatory success is what I think generates philosophical optimism. It is what is felt to make the physical sciences uniquely effective as a criterion of reality that will eventually exclude colour and many other would-be qualities from the world as it is independently of us.

Bernard Williams in his study of Descartes explains how and why the claim that the scientific conception of the world exhausts the way the world "really is" must rest on its explanatory power. That is what he thinks is essential to the project of showing that some of our beliefs represent the world as it really is independently of us, and that certain others do not. To try to make some such distinction without appeal to the explanatory power of some of the things we believe would leave us in the dilemma presented in chapter 2.[1] There would be no way of posing a challenging philosophical question about part of our everyday conception of the world.

If we ask which of our beliefs represent the world as it is independently of us and which do not, and we think of "the world" we are asking about as whatever is described by all our current beliefs, then we will find, not surprisingly, that *all* our beliefs represent that world as it is. As Williams puts it, if we think of the world in that way, "our conception of the world as the object of our beliefs can do no better than repeat the beliefs we take to represent it".[2] If, by contrast, we subtract all determinate content from our conception of "the world" and think of it purely abstractly as simply "what all systems of belief and representation are trying to represent", we will have no fixed notion of "the world" against which our current beliefs can be assessed. That would leave us with only the question of what to believe, or which of our beliefs are true:

---

1. See pp. 25–28.

2. B. Williams, *Ethics and the Limits of Philosophy*, Cambridge, Mass., 1985, p. 138.

Each side of this dilemma takes all our representations of the world together, in the one case putting them all in and in the other leaving them all out. But there is a third and more helpful possibility, that we should form a conception of the world that is "already there" in terms of some but not all of our beliefs and theories.[3]

Williams thinks that such a restricted conception is to be found in that austere scientific portion of everything we believe that is expressed in "absolute" or "nonperspectival" terms. But it gains its special standing not only because of how it is expressed but also because of its explanatory power. The austerely scientific conception is held to be unique in being able to explain what happens in the world and in being able to explain it as it presents itself to those of us who form that very conception. It can succeed as a criterion of reality if it can explain in its own scientific terms how our rich and complicated conception of the world has come about: "how creatures with our origins and characteristics can understand a world with properties that this same science ascribes to the world".[4] But in doing that, it will also explain how we have developed a partly false or distorted conception of the world as well: how we come to understand the world partly "anthropocentrically" or "perspectivally", as having many features which that science does not ascribe to the world. All those beliefs and perceptions that represent the world as the scientific account says it is, and all our other beliefs and perceptions that go beyond that austere scientific story, must be explained by nothing more than what that scientific portion alone says is true of the world.

The prospect of such explanations is what reveals the unique standing of the scientific conception. It is what avoids the "all or nothing" dilemma and so enables us to ask a significant question about the relation between the world and our conception of it. The explanatory potential of a conception of the world is what is "necessary to give substance to the idea of 'the world'" as it is put to work in the philosophical project.[5]

The content it supplies to that idea of "the world" is roughly this: the world as it is independently of us is whatever best explains everything that is so, including all human and other animal responses to what is so. What does not have to be so in the world for those responses to occur as they do is not part of the independent world. Human beings have developed an elaborate scientific account of the world. What shows

---

3. Williams, *Ethics and the Limits of Philosophy*, p. 138.
4. Williams, *Ethics and the Limits of Philosophy*, pp. 139–140.
5. Williams, *Ethics and the Limits of Philosophy*, p. 140.

that that scientific conception holds pride of place is the fact that our acceptance of that conception is thought to be best explained, scientifically, by the fact that the world is (at least roughly) the way that account says it is. If our accepting the remaining body of lore whose content goes beyond the strictly scientific account could also be explained by no more than the fact that the world is as that austere scientific account says it is, then "the world" or "reality" would have been shown to amount to nothing more than what that scientific account asserts. Since nothing more would be needed, nothing more would have to be countenanced as part of reality. The world or reality as it is "anyway", independently of us, would be given in full by that "absolute", scientific description.

The explanatory sufficiency of the austerely scientific conception is therefore what connects the idea of the world as scientifically described with the idea of the world as it really is. It "gives the content to the idea, essential to the traditional distinction [between primary and secondary qualities], that the scientific picture presents the reality of which the secondary qualities, as perceived, are appearances".[6] What reveals that colour and other "secondary" qualities are mere "appearances" and are not part of "reality" is not simply that they are not mentioned in the austere scientific account. It is that objects do not have to be thought of as having such qualities to explain why the world appears to all of us as it does:

> In understanding, even sketchily, at a general and reflective level, why things appear variously coloured to various observers, we shall find that we have left behind any idea that, in some way which transcends those facts, they 'really' have one colour rather than another. In thinking of these explanations, we are in fact using a conception in which colour does not figure at all as a quality of the things.[7]

Thomas Nagel, too, sees the possibility of explanations of this kind as crucial to any attempt to transcend ourselves and our current conceptions and to understand more objectively and in more general terms what he calls "our mental relation to the world".[8] He thinks that most additions to our knowledge, even extremely fruitful and far-reaching improvements, simply add further information or fill in a framework of understanding that is already given. But a genuine "advance in objectivity" of the kind we aspire to in the quest for reality would give us a

---

6. B. Williams, *Descartes: The Project of Pure Enquiry*, Harmondsworth, 1978, pp. 244–245.

7. Williams, *Descartes*, p. 242.

8. T. Nagel, *The View from Nowhere*, New York, 1986, p. 75.

new and more "external" understanding of our present conception of the world. It would enable us to assess that conception in a new way and in relation to what we can now see to be the way things really are. To produce such illumination, Nagel holds:

> a self-transcendent conception should ideally explain the following four things: (1) what the world is like; (2) what we are like; (3) why the world appears to beings like us in certain respects as it is and in certain respects as it isn't; (4) how beings like us can arrive at such a conception. . . . What we want is to reach a position as independent as possible of who we are and where we started, but a position that can also explain how we got there.[9]

He thinks that when we undertake a move to greater objectivity and seek a more "external" understanding of our perceptions of and beliefs about the colours of things in this way, we will find that the best explanation of those perceptions and beliefs will not involve the ascription to things of any "intrinsic color properties".[10] We test the reality or independence of features of the world we believe in by asking whether they are indispensable in explaining all our perceptions, beliefs, and responses:

> The hypothesis that objects have intrinsic colors in addition to their primary qualities would conspicuously fail this test, for it provides a poorer explanation of why they appear to have colors, and why those appearances change under internal and external circumstances, than the hypothesis that the primary qualities of objects and their effects on us are responsible for all the appearances.[11]

J. L. Mackie puts this same idea of explanatory parsimony at the centre of his defence of the distinction between primary and secondary qualities and of a purely physical reality which lacks all colour. He thinks "the literal ascription of colours as we see colours . . . to material things, to light, and so on, forms no part of the explanation of what goes on in the physical world in the processes which lead on to our having the sensations and perceptions that we have".[12] But the various qualities ascribed to objects in the physical sciences do form part of such explanations. Not only do they account for happenings throughout the physical world, but they also help explain the processes which lead to human beings' perceiving and believing in those very objects and properties. What is special about the physical story is not that it is

9. Nagel, *The View from Nowhere*, p. 74.
10. Nagel, *The View from Nowhere*, p. 75.
11. Nagel, *The View from Nowhere*, p. 76.
12. J. L. Mackie, *Problems from Locke*, Oxford, 1976, pp. 17–18.

restricted to certain properties that physicists happen to be interested in. "The physical considerations do not concern merely features which are scientifically interesting and important; they show that there is no good reason for postulating features of a certain other sort, namely thoroughly objective features which resemble our ideas of [colours and other] secondary qualities".[13] There is no reason to "postulate" such features because physical explanation alone, which makes no use of them, is sufficient to account for all our perceptions and beliefs about them.

What is at work in all these views is what could be called an "explanatory" criterion of the limits of "reality" or "the world", as those notions are to be understood in the philosophical question. What is to be thought of as real or as part of the world is only whatever is needed to explain everything that is so, including our having all the beliefs and responses to the world that we do. The minimum story that suffices to explain our acceptance of that story and our acceptance of everything else we accept will give us the whole truth about what reality or the independent world is like.

This does not mean that we can be sure at any point that we have found the true account that is adequate to explain all the rest. And there is no suggestion that we will ever possess a story that explains everything. The point is not epistemic, about what we are or will be in a position to believe. It is not a claim about how we can confirm scientific theories on the basis of observation, or how in general we come to have justified beliefs about the world. It is an explanation of the metaphysical idea of "reality" or "the world" that is put to work in the philosophical question about the degree of correspondence between our rich everyday conception of the world and the independent world or reality that that conception is about. That is not a question about the support for our beliefs. Theories we accept which go well beyond all the evidence we have so far found for them will nonetheless describe reality if their (presumed) truth is what we must appeal to in order to best explain our having all the perceptions and beliefs about the world that we do.

But not just anything that would be sufficient to explain all our responses would be enough. It will not do for us simply to dream up stories which, if true, *would* explain our responses and beliefs. It is a question of what does, in fact, explain them. That is a question about us and the world we actually live in. If we are going to try to apply this crite-

---

13. Mackie, *Problems from Locke*, pp. 18–19.

rion of reality and come up with a conception of the world as it really is independently of us, we must answer the question for ourselves here and now. We have to start where we are, and we have to answer the question with whatever we already believe or can find reason to accept. This brings out in another way why the conception of the world as it is independently of us, which we need for the philosophical question, must be carved out of everything that we already believe.

Something like Descartes's evil demon, for example, would explain all the same responses that our current scientific story is said to explain. The demon's goal is to deceive me into believing that I live in a complex world filled with physical objects and governed by scientifically discoverable laws, even though no such thing is true of the world. That would explain my believing everything I believe, and it would explain it more economically than the kind of world I believe in now. There would just be me and the demon. But, of course, we do not in fact believe in Descartes's demon. His machinations do not best explain my or anyone else's responses because no such demon exists. What we can appeal to in order to explain our beliefs and responses, and so what is to be regarded as part of the world, must be something we believe in. It must be part of our conception of the world. It is what we think *does* explain our responses that is to be reckoned as part of reality, not just whatever *would* explain them if it were so.

The philosophical project understood in this way might seem at first glance to differ only in its greater generality from what we recognize as a very natural and familiar task. I will call an explanation that explains away the appearance of something, or explains the belief in it without having to suppose that that belief is true, an "unmasking" explanation. It reveals the basis or source of a belief as not connected in the right way with its truth. It thereby unmasks or exposes a belief or appearance for what it is—an illusion, a false belief, or a mere appearance.

We rely on such explanations in a wide variety of circumstances in everyday life and find them illuminating and convincing. Not only are they used to account for familiar perceptual illusions and other forms of ordinary error or distortion, but they are given much wider currency in our culture, from talk of gods and other spirits and forces to various forms of social and political false consciousness. We explain why a person wearing sunglasses believes that the white paper in front of him is yellow by appealing to the effects of the glasses on the way the paper looks to him, together with his having forgotten that he is wearing them. We unmask that belief by explaining its origin without attributing yellow to the paper. Those of us who do not believe in ghosts, or in flying saucers from distant planets, think there are explanations of all the alleged appearances of them which do not imply that there are such things. We understand how certain social institutions exploit natural fears of death and lead people to believe they will enjoy eternal life. We could expose or unmask that belief by explaining why those people hold it, even though it is not true.

These and countless other familiar unmaskings do not all work in the same way. It is not always clear exactly how they do work, when they do. In many cases, it is difficult even to find a fully coherent belief that might be exposed as false; we discover, at best, obscurity or perhaps confusion. What do those who believe in eternal life believe? What exactly do they think endures? Do we really understand what sort of thing a ghost is supposed to be, insofar as it is something to be avoided? To think that those who believe in such things are wrong, we must have a fairly definite idea of what their belief amounts to. And when we do succeed in unmasking a belief as false, we do not always do so simply by ignoring its truth but sometimes by explicitly or implicitly denying it. If we show that what a frightened person saw in the attic on a particular occasion was a rippling reflection of the moon through the window, we implicitly deny the presence of a ghost in giving the explanation of the person's belief and fear.

These questions about familiar, everyday unmasking explanations must be kept in mind in understanding and assessing a philosophical unmasking of the colours of things. The appeal of that strategy comes from its apparent similarity to procedures we rely on without question in science and in everyday life.

We take the first steps towards a philosophical conception of a colourless independent world by starting off with all our beliefs and perceptions and asking ourselves how they arise from the world that produces them and that they are in some sense about. In asking in particular about our beliefs about the colours of things, we try to single out a certain subportion of the immense totality of things we believe that does not include any beliefs about the colours of things. If we could then find that that core of truths alone is sufficient to explain why we perceive and believe everything we do about the colours of things, we would see that those beliefs do not have to be true to explain how we come to have them in the first place. In giving those explanations in terms of that core of beliefs, we would, of course, be invoking the truth of some of our beliefs: all those in that core. So we would see that there being a world of the kind expressed in the core beliefs explains why we believe there is a world like that. But if we found that those beliefs alone are enough to explain all our other responses as well, we would see that there does not have to be a world of coloured things to explain why we believe there is one. Colours, therefore, would be exposed or un-masked as not part of the world as it is independently of us. They would fall at best on the side of "appearance", or as something "subjective".

The prospect of the explanatory sufficiency of some "absolute" core of beliefs is what I think is at work in the philosophical conception of an austerely restricted "reality" or world that excludes "anthropocentric" or "perspectival" materials supplied only by perceiving and thinking subjects. It is a very powerful picture. But for all its appeal, I think it is difficult to articulate the idea clearly and persuasively.

For one thing, it is enormously complicated, and the complications affect the way in which the explanatory criterion is to be applied in arriving at any such restricted conception. Suppose we wanted to restrict our view of reality to physical reality alone. To arrive at a reasonable belief in an exclusively physical world along the lines we are now imagining, we would have to be able to understand the presence in that purely physical world of such things as human perceptions, beliefs, and reactions. To arrive at a view of the world without colour, for instance, we must explain how in that world there come to be perceptions of and beliefs about the colours of things and, in particular, how human beings come to see yellow on particular occasions, or see a yellow lemon, or see that there is a yellow lemon in front of them. It is not just a matter of perception. It must also be possible to explain in physical terms how people come to believe on a particular occasion that a yellow lemon is in front of them, how people come to believe that there are yellow things at all, to believe that there are yellow lemons, that lemons get yellow as they ripen, that lemons are a different colour from ripe tomatoes, and so on. The whole rich complex of all our colour beliefs and perceptions would have to be fitted into and explained in a world described by nothing more than the statements and laws of physical science.

For one perfectly straightforward reason, it is clearly impossible to do that. We have conceded that no colour facts are to be found in a purely physical world; the physical vocabulary does not contain the resources for saying anything about the colours of things. But the physical vocabulary does not contain the resources for saying anything about anyone's perceiving or believing or thinking anything either. No psychological facts are to be found in a purely physical world. So the facts we are supposed to explain—that people perceive and hold beliefs about the colours of things, that Smith sees a yellow lemon, that Jones believes that there is a yellow lemon in front of her, and so on—are not themselves facts of the physical world, if that "world" is understood as everything that is true and is expressed in exclusively physical terms.

By restricting ourselves to the physical facts alone, we would not even be able to acknowledge such facts of perception and belief. But they must be acknowledged by anyone who is going to explain them. They are the facts which on this strategy are to be given an unmasking explanation that exposes the contents of our beliefs as not accurately representing the independent world. That is what is supposed to reveal that the world is a purely physical world and that nothing in it as it is independently of us is coloured.

An explanation, even an unmasking explanation, needs an *explanandum*. By restricting ourselves exclusively to the language of the physical sciences, the *explananda* we wish to account for would not even be part of the only world we accept. We could not state or acknowledge those facts the explanation of which is essential to the success of the unmasking explanation. Of course, we all know that human beings perceive colours, perceive that things are coloured, come to believe that things are coloured, and so on. But as they stand, those are not facts of the purely physical world. So in trying to restrict our thinking from the beginning to the body of physical truths alone, we would lose the very *explananda* involving human beings' perceptions and beliefs that the goings-on in that purely physical world are supposed to be enough to explain. This means that an unmasking explanation that has anything to explain away must countenance something more than purely physical facts as part of the world. We cannot regard the world as exclusively physical and at the same time offer unmasking explanations of psychological facts.

This might seem to present no difficulty for an exclusive physicalism which holds that what we take to be psychological facts are really physical facts. What must be explained—why and how human beings come to perceive and believe what they do about the colours of things—is admittedly not expressed in purely physical terms and so is in that sense not part of the physical world. But if those facts of human perception and belief are re-expressed in purely physical terms, they will then be seen to be part of the physical world after all, and a physical explanation will be available to account for them. And there will be no mention of colour anywhere in that explanation.

This suggestion as it stands will not do. What the unmasking explanation is supposed to explain is why we perceive the colours we do and why we believe that lemons are yellow, tomatoes are red, and so on. And there *is* no way of expressing or re-expressing just those facts in physical terms. There would be, if the whole psychological vocabulary could be translated into equivalent physical terms. But I am assuming that full semantic reduction of the one to the other is not available.

Without full translation of the psychological into the physical, there remains the physicalist thought that in some sense all that is "really true", or all that is "really going on", when human beings perceive colours and come to believe what they do about the colours of things, is that certain physical events and processes are occurring. Light is travelling in certain directions, various nerves are being stimulated, brains are functioning in certain ways, and so on. These are all just physical facts, and all of them can be explained physically. That is true, but the question now before us is how that exclusive physicalism is to be reached in the first place. How is it to be established that "*all* that is really going on" when human beings perceive colours are certain physical processes?

What does it even mean to say that certain physical processes and events are "all that is really going on" whenever we perceive colour and come to believe what we do about the colours of things? It cannot be said that on those occasions only the physical processes are going on, if that means that only the sentences expressed in physical terms are true. The psychological sentences about perceptions and beliefs are true as well; only because that is so is there anything psychological for the unmasking explanation to explain. Given that the physical sentences do not mean the same as, or are not equivalent to, the psychological sentences, the physicalist idea is perhaps that the physical facts in question are all that it takes to "make it true" that human beings perceive colours and come to believe what they do about the colours of things, or that they are all there is in the world "in virtue of which" those psychological sentences are true. And a purely physical explanation that does not mention colour could be given of all those purely physical facts.

This thought relies on the same obscure idea we encountered earlier: a fact or state of affairs expressed by a physical sentence that somehow "makes true" a different and nonequivalent psychological sentence. To overcome the present difficulty, the phrase "makes true" cannot be understood causally. We cannot say the physical goings-on *cause* our perceptions and beliefs about colour—not because that is not true, but because if it is true, the physical processes cannot be *all* that is going on. Psychological events and processes would be going on as well, if they are effects of what goes on physically. On that understanding, the world would include both physical and psychological facts.

The exclusive physicalist thought is perhaps that the physical facts "make" the psychological sentences true or are that "in virtue of which" they are true, because there is nothing else in the world that could make them true; the physical facts are the only facts there are. This still involves the obscure idea of one sentence "making true" a different non-equivalent sentence which it does not imply. But it does not avoid the difficulty. There is still the question of how an exclusive physicalist position is to be reached. We are now exploring the possibility of reaching it by an unmasking physical explanation of our believing everything we believe. But if we accepted only purely physical truths from the outset, we could not even acknowledge the psychological facts that it is the goal of the unmasking strategy to explain.

We are faced with a kind of dilemma. For a potentially unmasking explanation to have anything to explain, we have to admit it as a fact that people do have perceptions of and beliefs about the colours of things. But then we are countenancing a more than purely physical reality. If we admit only physical phenomena and acknowledge no such psychological facts at all, we will find nothing for a potentially unmasking explanation to explain away. This is an unavoidable feature of the unmasking explanatory strategy. It must take us beyond a strict and exclusive physicalism. In addition to the restricted core of facts in terms of which everything else is to be explained, we must acknowledge at least certain psychological facts.

This raises the question of what is involved in acknowledging the presence in the world of psychological facts of perception, thought, and belief. Just as with the physical facts, we can think of those additional psychological facts as identified so far only in terms of the vocabulary in which they are stated. They contain what we recognize as psychological verbs: 'Human beings *perceive* colours and *believe that* things are coloured', 'Smith *sees* a yellow lemon', 'He *sees that* there is a yellow lemon there', 'Jones *believes that* there is a yellow lemon in front of her', and so on. Perhaps something more can eventually be said about what is meant by calling such facts "psychological". For now, I note only that they go beyond what can be expressed in an exclusively physical vocabulary, just as colour words also go beyond the physical vocabulary. What are we admitting into our conception of the world when we add psychological facts to the exclusively physical conception with which we began? What are the conditions of admitting them, and what else do we have to admit to make the kind of sense of them that we do?

Williams is more sensitive than most defenders of the unreality or "subjectivity" of colour to the need to include the psychological in the world, and to the difficulty it creates for reaching a satisfactorily austere "absolute" conception of reality. He sees that the demands of explanation require that the purely physical conception "must be capable of being extended so as to have a place for consciousness within the world".[14] There is every reason to think that it will not be a small or simple extension. To include the fact that people perceive and believe what they do about the colours of things, we must acknowledge that they can perceive and believe many other things as well. And what else must we add to our conception of the world to admit human beings who perceive, believe, and act in ways that we can understand and identify? Everything that is needed for us to make sense of human beings with the particular thoughts and responses we attribute to them must also be reckoned as part of a world that contains the psychological facts we acknowledge.

Without some idea of the rich variety of facts we "add" to the world in "adding" psychological facts to it, we cannot begin to assess the prospects of explaining away some of our perceptions and beliefs by appeal to facts drawn only from a physical or otherwise suitably restricted subportion of everything we believe. With a rich body of psychological facts on the scene, it is a real question whether satisfactorily austere explanations of them will be available.

This considerably strengthens the requirements that Williams sees any successful unmasking metaphysical project must meet:

> One requirement is to produce, or at least to show the possibility of, the explanations which will link the material world as conceived under primary qualities with psychological phenomena such as the perception of secondary qualities, and, further, with cultural phenomena such as the local non-absolute conceptions of the world and indeed the absolute conception itself, including in that the possibility of physical science.[15]

That is obviously a tall order. But nothing less would do the philosophical job of explaining in general how human beings have come to have, and in certain respects to fail to have, a conception of themselves and the world that accurately represents the way things really are. Williams concedes that the extent to which such historical, social, and psychological phenomena can be characterized and explained in appropriately "absolute" or "nonperspectival" scientific terms is "a central philosophical question".[16] It stands as a challenge to the unmasking metaphysical project.

The question is not just whether explanations in purely physical, or some other appropriately restricted, terms will be available. It is at least

---

14. Williams, *Descartes*, p. 245.
15. Williams, *Descartes*, p. 246.
16. Williams, *Ethics and the Limits of Philosophy*, p. 140.

equally a question of what those explanations are meant to explain. How are those psychological *explananda* themselves to be thought of and fitted into the world, even before there is any thought of explaining them? The two questions are connected; they cannot be answered in isolation.

Success in the metaphysical project is not just a matter of our finding some physical explanation or other of our perceptions and beliefs about the colours of things. To reach the conclusion that objects are not coloured, we must find physical explanations that are superior to all others. They must therefore be recognizably better than the kinds of explanation we give of our perceptions and beliefs about the colours of things in science and in everyday life, when we are not engaged in the philosophical project. That is required for successful application of the criterion of reality on which the unmasking strategy is based: what does not have to be regarded as true in order to give the best explanation of why we believe that the world is a certain way is not part of the way the world really is.

How optimistic we can be about fulfilling this condition depends on some understanding of what makes one explanation of something better than another explanation of that same thing. And that, in turn, depends on what an explanation is, or what it is meant to do. We speak in many different ways and in many different contexts of explaining things. I can explain a fall in the market, I can explain Robinson's presence, I can explain a proof to someone, or astrology, Freud, last week's hurricane, the rise of the middle class, or why there is no milk in the refrigerator. In some of these cases, we appear to speak of explaining an individual—a thing, an event, a state, even a series of statements or a theory. In explaining a proof, or astrology, or Freud, I try to make a certain subject matter or body of doctrine more intelligible to someone; I expound it or explicate it. The other examples are explanations of facts, of why something or other is so. I explain why the market fell, why Robinson is present, why a hurricane occurred last week, why a middle class grew in size and power, why there is no milk. There is a fact, stated in a full sentence that I take to be true, which gets explained by a successful explanation. In explaining it, I appeal to other things I take to be true. Explanation of facts, or of why something is so, is the kind of explanation that concerns us here.

What is to be explained in the metaphysical project is why human beings perceive and believe what they do about the colours of things. Do we have reason to believe that the best explanations of all those facts will be given in purely physical terms, or even in terms which do not mention the colours of things? There are, of course, many things about ourselves that we could explain by appealing to physical facts alone.

We are physical beings, and many physical events and processes occur in us all the time, including the times at which we perceive and come to believe the things we do. We could, in principle, explain in physical terms why those physical processes and events occur as they do. But explaining those processes is not the same thing as explaining why we perceive and believe what we do about the colours of things. It is equally true that there are a great many physical processes going on when one person buys a house from another, for example, but explaining in a particular case why those processes are going on is not to explain why that person is buying that house from that other person.

It is a truism that an explanation needs an *explanandum*; it must be the explanation of something. Whether a given set of facts succeeds as an explanation depends, in part, on what was to have been explained. With physical facts and psychological facts, the *explananda* are different. The sentence in purely physical terms, 'Processes P1, P2, P3, . . . are occurring', does not imply the sentence 'Smith is buying a house from Jones'. Nor does the second imply the first. The same is true of physical statements about processes going on in a human body at a certain time and such sentences as 'Jones saw something yellow' and 'Jones came to believe that there is a yellow lemon in front of her'. The physical truth and the psychological truth are not equivalent. But whether an explanation succeeds depends in part on what was to have been explained. So what explains the one truth will not necessarily explain the other.

Again, this might be felt to present no obstacle to the prospect of physical explanation of psychological facts, since seeing something yellow, and coming to believe that there is something yellow in front of you, are, after all, things that go on in the physical world. And physical occurrences can be explained physically. This appears to be the way J. L. Mackie thinks of it. He says that the literal ascription of colours to things "forms no part of the explanation of what goes on in the physical world in the processes which lead on to our having the sensations and perceptions that we have".[17] If the phrase 'what goes on in the physical world' is taken to mean 'what is said in purely physical terms to be going on', then it is quite true that the ascription of colours to things forms no part of the explanation of any such processes, given that no colour words appear in the physical sciences. But if those physical processes get physically explained in that way and they do, in fact, "lead on to" our getting the perceptions we get, it cannot be said that

---

17. Mackie, *Problems from Locke*, p. 18.

either those processes or what physically explains them also explains our getting those perceptions of colour. That we get the perceptions we do is not something that goes on in the physical world at all, in that sense. It is not something that is said to be so in purely physical terms.

But if 'what goes on in the physical world' as Mackie understands it means only 'what goes on in the world that the physical sciences describe', it is equivalent simply to 'what goes on'. That includes everything that happens, everything that is true, in whatever terms it is expressed. Some of the things that go on in the world in that sense are that people see yellow things and come to believe that there is a yellow lemon in front of them. And can it be said that the purely physical story which includes no ascriptions of colours to things best explains psychological facts like that?

Mackie would no doubt say "Yes" and defend the superiority of the purely physical explanation on grounds of simplicity or economy. What he calls the "philosophical principle" of "the economy of postulation" says that one should not postulate or introduce into one's account of the world "supposedly objective qualities of kinds for which physics has no need".[18] That principle is said to be "philosophical" because it is not itself part of physics. The denial of colour to which it leads is not part of physics either:

> admittedly physics does not itself tell us that no such properties are there. This denial is a further, philosophical, step; but it is one which is at least prima facie reasonable in the light of the successes of physical theory.[19]

But the "principle" that is said to license that further step needs explanation and defence.

Certainly, we should not introduce into the physical sciences something for which those sciences have no need. More generally, we should not postulate or introduce into any explanatory enterprise something that is not needed for the explanatory task at hand. "Economy of postulation" in that sense sounds like a good idea. But then what is or is not to be postulated or introduced will depend on the particular explanatory task—on what needs to be explained. We cannot assume without further argument that the things or qualities needed for physical explanation are all that are needed for *all* explanatory purposes. The physical sciences cannot explain everything. That is no defect. They might be capable of explaining everything they are supposed to explain.

---

18. Mackie, *Problems from Locke*, p. 20.
19. Mackie, *Problems from Locke*, p. 19.

They could explain all the physical facts—everything that is true and expressed in purely physical terms. But that would not be to explain everything that goes on in the physical world in the sense in which it is equivalent to everything that is so.

There is even perhaps a way to admit that all the events and processes involved in our perceiving and coming to believe what we do about the colours of things are physical events and processes. Taking a psychological sentence like 'Jones sees something yellow' or 'Jones came to believe that there is a yellow lemon in front of her', we can nominalize the sentence to get a term for a kind of event: 'Jones' seeing something yellow', or 'Jones' coming to believe that there is a yellow lemon in front of her'. With specifications of time and space added, we could think of such terms as referring to particular events. We could do the same with physical sentences stating that such-and-such processes and events occurred at that same time and place. And we could perhaps grant in each case that the event referred to by the physical term is the same event as the event referred to by the psychological term.[20] That view has its difficulties, not the least of which are what an event is and what it is for something to be the same event. But if we agree that they are one and the same event, we must agree that that event is a physical event. In that sense, it could be that all events are physical events. But that does not imply that the physical explanation of the occurrence of that physical event also explains the occurrence of the psychological event. That is because the kind of explanation relevant to the unmasking strategy is an explanation of facts, truths, or something's being so, not of individuals or objects.

What is explained by the physical story is why the physical event occurred. To explain that is to explain why the truth stated by the physical sentence is true. And that explanation does not necessarily explain why the psychological event occurred, or why the truth stated by the psychological sentence is true, even if it is one and the same event. We could perhaps even concede that the physical explanation explains why the truth stated by 'There occurred physical event P, which is in fact the same event as Jones' seeing something yellow' is true. But that would not mean that the physical facts explain why that psychological event occurred.

If it did, and if it is allowed that there are such things as psychological explanations as well, it would be possible to give psychological

---

20. See, e.g., D. Davidson, "Mental Events", in his *Essays on Actions and Events*, New York, 1980.

explanations of physical events. If the event of Smith's buying Jones' house is the same event as the occurrence of certain physical processes P, then a psychological explanation of why Smith is buying Jones' house would be a psychological explanation of why there occurred that event of Smith's buying Jones' house, which is, in fact, the same event as the occurrence of physical processes P. If we hold that that psychological story does not explain why those physical processes occurred, we cannot hold that physical facts alone explain why the truths stated by psychological sentences are true. The different sentences are not equivalent. And psychological facts are what a successful unmasking physical explanation must explain.

It would be to no avail to protest on physicalist grounds that the physical explanation must be sufficient because the event in question is *only* a physical event: that the event of Jones' seeing something yellow, or the event of Jones' coming to believe that there is a yellow lemon in front of her on that occasion, is *nothing more than* a physical event. If that is intelligible at all, it must mean that only the physical and not the psychological singular term refers to something, or that only the physical and not the psychological sentence is true. If that were so, the *explanandum* would once again have disappeared, and there would be nothing psychological in the world for the physical explanation to unmask. But the response makes no sense. The whole point of the idea that mental events are identical with physical events is that a single event has both sorts of characteristics; there are no separate nonphysical events. That is what enables us to say that some physical events are also psychological events, so it would be absurd to go on to say that all physical events are nothing but physical events. A physical event that is also a psychological event cannot be said to be *nothing but* a physical event.

To say that an event is physical is presumably to say that predications in physical terms are true of it; it has physical features. But to say of an event that it is psychological or economic or political or athletic is to say that predications in psychological or economic or those other kinds of terms are true of it. If predications of all those kinds are true of one and the same event—as they might well be, if the idea of the identity of an event is clear enough to sustain it—it cannot be said that the event in question is exclusively physical, or that only the physical predications are true of it. But that is presumably what it would mean to say that it was *nothing but* a physical event.

This is the analogue for events of what we saw earlier about physical objects. Even if every object that exists is a physical object—on some recognized criterion of 'physical'—it does not follow that every fact is a physical fact, that everything that is true of those objects is express-ible in the terms of the physical sciences alone. The physical descrip-tions of those objects would give us no more than certain aspects of the world containing them, possibly not the whole truth. Similarly, if we knew that every event that occurs has physical features, or that a de-scription in purely physical terms is true of them, we could draw no conclusion about what else might be true of those very same events, or what other aspects of the world there might be. We could not conclude that all the facts we acknowledge to be part of the world can be ex-plained by appealing to only a few of the things we believe to be true of the objects or events in the world.

Whether physical explanations that fulfill the requirements of the philosophical project can really be given of our perceptions of and be-liefs about the colours of things, and, if so, whether they would be the best explanations we can find, is therefore still very much an open ques-tion. It is not settled, even if every object is a physical object and every event or process is a physical event or process. The prospect of suc-cessful unmasking explanations depends as well on our understanding of the psychological facts they are meant to explain.

I think the aspiration of this explanatory philosophical project en-courages us to think of the psychological facts of perception and belief in a certain way. We are led to think of them as separated, isolated ef-fects of strictly physical happenings, and so as mental or psychological by-products merely added on to an otherwise purely physical picture of the world. That can come to seem the only possible way to think of them. And then physical explanations of them seem to be the best we could do, and all we would need.

I do not think the psychological phenomena relevant to the philo-sophical project can be properly understood in that way. In the chap-ters that follow, I will try to explain why. For now, I want to try to bring out a way in which this picture of psychological facts and their rela-tion to an otherwise physical world would leave the only available "ex-planations" of them strikingly unsatisfying. Even at their best, they would not eliminate a feeling of mystery or miracle.

The feeling was well known to Berkeley. He thought the idea of ex-plaining our perceptions by the operations of matter alone was ludi-crous. Philonous in his *Three Dialogues between Hylas and Philonous* observes that:

> this way of explaining things . . . could never have satisfied any rea-sonable man. What connexion is there between a motion in the nerves,

and the sensations of colour or sound in the mind? or how is it possible these should be the effect of that?[21]

Berkeley was an idealist. He thought there were only ideas and minds, and that only minds, and not ideas, could cause anything. But it was not just his idealism and his conception of causality that led him to find no intelligible "connexion" between matter in motion and perceptions in the mind.

Descartes notoriously could find no connection between the movements of an extended body and something's happening in the mind either, but not because he was an idealist. He thought two distinct objects or substances were involved, only one of which was a mind. To reach the mind and produce a perception, physical motions would have to send a "spark" across a gap that is physical on one side and mental on the other. Descartes could not deny that the "spark" gets across there somehow, since interaction obviously occurs. But what the connection is, or how it occurs, would have to remain a mystery, something completely unintelligible to us. That is why occasionalism and parallelism look like equally plausible theories, given dualism. Nothing in the observable facts seems to favour one kind of "connection" over the others.

But neither idealism nor mind-body dualism is essential to finding mysterious the production of mental effects by nothing more than events described and explained in the physical sciences. Even Locke insisted that the effects of "mechanical affections of bodies" on perceivers who get sensations or ideas "perfectly surpass our comprehension".[22] We can perhaps understand how the size, figure, or motion of one body causes a change in the size, figure, or motion of another, but there is no intelligible connection between those primary qualities of things and the sensations and ideas that they produce in us:

> We are so far from knowing *what* figure, size or motion of parts produce a yellow colour, a sweet taste or a sharp sound, that we can by no means conceive how *any* size, figure or motion of any particles, can possibly produce in us the idea of any colour, taste or sound whatsoever: there is no conceivable connexion between the one and the other.[23]

Locke does not mean that there is no connection at all between physical motions and the appearance of ideas. He thinks the one produces

21. Berkeley, *Three Dialogues between Hylas and Philonous* in *Berkeley: Philosophical Works* (ed. M. Ayers), London, 1975, p. 166.
22. Locke, *An Essay concerning Human Understanding* (ed. P. H. Nidditch), Oxford, 1975, IV, 3, xxviii (p. 559).
23. Locke, *Human Understanding*, IV, 3, xiii (p. 545).

the other. What he is denying is any *understanding* of that fact, any explanation of the link between the physical and the psychological. We can find no "natural connexion" between them. All we can do is ascribe it to "the arbitrary will and good pleasure of the Wise Architect", who for reasons of his own which are not intelligible to us simply "annexes" certain ideas to certain motions and not to others.[24]

Locke did not think that the unintelligibility of a link between matter and thinking is due to there being two distinct substances involved. He thought that it was "not much more remote from our comprehension" to conceive of God as "superadding" a faculty of thinking to a material thing than to conceive of him as "superadding" or joining a thing that thinks to a material thing that does not.[25] Locke remained on the fence about one substance or two; what he saw as common to both sides of the fence is the inexplicability of psychological facts in purely physical terms.

I think these philosophers were right to find no satisfying natural explanation here. Given their conception of the psychological facts involved, any discoverable connection between those facts and goings-on in the purely physical world could seem only "arbitrary" and "remote from our comprehension". A successful explanation should provide some intelligible link between the explanation offered and the fact to be explained. But it seems that no such link would be available if psychological facts are thought of as simply added on to purely physical facts and "explained" as effects of them in the only way that seems possible.

A full account of what goes on physically in a certain area during a certain period of time, along with knowledge of physical laws which those events instantiate, would enable us to explain why, given the earlier events, the later events occur. If we restrict ourselves to that physical story alone, we will not know whether anything psychological occurred during that period at all. If we are then informed that something psychological also occurred, we would not know from the physical story alone even what kind of psychological event or fact it was, let alone why it occurred. To be told that what happened psychologically was that a certain person Jones saw something yellow and came to believe that there is a yellow lemon in front of her would not be to understand why those psychological events occurred. Even if we know the precise time at which that particular perception and that particular belief arose, we would be no closer to understanding why they occurred. We would

---

24. Locke, *Human Understanding*, IV, 3, xxix (p. 560).
25. Locke, *Human Understanding*, IV, 3, vi (p 541).

know everything that happened physically up to and including the time at which the perception and belief occurred, but that would not make those psychological facts any more intelligible to us. They are facts of a completely different kind from physical facts, and we would need to see the two kinds of facts as connected in some way. Physical laws alone serve only to connect physical facts with one another; they say nothing about a connection with anything psychological.

This seems to force us towards what has come to be a more or less standard picture of how psychological phenomena are to be fitted into the physical world. It sees laws or generalizations as essential to explanation, but since psychological facts are not part of a purely physical story, we need, in addition, some laws or generalizations that connect physical with psychological phenomena. These "bridge" laws or generalizations could then be combined with purely physical information to explain psychological facts.

It is worth noting that this familiar conception, which is an expression of a certain primacy of the physical sciences, in no way supports an exclusive physicalism. It is not a view on which psychological facts are explained by physical facts alone. Psychological facts are explained on this view, if at all, only by physical facts combined with "bridge" laws or generalizations which are not themselves expressed in purely physical terms. If laws combining physical and psychological terms are needed to forge an explanatory link between the physical and the psychological, then any higher-level explanations of why such "bridge" laws hold would also have to be couched in a combination of physical and psychological terms. Laws that are purely physical assert no such connection. So on this conception, physical-psychological connections must be accepted as features that cannot be eliminated from any world in which psychological facts can be explained.

The first question this raises is the extent to which we can realistically hope to find physical-psychological laws or generalizations of this kind that serve to explain familiar psychological phenomena. For psychological facts in general, the prospects seem far from good. Take the broadly psychological phenomenon of one person's buying a house from another. It seems absurd to look in the vocabulary of the physical sciences for a minute description of a correlate or antecedent of such a type of action. It seems almost equally absurd to look for a "bridge" law linking a determinate physical condition in general with a person's believing that there is a yellow lemon in front of her. Buying a house and believing that there is a yellow lemon there are complex psychological phenomena that can be manifested in many different physical ways.

But to many, it has not seemed absurd to seek such laws in the case of apparently simpler psychological phenomena such as sensation. A physical correlate of pain or of a particular kind of pain has seemed far from an absurdity. And if perception is likened to sensation or is thought to be equally simple and direct, perception, too, can perhaps be thought of as susceptible of this kind of physical explanation.

This raises complicated questions about the relation between sensation and perception, and about the relation between both of them and thought, belief, and knowledge. I take up some of those matters in the chapters that follow. But it is worth pausing to notice the fundamental dissatisfaction that I believe is inherent in this more or less traditional picture.

Suppose we did discover significant correlations between certain physical conditions and certain kinds of sensations or perceptions. Part of what I think Locke was responding to in his invocation of "the arbitrary will and good pleasure of the Wise Architect" is that, even so, there would be a way in which the psychological phenomena in question would forever remain unexplained. The most we could find is that certain psychological phenomena happen to be "annexed" to certain physical phenomena, and certain others to others. We could perhaps find correlations or generalizations, but they alone would not provide satisfactory explanations of particular instances that fall under them. To say that Jones, in whom certain physical events are occurring, sees something yellow, because everyone in whom physical events of just that kind occur sees something yellow, does not really explain why Jones sees what she sees. We understand that Jones is like others, but it remains "remote from our comprehension" why just those psychological goings-on are "superadded" to just those physical goings-on.

To try to increase our understanding by moving to a higher level and explaining why the mixed correlation or generalization holds would be to no avail. That correlation could not be explained in purely physical terms, for the same reason that physical facts alone were originally insufficient to explain psychological facts. And to try to explain it by appeal to some even higher-level correlation would still leave us with an equally "arbitrary" generalization in which certain kinds of psychological phenomena are simply said to be "annexed" to certain physical conditions as inexplicably as they were in the lower-level correlation. Of course, a well-established correlation would put us in a position to predict the occurrence of certain kinds of psychological event, given a purely physical account of what has gone on. But still we would see no intelligible connection between the two. We would not understand *why* the psychological events we expect will occur, or *why* the correlations we have discovered actually hold. We would simply have to accept the correlations as brute facts which cannot be explained further. The only alternative would seem to be a more encompassing theory that goes beyond both the physical and the psychological vocabulary and somehow explains the connections between phenomena of the two kinds. But no one has any idea what that would be.

It is true that in any attempt to understand something we will eventually be faced with some brute facts which we must accept as simply part of the way things are. To explain them, we could only appeal to further facts, which, in turn, would have to be accepted for what they are. There is no prospect of explaining everything by appealing to higher and higher levels of generalization. That kind of fundamental inexplicability must be granted for everything, not just psychological phenomena. But I think the kind of dissatisfaction I have in mind here is specific to "explanations" of psychological phenomena as understood in this way. It could be put by saying that mere correlations between psychological and physical facts, however well supported, cannot explain psychological phenomena as the psychological phenomena they are.

Locke was struck by the fact that whatever physical conditions in fact produce a perception of yellow could have produced something else instead, or nothing at all. For all that is true of the physical movements alone, "the Wise Architect" could simply have "annexed" a different kind of psychological item to those movements, or no psychological item at all. The correlation therefore provides no explanation of why the kind of perception correlated with certain physical movements is a perception of what it is a perception of. Why is it that what arises from just these physical conditions is a perception of yellow? That is what we want to know. Even if we grant that *something* psychological arises from just these conditions, why is it not a perception of red, or a perception of something cubical, or a pain—or a thought of the square root of minus two, for that matter? Why is it just that particular psychological phenomenon that does, in fact, arise here? That is what we could not understand further, on this picture. It would simply have to be accepted that certain kinds of physical and psychological items are correlated in the world as it is.

That would leave our perceptions inexplicably related to the world we take them to be about. We could not deny that something in the world produces those perceptions under certain conditions, but the fact that what are produced in those conditions are perceptions at all, rather than some other psychological phenomena, and that they are perceptions of just those features that they are perceptions of, would not be something we could understand from the physical facts and the correlations alone. And if that remained inexplicable or could be attributed at best only to "the arbitrary will and good pleasure of the Wise Architect", this view would always leave us with a less than fully satisfactory understanding of our perceptions and beliefs about the world. The philosophical quest for reality as we have been understanding it requires fully satisfactory explanations of those psychological phenomena. That is essential to any unmasking explanatory strategy that could lead us to a conception of a colourless world.

For the defender of a conception of a world that lacks all colour, it might seem to be a virtue of this kind of view that it would leave our perceptions of colour inexplicably related to the world we take them to be about. That is just what is to be expected of perceptions of colour if nothing in the world has any colour at all. Perceptions of colour would *not* be related to the world in any satisfyingly intelligible way; there would be nothing in the world that they are perceptions of. The only intelligible relation we could then discover between our perceptions of colour and the world that produces them would be that certain kinds of perceptions always arise under certain kinds of physical conditions. But since the specification of those physical conditions would include nothing about the colour of anything, there would be nothing in the world that would explain why the perceptions are perceptions of colour at all, or perceptions of this or that particular colour. There would be no intelligible link whatever between perceptions of colour and the world that causes them.

But on this view of perceptions as mental effects of interaction with an otherwise physical world, that would be true of all our perceptions. They would all be nothing but end products of certain physical processes. So our perceptions of shape, size, motion, and so on—all those features that are mentioned in the physical sciences and so are thought really to belong to objects in the independent world—would also be explained as arising when they do only by discovering the conditions in which they, in fact, arise. As before, there would be no satisfactory explanation of why a perception that has been found to be correlated with a certain physical condition is a perception of what it is a perception of.

If it had been discovered that a perception of something cubical arose only when a cubical object is present to a perceiver, for example, there would be no further understanding of why it was a perception of something cubical that arose in just those circumstances. Why does that kind of perception arise just then? Why not a perception of yellow, or a pain, or the thought of the square root of minus two? That would not be something we could understand further, on this view of perceptions. We could appeal to nothing more than the correlations we could discover.

That perceptions of something cubical are correlated with the presence of cubical objects would be just as much subject to "the arbitrary will and good pleasure of the Wise Architect" as the correlation between perceptions of yellow and the presence of certain physical conditions. The relation between perceptions and the world would be no more intelligible in the one case than in the other. For all that the correlations alone could tell us, each kind of perception could have been "annexed" to quite different objects or conditions while remaining the kind of perception that it is.

This view has this consequence because the perceptions in question are identified as perceptions of a particular kind independently of the conditions or states of affairs which they are perceptions of. Discovery of a correlation between things of two kinds requires that things of each of the two kinds be identifiable independently of any correlation between them. To find that As are correlated with Bs, we must be able to recognize an A independently of recognizing a B. So if the occurrence of perceptions can be explained only by finding conditions in the world with which they are correlated, a perception of a certain kind must be identifiable as such independently of the conditions in the world that can be found to give rise to it.

That has been widely thought to be true of sensations. The idea is that we simply know when we have a pain, for example, and we can then try to discover what produced it. This view says the same thing about perceptions in general. Independently of discovering anything that is so in the world around us, we are said to be able to recognize a perception as a perception of yellow, or as a perception of something cubical. We can then look to see what is true in the world that produces perceptions like that. Even if we find that a cubical object is present every time a perception of something cubical appears, that amounts to nothing more than a contingent correlation. There would be nothing about perceptions of something cubical that prevents them from being produced by, or "annexed" to, different physical conditions from those that happen to produce them now. Even if they were universally correlated with the presence of spherical objects, say, this view implies that they would still be perceptions of something cubical, and that we could recognize them as such.

Free of the philosophical explanatory project, and of the conception of psychological facts that it seems to encourage, I do not believe that this is the way we think of perception. We think that, in general, the reason we perceive something cubical in the presence of a cubical object (given the right conditions) is that there is a cubical object there, and we perceive it. What we think of perceivers as perceiving depends, in general, on what we think is there to be perceived. That makes for a more intelligible link between perceptions and the world we take them to be perceptions of. We can then understand why a perception of just that kind arises in just those conditions. No view which sees perceptions as identifiable independently of what they are perceptions of, as this view sees them, can provide such an understanding. It would leave room for perceptions of colour in a world which nonetheless lacks all colour; that is what makes it congenial to the conception of a completely colourless world. But it could not satisfactorily *explain* the presence of those perceptions in that world. That is because it could give no fully satisfactory explanations of the presence of any perceptions at all, so conceived—not even perceptions of something cubical in a world filled with cubical things. But satisfactory explanations of our perceptions of colour are essential to the success of the unmasking philosophical project.

5

Perception, Predication, and Belief

It is difficult to assess the prospects of finding philosophically satis-factory unmasking explanations that will reveal to us the true nature of reality. One difficulty is the enormous richness and complexity of what is to be explained. It is nothing less than all of human knowledge, thought, and experience. How we have come to possess a set of beliefs amounting to an elaborate picture of an independent world, how we have developed a scientific account of that world which in broad out-line is correct as far as it goes, and how we experience and naturally come to believe so many things which seem to go beyond that strictly scientific account—all this must be explained by only part of what we already take ourselves to know about the world. The limits of that priv-ileged core of facts that will constitute reality cannot be defined or iden-tified in advance. Where the limits lie depends on what turns out to be needed to explain everything that must be explained. And the expla-nations that are to lead us to reality must be the best we can discover.

I have indicated why I think no view of reality reached by such an explanatory route could be an exclusively physical reality. Something more than physical facts alone must be acknowledged from the outset if there is going to be anything for the potentially unmasking explana-tions to explain. Even on the conception of explanation that seems most congenial to the philosophical project, correlations between physical and psychological phenomena must be accepted as ineliminable fea-tures of any world in which psychological facts can be explained. That takes us beyond physicalism. But if we must go beyond physicalism, where can we stop? Can we arrive at any significantly restricted and so still partly negative conclusion about the contents of the world? Can it be shown, in particular, that although the independent world is richer than all the physical facts, it still contains nothing that has any colour, or that whatever colour objects have is something "subjective" or dependent upon us? That depends on what is needed to give the best explanations we can find of our getting all the perceptions and beliefs about the colours of things that we do.

That raises the question of how psychological facts are to be explained and what makes one explanation better than another. But before that, there is the more fundamental question of what psychological facts are and how they are to be understood. You cannot hope to explain something unless you grant that there is such a thing and you have at least some idea of what it is. So even to think of explaining how colour perceptions and colour beliefs arise, we need some way of understanding them as the psychological facts we take them to be. Perceptions and beliefs are not all that are at stake. There are also hopes, fears, wishes, imaginings, memories, and fantasies involving the colours of things—in fact, every way in which colour figures in our mental lives. But I will stick to thoughts, beliefs, and perceptions. The question is how they are to be understood.

Can we understand and accept all the psychological facts of perception and belief concerning the colours of things as we do and still arrive at the conclusion that no object in reality has any colour or that colour is something "subjective" or dependent upon us? Among all the issues crucial to the success of the unmasking project, this is the question I want to concentrate on the most.

Those who defend the unreality or subjectivity of colour have tended to concentrate on the *perception* of colour. We have seen that there are good reasons for that. We have also seen how perceptions of colour have come to be thought of as simple "sensations" somehow added on to an otherwise purely physical story. That is one of the things that has made "subjectivism" about colour look not only plausible but also, with certain added assumptions, virtually inevitable. The idea is that perceiving yellow, for example, involves the presence or occurrence of something called a "sensation" (or sometimes an "idea" or "impression" or "sense datum" or even just an "experience") of yellow. Such a thing is said simply to appear "before the mind" on certain occasions, most often as a result of a physical interaction between something in front of a person and that person's functioning open eyes and brain. The view is not simply that a person sees yellow on a certain occasion because of a physical interaction between something in front of him and his eyes and brain; everyone would presumably accept that. This theory crucially adds that what happens whenever a person sees something is that something called a "sensation" (or "perception" or "idea", etc.) with a certain character appears.

It is easy to see why this seems to hold out the best prospects for explanations of psychological phenomena in physical terms. The "explanations" might be less than fully satisfying for the reasons I have suggested, but if there were such things as these "sensations" or "perceptions", and their occurrence were, in fact, correlated with certain physical conditions in the way imagined, then whenever we knew what the relevant physical conditions were, we could predict pretty reliably when a "sensation" of a certain kind was going to appear. We might not fully understand *why* a "sensation" of that particular type occurs in those circumstances, but knowledge of the physical conditions would enable us to predict it. To do so, we would not need to know anything about the colours of any objects. So colour perceptions would not have to be understood as perceptions of something that is present in objects.

In this respect, colour "sensations" are to be thought of as just like more familiar sensations—for example, pains. That is what encourages the idea that there is no colour in objects which act on us to produce "sensations" of colour. There is no pain in a pin which acts on us to produce a sensation of pain. A pin divides the flesh to a certain depth, and we have a certain sensation with a quite special and distinctive character. Why a painful sensation occurs in just those circumstances rather than a perception of yellow or a perception of something cubical is, on this view of sensation, perhaps not fully explainable. Perhaps only "the Wise Architect" knows. Or maybe he even brings it about. But there is no doubt that a certain sensation occurs. Purely physical processes occur between pin and brain, with no pains anywhere among them, and then at the last step, as it were, a sensation with a certain character appears. We are aware of that character; we feel it. But that is the only place that that felt character comes into the story of sensation. The only place the pain—what we feel—fits into the physical world is as a feature of one of the effects of what is otherwise nothing but a physical process.

If there were an exact parallel between sensations of pain and "sensations" of colour, the only place colour—what we see—would fit into the physical world would then be as a feature of one of the effects of what is otherwise nothing but a physical process. Physical objects would not have to be thought of as having colours on this view, any more than they are thought of as having pains. Objects can *cause* pains—that is to say, sensations of pain—and in the same way objects are said to cause "sensations" of colour. But they do not themselves need to have any pains or any colours in order to do that.

This view of perceptions of colour is not easy to understand, despite its long and distinguished history. I think I have a pretty good idea of what sensations are and some idea of the great variety of sensations it is possible for human beings to have. I think I have had my share. But I really do not know whether I have ever had a sensation of yellow or not. According to this view of "sensations", I have had one every time I have seen the yellow of a lemon, or of a buttercup, or of anything else that is yellow, as I have certainly done many times.

One thing that makes this view difficult to understand is how we are to understand the differences among different colour "sensations". A "sensation" of yellow is presumably different from a "sensation" of green. What is the difference? It might seem easy to explain it as simply a difference between "sensations" with different qualities or features. But *what* difference? *What* features? Two "sensations" can differ in some ways without differing in all. Even two "sensations" of yellow presumably differ from each other in some ways. And a "sensation" of yellow would seem to have *some* features in common with a "sensation" of green, despite their differences. Obviously, the relevant similarity or difference is to be specified as similarity or difference *in colour*. But how is that to be described? What is a difference in colour as applied to "sensations"?

If "sensations" of colour differ from one another only in having or lacking certain qualities or features, there is a temptation to say that we understand what "sensations" of yellow are simply by having them. We know they are different from "sensations" of green by having some of those, too, and recognizing the difference. In each case, we are simply aware of certain distinctive features of our different "sensations" of colour, just as we sometimes have the painful sensation of a pinprick and at other times the recognizably different and pleasant sensation of taking a cooling drink. We know the difference. Each of us knows by direct experience "from his own case", as the saying goes, and so in that way we understand what we ascribe to others when we say they have a painful sensation or a "sensation" of yellow.

I do not believe that this way of understanding perceptions of yellow or perceptions of green can be made to make sense. The reasons are by now familiar. The view assimilates perceptions of colour to sensations of pain, but I do not think our understanding of sensations of pain can be accounted for in this way either. The idea appears to be that no one who has not felt one could know what a pain of a certain kind is, and that all it takes to know what pains of that kind are is to have felt one or several of them. The first point is at best dubious, and the second is completely implausible. Even if you cannot know what a sensation of a certain kind is without having one, it is not sufficient simply to have one, or five, or a million of them, to understand what a sensation is or what a sensation of that kind is. From those experiences alone, you would not acquire the capacity to ascribe sensations of that kind to yourself or to others, or to understand what they are. Having sensations is one thing; knowing what sensations are and being able to think of yourself and others as having them is another matter.

The main difficulty for this way of thinking of our understanding of sensations is that there is no way of simply having or experiencing or gazing at—or, for that matter, even holding in your hand—a particular object or item from the mere "possession" of which you can arrive at an understanding of it as a thing of a certain kind rather than of some other kind. Nor is there therefore any possibility, on the basis of that purely nondiscursive "possession" or "acquaintance", of asking whether you have got something of the same kind again on a second occasion. Every two things are the same in some respect or other, and also different in other respects, so whether the things are of the same kind or not will depend on which respects are relevant to the question of similarity. And that cannot be fixed simply by the presence of an object or item or experience which you merely "have", without being able to think of it in any one way rather than another.

This makes it almost irresistible to appeal to *simple* sensations or experiences whose distinctive character can be fixed by "acquaintance" alone. If certain experiences had only one feature or perhaps only one salient feature, something that, in turn, had no complexity of its own, there would seem to be no possibility of indeterminateness about what kind of thing is present in such an experience, or whether something of the same kind is present again on a second occasion. We might then hope to learn what a thing of that kind is directly from our awareness of our repeated acquaintances with it. The theory of perceptions as "sensations" of a certain distinctive character goes naturally together in this way with a distinction between simple and complex features of things and with a need for the presence in our experience of instances of unmistakable simplicity.

The simplicity in question would have to be absolute. It would not be enough for perception to present us with combinations of features which can be distinguished from one another and so must each be "simpler" than the combination itself. The colour, the taste, and the smell of an apple,[1] for example, can each be distinguished from the other qualities, so each can be said to be "simpler" than that "complex" combination. But it does not follow that the colour, the taste, and the smell are themselves simple and have no further distinguishable aspects. Relative simplicity—or one thing's being simpler than another—is not enough to avoid the difficulty of indeterminateness. That is why experience must present us with instances of absolute, not just relative, simplicity if we are to get an idea of something simply from direct acquaintance with it. Locke saw the need. He thought there must be "simple" ideas of sensation, "which being each in it self uncompounded, contains in it nothing, *but one uniform Appearance, or Conception* in the mind, and is not distinguishable into different *Ideas*".[2]

That quest for absolute simplicity seems to me no more than a dream.[3] But even if each person's experience did contain such simple objects or features, that would still not explain how it is possible for people to think that they have such sensations or to attribute them to others. Having sensations with a certain simple character is one thing; thinking of oneself and others as having them is something else. It is thinking of human beings as perceiving colour that is essential to the unmasking philosophical project. Only someone who acknowledges that we have perceptions of colour could think of explaining away those perceptions.

Another thing that makes the view difficult to understand is uncertainty about how closely or in what respects "sensations" of colour are supposed to be analogous to sensations of pain, if pains are understood in that same way as "simple" sensations. The analogy must be close to support the idea of a world of colourless objects accompanied only by "sensations" of colour. But the closer the analogy, the more obscure the view becomes. That is because colour figures in perception in ways that are not easily captured in the idea of a "sensation" with a certain distinctive character.

The view speaks of perceptions of colour, and there is no question that we have such things. That is to say, it is often true that a person sees yellow or sees green. That way of thinking of perceptions perhaps comes closest to thinking of them as "sensations". But more typically, when we see colours, we see coloured objects. Someone sees a yellow

---

1. See, e.g., D. Hume, *A Treatise of Human Nature* (ed. L. A. Selby-Bigge), Oxford, 1958, p. 2.

2. Locke, *An Essay concerning Human Understanding* (ed. P. H. Nidditch), Oxford, 1975, II, ii, 1 (p. 119).

3. Here I draw on Wittgenstein's treatment of the demand for simplicity and simple "private objects" in his *Philosophical Investigations* (Oxford, 1953). The issues involved lie at the heart of this subject; I rely heavily on his discussion of them.

lemon nearby in good light, for example. That is not just a case of seeing yellow. The person does see yellow, but the yellow he sees is the
yellow of a lemon, and he sees the lemon to be yellow. He sees the
colour to be a property of an object that he sees. Even if he does not
see or know that the thing he sees is a lemon he sees something yellow, and sees it to be yellow. Of course, it is also possible to see something yellow without seeing yellow. You might see a ripe lemon in a
largely darkened room; what you see is yellow, but you do not see any
yellow at all.

It is also possible, perhaps, to see a colour without seeing anything
at all to be that colour. If you look straight up on a clear day you will
see nothing but blue. But almost always when we see colour we see
something to be a certain colour. This could be called "predicational"
seeing. It is reported in a sentence with a modified noun or noun phrase
as complement to the verb 'see'. It involves seeing an object, but the
person does not just see an object that, in fact, has a certain property;
he sees an object to have a certain property. That involves more than
seeing a colour, and there is a question whether the view of colour perceptions as simple "sensations" can account for it.

The sentence 'Jones sees a yellow lemon' appears to imply that there
is a yellow lemon that Jones sees. It is tempting to say that if there is
no yellow lemon there, then that cannot be what she sees. That implication would also explain how it is possible for someone to see a yellow lemon without seeing any yellow; what is seen is, in fact, a yellow
lemon whether it is seen to be yellow, or a lemon, or not. But it is also
possible, if rare, for someone to be said truly to see a yellow lemon
when there is, in fact, no yellow lemon near the person to be seen. A
hallucination or a hologram can provide just such an experience. That
can happen even if the person knows what is going on and does not believe that there is a yellow lemon where he sees one. It remains true
that the person sees a lemon (not a banana), and he sees it to be yellow
(not green). In such cases, the person typically, perhaps necessarily, sees
yellow and sees a lemon, despite the fact that there is no such thing,
and therefore no such yellow lemon, as the thing the person sees.

"Predicational" seeing also occurs in more familiar illusions. We can
sometimes see what is, in fact, a green lemon to be yellow, and see what
is, in fact, a white egg to be a lemon and to be yellow. But "predicational" seeing is not restricted to nonveridical seeing. It occurs in mundane, normal cases of seeing a coloured object in plain view in good
light. We do not simply see colour; we see objects to be coloured.

Perception is most useful to us when we see that something or other
is so—we see that a lemon on the table is yellow or that there is a yel-

low lemon on the table. This could be called "propositional" seeing; it is reported in a sentence with a sentential or propositional complement to the verb 'see'. In these cases, too, the perceiver typically sees yellow, sees a yellow lemon, and sees a lemon to be yellow. But again, that need not be so. It is possible to see that a certain object has a certain property without seeing an instance of that property or even seeing the object. You could see that there is a yellow lemon on the table by seeing something that reliably indicates that there is a yellow lemon there, but without seeing anything yellow at all. You can see that the Pope has been elected by seeing smoke coming from a chimney.

The relations among propositional seeing, predicational seeing, and seeing an instance of some property are obviously complex. The perceptual possibilities are rich and complicated. They are at least as rich as the enormous variety of English sentences that have ever been true which contain a main verb of perception and some mention of colour in the specification of what is perceived. It looks as if it would be courting trouble to speak without qualification of "a perception of yellow" or "an experience of yellow" or even "an experience of seeing something yellow", as if there were only one kind of thing it could be. That oversimplification would make it difficult to accommodate all the perceptual facts.

Some of the facts that any attempt to establish the unreality or "subjectivity" of the colours of things must account for can be expressed in English sentences such as these:

(1) Jones sees yellow.
(2) Jones sees something yellow.
(3) Jones sees something to be yellow.
(4) Jones sees a yellow lemon.
(5) Jones sees a lemon to be yellow.
(6) Jones sees that a lemon on the table is yellow.
(7) Jones sees that there is a yellow lemon on the table.

These all state facts of perception, but it is not only a matter of perception. The variety of thoughts we can think about colours and the colours of things is at least equally rich. And colour as it figures in perception is connected with colour as it figures in thoughts and beliefs. I believe that ripe lemons are yellow, and I can believe on a particular occasion that a lemon on the table is yellow. I can believe such things whether I am perceiving anything at the time or not. When I believe, with my eyes closed, that there is a yellow lemon on the table, what I believe to be so is just what I can see to be so if I open my eyes and see that there is a yellow lemon on the table. "Seeing is believing", we are told, and that must be propositional seeing. Propositional seeing can have the same content or "object" as believing. It can share its objects not only with believing but also with inquiring, hoping, fearing, and any other attitudes that take something with a truth value as their objects. We understand perception to be connected to other attitudes in these ways.

So we can add to the list of psychological facts to be explained such sentences as:

(8) Jones believes that there is a yellow lemon on the table.
(9) Jones hopes that there is a yellow lemon on the table.
(10) Jones wonders whether there is a yellow lemon on the table.

This is a ludicrously short list, given the huge variety of psychological facts, but it is enough to give us something simple and concrete to focus on.

We understand these and similar sentences. We know that many things like these involving colour are often true. Our conception of the world before we engage in philosophical reflection about it includes such facts of human perception of colour and thought and belief about the colours of things. The unmasking metaphysical project must understand and accept such facts and do justice to the differences and interconnections we recognize among them. The question is whether it can do that and still reach the metaphysical conclusion that objects are not really coloured or, if they are, that their colour is "subjective" or somehow depends on what we perceive.

Our understanding of each of these sample sentences is not independent of our understanding of the others. They are connected in their internal structure, so the different psychological facts they state if they are true are similarly interconnected. In (1), Jones is said to see a certain colour, in (2) that same colour is ascribed to the something Jones is said to see, and in (3) she is said to see something to be that colour. That same colour is ascribed in (4) to the lemon Jones is said to see, she is said to see a lemon to have that colour in (5), and in (6) and (7), she is said to see that a lemon on the table has that colour. In short, the word 'yellow' appears to function here as a predicate used to ascribe a property to something. If the belief reported in (8) is true, there is a yellow lemon on the table. Yellow in that case is a property of a lemon. If we ask what it is seen or believed to be a property of within the scope of Jones' seeings and believings as reported in sentences (2)–(8), the answer again would appear to be "a lemon", or at least "something".

I say "would appear" because whether these sentences can ultimately be read as related to one another in this straightforward way remains to be seen. But they must be understood as interconnected in some way or other. We understand what we perceive to be related in some way to what we can think about, believe, know, want, hope, fear, and so on. And what we can believe, know, want, and so on is, in general, what can be so in the world. It is perhaps obvious that perception is connected in some way with the rest of our mental life, given that perception is above all a way of getting information about the world. What we perceive is available and somehow put to use in thinking and believing and acting on the world around us. But the point is worth stressing. There must be some intelligible relation between what we perceive and what we think or believe.

The view that likens perceptions of colour to sensations with a certain distinctive character makes it difficult to understand these sample sentences. At the very least, it means that we cannot read them as related to one another in the most straightforward way. 'Jones sees yellow' would presumably report the occurrence of a "sensation" of yellow on that view. The word 'yellow' would serve to identify the kind of "sensation" Jones has, just as 'Jones feels a sharp pain' identifies another kind of sensation. It seems clear that 'yellow' cannot be read that way in sentences (8), (9), and (10). In 'There is a yellow lemon on the table', it is a predicate ascribed to a physical object. That sentence states what Jones is said to believe in (8), so it has the same role there. But what (8) says Jones believes to be so is just what (7) says she sees to be so, so it must have the same meaning there, too. Similarly for (6): 'Jones sees that a lemon on the table is yellow' attributes to Jones a perception which is veridical if 'There is a yellow lemon on the table' is true. And there again, 'yellow' is predicated of a physical object. The only way it could stand for a feature of a "sensation" in (1) and for a property of a physical object in (6)–(10), while retaining the same meaning throughout, would be if it stood for a property that can belong both to "sensations" and to physical objects. The analogy with sensations of pain would then have broken down.

To try to sustain the analogy and say that having a "sensation" of yellow is just like having a sensation of pain, except for the difference in the kind of sensation it is, we would have to distinguish the role of 'yellow' in reports of "sensations" from its role in sentences such as (6)–(10). It looks as if it would then be incoherent to think that a certain lemon is yellow in the sense of 'yellow' that it bears in 'Jones sees yellow', just as it is incoherent to think that a certain pin has a pain. What we feel when a pin divides our flesh—the pain, or the painfulness of the sensation—is not something we can intelligibly think is a feature or property of a pin or any other physical object. It is a feature or property of a sensation. To understand a perception or "sensation" of yellow in the same way would mean that yellow is simply a feature or property of the "sensation" we get, for example, when we are appropriately placed in good light before a ripe lemon. What we then see or "sense" would not be something we could intelligibly think is a feature or quality of a lemon or any other physical object.

This would not mean that the word 'yellow' as applied to physical objects is unintelligible. It would mean only that the word does not have the same meaning in all the other sample sentences as it does in characterizing a certain kind of "sensation" in sentences like (1). But then some account would be needed of its role or meaning in those other sentences and of how they are related to 'Jones sees yellow', so understood. Anyone who would unmask our perceptions of and beliefs about the colours of physical objects as illusory or in some sense "subjective" must at least acknowledge and have some understanding of those facts of perception and belief.

Descartes regarded both colours and pains as sensations or qualities of sensations. He thought colours are unintelligible, considered as qualities of physical objects. It was not just that thoughts about the colours of objects are never true; there was not even a coherent thought to the effect that a physical object is coloured. Given his view of colours as sensations, I think he was right to draw that conclusion. To think that a lemon is coloured would be as incoherent as thinking that a pin is painful, or has a pain. Descartes admitted that we do call physical objects coloured, but he thought that in doing so we are simply confused. We have not freed ourselves from certain "prejudices of youth" that continue to bedevil the mind.[4] Unfortunately, he never explained exactly what our confusion is, or how it is even possible for us to make it. That would be to explain the relation between "sensations" of colour and our thoughts and beliefs about the colours of objects.

One thing he thought we might be doing when we think that a lemon is yellow is to suppose that it somehow resembles our sensation of yellow. That is one way in which 'yellow' predicated of a physical object would mean something different from what it means when predicated of a "sensation". To call a "sensation" yellow is presumably not to say that it resembles a "sensation" of yellow. For Descartes, a resemblance between "sensations" and objects simply makes no sense, in part be-

---

4. Descartes, *Principles of Philosophy*, I, 71, in *The Philosophical Writing of Descartes*, vol. I (tr. and ed. J. Cottingham, R. Stoothoff, and D. Murdoch), Cambridge, 1985, pp. 218–219.

cause "mental" things like sensations are completely distinct from physical things like lemons.

But it is not strictly true that a sensation and a physical object can
have no properties at all in common. "Having begun to exist in the twen-
tieth century", for instance, might be true both of my current "sensation" of a lemon and of a lemon I see. The main trouble with the suggestion is rather that the mere idea of resemblance is too general. To
help in this case, it would have to be resemblance in a certain specific
respect. The thought would have to be that the lemon resembles the
"sensation" *in colour*. And it is just the thought of a physical object's
being coloured that the appeal to resemblance is supposed to explain
in the first place. If it is incoherent to think that an object is coloured
in the way that a "sensation" is coloured, then to think that an object
resembles a "sensation" in having the same colour would be incoherent as well.

When Locke denied that the colours we see are qualities of physical
objects, he put the point by saying that the "ideas" of colour that we
receive in perception do not "resemble" anything existing in the objects
around us. In this respect, ideas of so- called secondary qualities were
thought to differ from ideas of "primary" qualities like shape, size, motion, and the like.[5] This, too, might be taken to suggest that what we
think when we believe that the objects around us are coloured is that
they resemble in some way the "sensations" or "ideas" of colour that
we get in perception. If that were the real content of the thought 'The
lemon is yellow', then to deny that colours are qualities of physical objects would be to deny that there is any relevant resemblance between
our "ideas" of colour and the physical objects that cause them. We saw
that there is good reason to deny that.

But that cannot be Locke's reason for denying that objects are
coloured. In the case of the "primary" qualities, he said there *is* a "resemblance" between our "ideas" and the objects that cause them. He
meant that we get "ideas" of the shape, size, motion, and so on of objects in perception, and we are right in thinking that objects have shape,
size, motion, and so on. If in predicating an ovoid shape of a physical
object, we were really thinking that our "idea" of an ovoid shape resembles that object, and if there can be no relevant resemblance between "ideas" and physical objects, then our thought in that case would
also be false at best. But on Locke's view, our beliefs about the primary

---

5. Locke, *Human Understanding*, II, 8, xv (p. 137).

qualities of objects are often true. Predicating properties of physical objects therefore cannot be understood as simply asserting a resemblance between an "idea" and a physical object.[6]

Hume tried in a way to save the idea that the property we think belongs to an object when we think it is coloured is the same property that we find in our perceptions or "impressions" of colour. 'Yellow' could have the same meaning in sentence (1) and sentence (8) on that suggestion, even though it stands for a feature of an "impression" in (1). He thought we can take the properties of our "internal impressions" and somehow "transfer" them in thought to objects we think about. Colours, sounds, tastes, smells, and heat and cold, he thought, are all "nothing but impressions in the mind, deriv'd from the operation of external objects, and without any resemblance to the qualities of the objects".[7] In that respect, they are like a feeling produced in us by certain kinds of objects. But we can "transfer that feeling to the objects; as nothing is more usual than to apply to external bodies every internal sensation, which they occasion".[8] That is because:

> the mind has a great propensity to spread itself on external objects, and to conjoin with them any internal impressions, which they occasion, and which always make their appearance at the same time that these objects discover themselves to the senses.[9]

The objects "as they really stand in nature"[10] do not actually have the qualities we attribute to them in this way. We only mistakenly, but understandably, think they do. We have a "great propensity" to think that objects have many qualities that they do not really have.

---

6. A more innocuous understanding of Locke's view puts no special weight on the "resemblance" he speaks of between "ideas" or "sensations" and physical objects. To say that the "ideas" of the primary qualities of bodies "are Resemblances of them, and their Patterns do really exist in the Bodies themselves", but that in the case of secondary qualities "there is nothing like our Ideas, existing in the Bodies themselves", could just be a way of saying that bodies do have shape, size, motion, and the other primary qualities, but not colour, smell, taste, and other secondary qualities. Our "ideas" of the primary qualities are "ideas" of what is true of objects; our "ideas" or secondary qualities are not. There is a "resemblance" or correspondence between what we think and what is so in the first case but not in the second. The distinction expressed this way relies on the notion of the truth of what we think to be so but not on a "resemblance" between "ideas" and objects.

7. Hume, *Treatise*, p. 226.

8. D. Hume, *Enquiries concerning the Human Understanding and concerning the Principles of Morals* (ed. L. A. Selby-Bigge) Oxford, 1966, p. 78n.

9. Hume, *Treatise*, p. 167.

10. Hume, *Enquiries*, p. 294.

This suggestion does not take us very far. We cannot find in Hume, or anywhere else,[11] any account of how we could manage to form an intelligible thought that a physical object is coloured, given that colours are nothing but impressions or features of impressions in the mind. We are said to "transfer" something we find only in our "internal impressions" or "sensations", but we presumably do not "transfer" the internal impression itself to the object. We do not suppose that a pin that pricks us has a sensation of pain, and we do not think that a lemon we see has an impression of yellow. That really is nonsense. And even if we did think that, it would be a poor candidate for what we think when we think that a lemon is yellow.

It is not much better to say that what we "spread" onto the object and so mistakenly think belongs to it is not an impression but a feature or quality of an impression. It makes no sense to suppose that the painfulness that is a feature of our sensation of pain is a property of the pin that causes it. And if the yellowness of an impression of yellow is like the painfulness of a sensation of pain, it would make no sense to suppose that it is a quality of the lemon that causes it either. If the thought of a physical object's having properties of that kind is unintelligible, as the parallel with pain suggests that it is, we get no help in understanding how we nonetheless can have thoughts about the colours of objects by being told only that we have a "great propensity" to think them. How *could* we think that the painfulness of our sensation is somehow a property of a pin?

Neither the idea that we think physical objects resemble our colour "sensations" nor the idea that in thought we "transfer" qualities of our "sensations" onto the objects that cause them explains how what we think when we think physical objects are coloured is related to perceptions of colour understood simply as "sensations" with a certain distinctive character. But the problem they fail to solve is real, and they at least have the merit of trying to solve it. The problem is to explain the relation between perceptions of colour and thoughts about the colours of things. Putting it in terms of our sample sentences, how is the word 'yellow' as applied to perceptions or "sensations" in sentence (1) related to its use in sentences (8)–(10) about beliefs and thoughts about the colours of physical objects? On the view of perceptions of

---

11. I have discussed this idea of Hume's in my " 'Gilding or Staining' the World with 'Sentiments' and 'Phantasms'", *Hume Studies*, 1993. A similarly "projectionist" account is proposed in P. Boghossian and D. Velleman, "Colour as a Secondary Quality", *Mind*, 1989, and elsewhere.

colour as "sensations" with a certain distinctive character, the word has a different meaning in the different contexts. The question is what the connection is between them.

The problem is not restricted to thoughts about the colours of things. Propositional seeing shares its objects with thought and belief, so colour terms in perceptual sentences like (6) and (7) must function as the word 'yellow' does in (8)–(10), where it stands for a property of physical objects. A shift in the meaning of 'yellow' must therefore make its appearance earlier in the series of sentences, somewhere between sentences (1) and (5). But even in predicational seeing ('Jones sees a lemon to be yellow') and objectual seeing ('Jones sees a yellow lemon'), colour terms appear to stand for properties of physical objects. It is difficult to resist the conclusion that if there is a change in the meaning of 'yellow' it comes right near the beginning of the series of sentences, immediately after 'Jones sees yellow'. But the understanding of even that sentence cannot easily be severed from all the rest. It would seem to leave us with no way of accounting for the familiar fact of seeing an object with a certain colour.

Someone who sees a lemon on the table and sees it to be yellow can thereby see that a lemon on the table is yellow. In that case, the predicational seeing reported in (5) involves seeing an instance of that property that is also seen or thought to belong to a lemon in the propositional perception or thought that a lemon on the table is yellow. The property in that case is understood as a property of a physical object, so that is how it must be understood in (5) as well. If (4) 'Jones sees a yellow lemon' is true, but Jones does not see yellow or see a lemon to be yellow, the word 'yellow' in (4) clearly stands for a property of a lemon. If she does see yellow and sees a lemon to be yellow, then (5) is true, so 'yellow' again must stand for a property of a physical object in (4). But if Jones sees a lemon to be yellow, she sees something to be yellow, so (3) is true, and 'yellow' must mean the same there as it does in (4).

It is just possible, I suppose, to read 'Jones sees something yellow' as reporting the occurrence of a "sensation" of a certain distinctive kind. Seeing something yellow is a recognizable kind of experience we can have. But 'Jones sees something yellow' is also true if Jones sees something that is in fact yellow, whether she sees yellow or sees it to be yellow, or not. On that reading it is less plausibly taken to report a certain distinctive kind of visual "sensation". You can see something yellow in the dark or when it is bathed in blue light.

I think we have to conclude that if 'yellow' is taken to stand for a distinctive feature of a certain kind of "sensation" in 'Jones sees yellow', it cannot be understood to have that same meaning in any of the other sample sentences. At best, the only place it could have that meaning is in sentence (1). But even there it is difficult to understand 'yellow' in that way, given our understanding of the facts stated by the other sentences. When Jones sees a lemon to be yellow by seeing yellow and seeing it to be a property of a lemon, Jones sees yellow, so sentence (1) is true. But then the very property she sees is also the property she sees the lemon to have, and predicational seeing of that kind attributes to the seen object the same property that propositional seeing and thinking can attribute to an object. In each case, it is a property of a physical object. Without taking 'yellow' in sentence (1) to stand for a property that can belong to physical objects, we seem unable to understand the simplest normal cases of seeing a yellow lemon in good light right before our eyes. How would it be possible to see yellow and to see a lemon to be yellow, if seeing yellow were simply a matter of having a "sensation" with a certain distinctive character?

Many philosophers have held that perception is the source of thought: what we get through the senses is what determines the limits and so the possibility of thought, belief, and knowledge. That assumption ought to strike us as more surprising and more questionable than it apparently does, at least with respect to predicational and propositional perception. Surely someone could perceive something to have a certain property only if the thought of its having that property made sense to him, and he could perceive that something or other is so only if he could have the thought of its being so. If you weren't even capable of having the thought of something's being F or the thought that p, how could you ever perceive something to be F or perceive that p? If you could not, then what you can think would be what determines or limits the scope of what you can perceive; the possibility of thought would be what determines the possibility of perception.

Most seventeenth- and eighteenth-century philosophers (and a great many more recently as well)[12] denied that, or appeared to deny it, and said in effect that it is the other way around. Kant was not among them, but Locke and Berkeley and Hume certainly were and, at least with respect to colour, so was Descartes. That is no doubt partly because they all took nonpropositional perception to be basic, and they understood nonpropositional perception in a certain way. They thought of it as the occurrence of a certain kind of "sensation", and they thought the

---

12. The idea is perhaps still present in, for example, Christopher Peacocke's insistence that "Nothing is more fundamental to understanding the content of psychological states than sense experience" in his *Sense and Content*, Oxford, 1983, p. 4.

ability to think thoughts of certain kinds was not needed for the direct acquaintance that a "sensation" of colour gives us.

Those philosophers nonetheless spoke without hesitation about such things as perceptions or "sensations" of a round, red apple, or an ovoid, yellow lemon. There is no doubt that we do have such perceptions. The question is how they are possible if perceptions are nothing more than "sensations" with a certain distinctive character. What is in question is predicational perception. It is not just a matter of seeing roundness and seeing an apple, but of seeing an apple to be round or, in general, seeing an object to have certain properties. What does it take for us to have perceptions like that?

It is not enough to say that we see an object to have certain properties whenever several perceptions of properties are presented "together". For Berkeley, for example, a cherry "is nothing but a congeries of sensible impressions, or ideas perceived by various senses; which ideas are united into one thing (or have one name given them) by the mind; because they are observed to attend each other".[13] But having a "congeries" or collection of "sensible impressions" of several different properties is not the same as having a "sensation" of one thing that has all those properties, even if we always see all those properties together. We might always simultaneously see one small, square, yellow thing and another large, ovoid, green thing "together" in the same experience. We see instances of the properties of being yellow and being ovoid, and we see them together, but we do not see one thing to be both yellow and ovoid.

Locke thought that when we notice certain ideas to "go constantly together" we suppose them to "subsist" in some "Substratum" that holds them together. That does not seem to be true in general, for the reason just given. But even if it were, he admits that no one has any idea of what that "Substratum" is except "a Supposition of he knows not what support of such Qualities".[14] This could be just a way of saying that we simply have the idea of an object with certain qualities, without being able to explain it further, and that perception is typically of such objects and is predicational. That would mean that we see things to have certain qualities and that the qualities we see, we typically see to belong to objects. In that case, the qualities we see objects to have, including their colours, would be the very properties we can think and believe them to have. Seeing yellow, as reported in sentence (1), would

---

13. G. Berkeley, *Berkeley: Philosophical Works* (ed. M. Ayers), London, 1975, p. 197. I have reversed the order of the two sentences.

14. Locke, *Human Understanding*, II, 23, i–ii (p. 295).

be seeing a property which we can attribute to a physical object. It would not be simply having a "sensation" with a certain distinctive character.

The "sensation" view of perceptions of colour splits off perception of colour from what we think of as belonging to an object when we think of it as coloured. It also leaves predicational seeing at best completely mysterious. What we are aware of in colour perception cannot be the property we see an object to have when we see it to be coloured, but we do see colours, and see them to belong to physical objects.

The difficulty presents itself in another way if we try to generalize this conception of "sensations" of colour. If *all* perception were understood on the model of undergoing sensations of pain, as we have so far been supposing that colour perception might be, then whenever we perceived any property at all we would simply be having a "sensation" with a certain distinctive character. If that character that we perceive, like the pain that we feel, is not something it would be intelligible to think of as a property of a physical object, we could have no thoughts or beliefs about physical objects' having any of the properties that we perceive. Whatever properties we could intelligibly think of objects as having would have to be different from all the properties available to us in perception.

That would then be true even of the shapes and sizes and motions of things. If it made no sense to attribute to an object the very feature we see when we see colour, just as it makes no sense to attribute to an object the very feature we feel when we feel pain, because in each case we are just having a certain characteristic "sensation", so it would make no sense to attribute to an object the very feature we see when we see shape, or size, or motion, or any other perceivable property. In every case, we would just be undergoing certain characteristic "sensations".

That would mean that we could form no coherent thoughts or intelligible beliefs about any *perceived* or *perceivable* qualities of physical objects. We could make no sense of physical objects' having perceivable properties at all, just as we can make no sense of a pin having a pain or having that quality of painfulness that we find in some of our sensations. If a sentence like 'Jones sees something ovoid' simply reported the occurrence of a certain characteristic "sensation", as the sentence 'Jones sees something yellow' was said to do, then the word 'ovoid' could not have the same role or meaning in that sentence as it does in 'Jones sees an ovoid lemon', 'Jones believes that there is an ovoid lemon on the table', and 'There is an ovoid lemon on the table'. What is predicated of the physical object could not be the same property that figures in the perception.

Accepting this view of all perceptions without exception would leave us with no way of intelligibly ascribing any perceived feature to any object that is not a "sensation" or perception. The only perceived properties we could think about (if we could think at all) would be properties of nothing more than "sensations" or "ideas" that we receive in perception. Berkeley saw that implication of the view—and (alas) drew the conclusion that we can think of nothing that is not perceived, and nothing is ever perceived but ideas. Even without going that far, the view implies that if we do intelligibly ascribe certain properties to objects that are not "sensations", they are not properties we ever perceive, or perceive objects to have. The properties we can think of as belonging to objects could not be perceived, or perceived to belong to objects. This would separate all possible "objects" of thought from all possible "objects" of perception.

It seems undeniable that we do intelligibly ascribe certain properties to objects that are not "sensations" and that we also sometimes perceive objects to have those very properties. It follows that at least *some* perceptions are perceptions of properties, or of objects' having properties, that we can also think belong to objects in the independent world. Those perceptions are in that sense "intentional". They are perceptions *of* a certain property or thing, or perceptions *of* a thing's having a certain property. What we can perceive in that way, we can also believe to be true of certain objects. We can accordingly perceive *that* such and such is so. The "objects" or contents of such perceptions are also possible "objects" or contents of other psychological attitudes. What we can perceive overlaps in that way with what we can think.

The idea of a perception's or a thought's being "intentional" or having an "object" in this sense is not easy to define. I think we all understand it, insofar as we understand psychological sentences like those I have given. We know how such sentences function, and to that extent we understand the kinds of psychological facts they state when they are true. But there is no hope of defining the idea in equivalent but non-"intentional" terms.

We speak of a perception of yellow, or a perception or thought *of* a yellow lemon, and that does express what we mean, but the appearance of the word 'of' is not enough in itself to identify the intentionality of a perception or thought. A pain, which is a sensation with a certain distinctive character, can also be described in English as "a sensation of pain". But that is not the same 'of' as in 'a thought of pain' or 'a thought of a yellow lemon'. Nor, I believe, is it the same 'of' as in 'a perception of yellow' or 'a perception of a yellow lemon'.

A sensation of pain is just a painful sensation, in the same way that what can be described in English as "the city of Chicago" is just the city Chicago. A picture of Chicago, which is an object with certain perceptible properties, is also a picture *of* something. A name of Chicago, which is an inscription with a certain shape, is also a name *of* something. But the city of Chicago, which is a city, is not a city "of" something in that way. Nor, I think, is a sensation of pain, which is a sensation, a sensation "of" pain in that sense either.[15] The present point is that, unlike sensations of pain, at least some of our perceptions must be understood to be perceptions *of* something in the "intentional" sense. And if we ever ascribe perceivable properties to objects, as it seems we do, some of the properties we perceive must be properties which it also makes sense to think of as properties of physical objects. The analogy with sensations of pain cannot hold across the board for all perceptions.

A perception of shape, or of something's having a certain shape, appears to be an "intentional" perception in this sense. It also appears to be a perception of that very property that we also ascribe to a thing in the thought that the thing has a certain shape. The same intentional "object" is present for both perception and thought. It is true that shape terms like 'ovoid' and 'rectangular' can be defined in purely geometrical terms, but that is no bar to our also perceiving things to have those properties. If we perceive things to be ovoid, or rectangular, as we do, those geometrically defined properties are the very properties we perceive objects to have. The same property is both perceived and also intelligibly thought or believed to belong to an object. This, of course, does not mean that we always believe things to have the shapes we perceive them to have, that our beliefs about the shapes of things are never mistaken, or even that whenever we perceive something of a certain shape there is always an object in the appropriate place that has some shape or other. It means only that the shapes we perceive things to have are shapes we *can* also think or believe objects to have.

Understanding perceptions of colour as "intentional" in this way would seem to make it more difficult than it would be on the "sensation" view to reach the conclusion that physical objects are not really coloured or that the colour they have is somehow dependent on us. Or at least it would be more difficult if colours are thought of as properties that can be the object of both perception and thought—that the

---

15. Pains might be thought of as perceptions *of* damage or disturbance in the body. If so, they would be "intentional" perceptions *of* something. But they are not in that sense perceptions *of* pain.

colours we see are the very properties we think physical objects have when we think of them as coloured. I think it is no coincidence that the defence of the unreality or "subjectivity" of colour has been so closely associated with the traditional view that likens seeing colour to having sensations of pain.

To understand the perception of shape as "intentional", with the same intentional object available for both perception and thought, means that we can perceive something to be ovoid and also intelligibly think or believe it to be ovoid. But an intelligible thought is true or false, and if we think that a certain object is ovoid and that thought is true, the object is ovoid. So if perceptions of colour are "intentional" in the same way, and when someone sees yellow or sees an object to be yellow, the property he sees or sees the object to have is the very property we can also think or believe an object to have, then if such a thought is ever true, the object in question is yellow. So much the worse, it would seem, for the unreality of colour. If intelligible thoughts about the colours of objects are sometimes true, objects are coloured.

To reach the conclusion that physical objects are not coloured, then, or to defend the "subjectivity" of whatever colour objects can be thought to have, we must argue along one or the other of several distinct lines. If we hold that perceptions of colour or of the colour of an object are not simply "sensations" with a certain distinctive character but are "intentional" perceptions *of* something, the first question is what sorts of things they are perceptions of. Here there are two alternatives.

If the "objects" of colour perceptions are the same properties that can also be ascribed in thought and belief to physical objects, perception and thought involving colour would be directly connected. 'Jones sees yellow' would report the "intentional" perception of a certain property, and the word 'yellow' would stand for that same property in 'There is a yellow lemon on the table' and in all the other sample sentences. To reach the metaphysical conclusion of a colourless reality along this line, we would then have to argue that physical objects do not really have the colours we perceive and believe them to have. None of our perceptions of the colours of objects would be veridical, and none of our thoughts or beliefs about the colours of objects would ever be true, or true in reality. This could be called an "error" theory of the colours of things. It would deny that physical objects are coloured.

A second alternative would be to argue that although perceptions of colour are "intentional" perceptions of something, and even perceptions of properties, they are not perceptions of the same properties that it is intelligible to think of physical objects as having. 'Jones sees yellow' would report the perception of a certain property, but 'yellow' would not stand for that same property in all the other sample sentences. This would not necessarily mean that our thoughts and beliefs to the effect that objects are coloured are unintelligible, or even that they are false. It would mean only that, in thinking that physical objects are coloured, the properties we ascribe to those objects are not the properties we see when we see colours. Perception and thought involving colour would be less directly connected than on the first alternative.

This second strategy would require that we explain what our thoughts and beliefs to the effect that objects are coloured amount to, and how they are related to the colours we perceive. One way of doing that might be to say that in thinking of physical objects as coloured we are thinking only of what kinds of colour perceptions they would produce in certain kinds of perceivers under certain conditions. Such thoughts might be largely true, so it would be true that objects are coloured on such a view. Since the colours of objects would depend on what sorts of responses they would produce in certain perceiving subjects, this could be called a "subjectivist" theory of colour.

A similarly "subjectivist" theory would be the natural outcome of continuing to hold that perceptions of colour are "sensations" with a certain distinctive character. On that view, perceptions of colour would not be understood as having contents or "objects" in the intentional sense at all. They would not be perceptions *of* anything in that sense and so not perceptions of properties that are also intelligibly ascribable to physical objects. I have tried to identify some of the obscurities and difficulties in that view. But to persist with it would also require that we explain the connection between colour as it figures in perception and colour as it figures in our thoughts and beliefs about the colours of objects. Since the word 'yellow' would not have the same role or meaning in reporting the occurrence of a perception of colour as it does in the other sample sentences, the connection between them would have to be explained. Some coherent understanding of the acknowledged psychological facts of perception and belief is needed before any unmasking explanation can begin.

Pursuing one or the other of these different strands of argument is a minimal condition of success for the unmasking strategy. To reach a convincing negative or "subjectivist" conclusion down any one of these routes is a pretty tall order. I think it is fair to say that it is more than anyone who has embraced the unreality or subjectivity of colour has so far actually achieved.

6

Perceptions of Colour and
the Colours of Things

Whatever strategy we pursue to reach a philosophical conclusion about
the colours of things, we must start with some understanding of perceptions of colour and of what we believe when we believe that objects
are coloured. The psychological facts of perception and belief concerning the colours of things must be acknowledged, so the contents of those
perceptions and beliefs must be understood in some way. That requires
some account of the relation between the objects or contents of those
perceptions and the objects or contents of the beliefs. To understand
beliefs about the colours of physical objects as ascribing to those objects the very properties that we see when we see colours is to accept
what I call a direct connection between them. The word 'yellow' would
stand for the same property in each of our sample sentences.

It looks as if reaching a negative conclusion about the colours of things
on that assumption would mean that all our perceptions of the colours
of objects are illusory and all our beliefs about the colours of objects are
false. That might be too paradoxical to be believed. I will examine the
prospects of reaching that conclusion in that way in chapter 7.

It is perhaps better to begin with the other alternative, which sees an
indirect connection between the objects of perception and the objects
of thought concerning the colours of things. On that view, perceptions
of colour are not perceptions of the same properties that we ascribe to
physical objects in the thought that they are coloured. 'Yellow' would
not stand for the same property in each of our sample sentences. This

appears to leave room for the possibility that our beliefs about the colours of things are largely true, even though the colours we see are not properties of any physical objects. That conclusion, if it could be reached, would be less paradoxical than what the first alternative seems to offer.

This second alternative can take either of two forms, depending on how perceptions of colour are to be understood. To think of them as "sensations" with a certain distinctive character would not be to think of them as perceptions *of* anything, so not perceptions of the properties of anything. They would not be thought of as "intentional" perceptions at all, but simply as "sensations" or experiences of certain kinds that occur under certain conditions. But a *thought* of a coloured object is to be understood as "intentional". When we think of an object as coloured, we ascribe some property to it in thought. On this form of the indirect view, the property we ascribe is not what we are aware of in perceptions of colour. This is one way in which our thoughts about the colours of objects could be indirectly connected with perceptions of colour.

A form of indirect connection between the objects of perception and of thought is also possible on an "intentional" view of perceptions of colour. That would be to regard perceptions of colour as perceptions *of* something, even perceptions of the properties of something, but not of the same properties that we ascribe in thought to physical objects. The colours we see on that kind of view might be nothing more than seen instances of colour properties, or perhaps seen properties of things that are seen (or "directly seen"), such as "sense data", or two-dimensional visual patches, or areas of one's "visual field". But if those seen properties could not be thought of as belonging to physical objects, what we ascribe to objects in our thoughts that they are coloured would be different from those properties that are seen. The word 'yellow' would not stand for the same property in each of our sample sentences on this conception of the objects of colour perception either.

A metaphysical project that endorses either form of such an indirect connection must explain the contents of our psychological attitudes towards colours and the colours of things. It must explain how the role of colour words in reports of perception is related to their role in ascribing colours to physical objects. By far the most promising way of trying to connect the two is to appeal once again to an alleged parallel with sensations of pain. In this case, it is a parallel with the connection between sensations of pain and our thoughts and beliefs about the objects that cause them.

A thumbscrew can be said to be a painful instrument. The sensation we get from putting it on and twisting it tight is a painful sensation.

But the word 'painful' obviously does not denote the same property in both of those sentences. What is said to be true of the thumbscrew is not that it has that feature which serves to identify a sensation as a painful sensation. What is true of the thumbscrew is, roughly, that some sentient beings get painful sensations if it is attached to them in certain ways. The suggested parallel is that something similar is true of those objects we regard as yellow: some sentient beings get perceptions of yellow if those objects are placed before them under certain conditions. If that were what we are saying of an object when we say it is yellow, the word 'yellow' obviously would not denote the same property in both applications. What it means in reports of perceptions would differ from what it means when predicated of a physical object. An object thought of as yellow would not be thought to have that feature that serves to identify a perception as a perception or "sensation" of yellow. But still, it would make perfect sense to say and think that an object is yellow, just as it makes sense to speak of a painful instrument. And that thought, so understood, could often be true.

This way of understanding our thoughts and beliefs about the colours of things would enable us to hold that the colours we *perceive* belong to nothing in the independent world. Depending on how perceptions of colour are understood, perceived colours would be either only features of our "sensations", or only properties of things that we see (or "directly see") under certain conditions, not including physical objects. What we call *the colour of an object* on this alternative could be nothing more than the object's disposition or capacity to produce certain perceptions of colour in sentient beings under certain conditions.

An object's capacities need not always, or perhaps ever, be exercised. Just as a thumbscrew remains a painful instrument even when it is not in use, so an object can be coloured in this sense when it is not actually producing any perceptions of colour, or even if it never produces any at all. It is a matter only of possible perceptions of colour—of whether the appropriate perceptions *would* occur under certain conditions. They are not expected to occur in sentient beings under all conditions—not in total darkness, for example, and not even in good light in beings whose eyes are closed or otherwise do not function properly. But on this view, the occurrence of perceptions of colour when the appropriate conditions are fulfilled would be essential to an object's being coloured, just as the occurrence of sensations of pain under the appropriate circumstances is essential to an object's being a painful instrument.

We know in rough general terms how human beings must be equipped and what the conditions must be like for them to perceive the colours of objects placed before them. It is certainly much more complicated with colours than it is with thumbscrews and sensations of pain, but even without being able to specify the details precisely, we have a pretty good conception of the general conditions of reliable colour perception. We know that the perceivers have to be more or less normal human perceivers functioning more or less normally. They have to be facing with eyes open an object that is within viewing distance, with sufficient illumination, no opaque object intervening, no coloured lights shining on the object, and so on. Under those conditions, such perceivers will normally get perceptions of the colour of the object that stands in that position. The present suggestion is not simply to remind us of all this knowledge but to put it to work in giving an explanation of what it is for an object to be coloured, or what we mean or what we believe when we predicate colour of a physical object.

To use this knowledge to express the conditions for an object's being yellow, for instance, we might begin with something like this:

> x is yellow if and only if normal human perceivers standing in certain relations R to x in certain kinds of perceptual circumstances C would get perceptions of yellow.

This is obviously only a general schema of an account as it stands. To give it determinate content, what is meant by 'normal human perceivers' would have to be explained, and the relations of orientation R and the surrounding conditions C would have to be specified concretely. There are different ways of making these specifications, and, as we shall see, the differences matter. But the suggestion is that with some such details filled in, a statement like this can tell us what it is for an object to be yellow, and so what our thoughts or beliefs about objects' being yellow amount to, and so in that sense what 'x is yellow' means, said of a physical object. I will call a fully specified version of a statement like this "the biconditional about yellow things". The suggestion is that this holds for colours of objects in general: there is a corresponding biconditional for each colour.

Many philosophers have offered an account along these lines as what they call an "analysis" of the colours of things. But there is considerable obscurity about what exactly a philosophical "analysis" of something is supposed to be. Many in the recent past who would have called themselves "analytic" philosophers thought they knew what a successful "analysis" would be, even if they had trouble coming up with many that were both interesting and correct. A successful "analysis" was said to issue in an "analytic" statement, true by virtue of meaning alone, which accordingly served to state or exhibit the meanings of certain of its terms, or the components of certain of its constituent concepts. Our knowledge of such meanings or concepts was said to be *a priori*, independent of all experience, even if our acquisition and possession of the concepts in question were not.

It has proven difficult to defend, or even understand, the general theory of *a priori* knowledge on which this conception of the "analytic" task of philosophy was based, and no reasonably satisfactory account of the special character of "analytic" truth has ever been given. Few today would explicitly defend it. But philosophers continue to offer what they call "analyses". What is a philosophical "analysis" of something supposed to be? Is it something specific and identifiable as such, or is the word 'analysis' now applied to virtually all attempts to understand anything? The question in this case is what the claim to have "analyzed" the colours of things amounts to. What is the suggested account trying to do?

The present suggestion is meant to explain the content of our thoughts about the colours of objects. It obviously does not purport to tell us in general what colour is or what the colour words mean wherever they appear. The word 'yellow' remains on both sides of the biconditional about yellow things; it is not eliminated. That is as it should be, on the assumption of an indirect connection between the objects of perception and the contents of our thoughts about the colours of things. The left-hand side of the biconditional about yellow things is restricted to predications of yellow to physical objects. It is meant to tell us only what an object's being yellow is, or the meaning of the phrase 'x is yellow', when 'x' stands for a physical object. That is how it will explain the link between perceptions of colour and our understanding of and thoughts about the colours of objects.

The colour of a physical object on this view is to be understood as a power or disposition the object has to produce perceptions of certain kinds in certain circumstances. Colour terms are used in specifying the kinds of perception in question, but the proposed "analysis" obviously cannot be applied in turn to colour terms as they occur in those specifications. The yellowness of a "sensation", or a perception's being a perception of yellow, is not a matter of its having the power to produce perceptions of a certain kind. The colour terms used to identify different kinds of perceptions are left unanalyzed or unexplained by the biconditional.

But still, the suggestion can be seen as taking a big step in the direction of a fully general understanding of colour. It would explain attributions of colour to physical objects solely in terms of the objects' dispositions to produce certain kinds of perceptions. That would be a form of reduction, and if it worked it would be a real advance. It would reduce what still needs to be explained to perceptions of colour alone. If we could understand what perceptions of colour are and how they differ from one another, and if we could identify them and the differences among them, independently of accepting any filled-in biconditional of this form, we might have all we need for understanding what it is for an object to be coloured, and so what our thoughts and beliefs about the colours of objects amount to and how their contents are related to the colours we perceive.

The colour of an object on this view is a different property from what we see when we see colour. The colour of a physical object is something relational, not a categorical feature that an object possesses independently of all possible human reactions to it. It is in that sense that on this view colour is something "subjective" or dependent on or relative to human or other sentient responses. The view does not imply that objects in the world are not coloured or that the only place for colour in the world is as something perceived or as a feature of a "sensation". Nor would there have to be systematic error or illusion involved in our beliefs about the colours of things. On the contrary: if the biconditional about yellow things does tell us what it is for an object to be yellow or what we believe when we believe that an object is yellow, and if what it says is in fact true of some objects in the independent world, then our beliefs about the colours of things would often be true. Many objects would be yellow.

This view would provide a way of retaining the commonsense belief that objects are coloured, then, while holding that colour is something "subjective" or dependent on us, and in two different ways. The colours we perceive would not be properties of anything in the world independently of us, no matter which way perceptions of colour are understood. If they are thought of as nonintentional "sensations", perceived colours would be simply distinctive features of such "sensations", just as the pain of a pinprick is a feature of a certain distinctive kind of sensation. Pains are subjective in the sense of depending for their existence on the existence of experiencing subjects; if no experiencing subjects existed, there would be no pains. Perceived colour would be subjective in the same way. If there were no perceivers, there would be no perceived colours.

If perceptions of colour are understood as intentional, but what they are perceptions of are properties only of things seen (or "directly" seen) and not properties of physical objects, perceived colour would again be subjective. It would be a property only of things that depend for their existence on being perceived. If there were no perceiving subjects, there would be no such things, and so no perceived properties of such things, and so no perceived colour in that sense. On either view of perceptions, all perceived colour would be something subjective.

The colour of an object, which on this view is a different property from colour that is perceived, is also "subjective", but in a different way. What colour an object is depends on the character of normal human perceivers' responses to the object. Specification of the colour of an object in a biconditional of this kind makes essential reference to perceptions of colour by certain kinds of perceivers. An object's being coloured does not require the existence of any actual perceivers or perceptions of colour, but it does depend on what kinds of perceptions certain kinds of perceiving subjects *would* get from it. On this view, an object does not have a colour independently of what is (perhaps only conditionally) true of human perceivers and their perceptions.

This seems to me a sufficiently robust version of "subjectivism" to deserve the name. There would be a significant human dependence or relativity involved both in the colours we perceive and in the colours of physical objects. Statements about colour would not be true or false independently of what is true of human beings. But it does not matter much what label we use. What matters is the contrast that this kind of view draws between the colours of objects on the one hand and their shape, size, motion, and other "primary" qualities on the other. The shapes of objects are not to be similarly understood as relational properties in the specification of which there is an essential reference to human perceptions of shape. An object's being ovoid is not to be a matter of its having a disposition to produce perceptions of something ovoid in experiencing subjects. Even if no perceptions at all would ever occur in the presence of an ovoid object under any circumstances, or if some perceptions would occur but they would not be perceptions of something ovoid, the object in question could still be ovoid. Thoughts and beliefs about the shapes and other "primary" qualities of objects are to be true or false independently of everything that is (perhaps even only conditionally) true of experiencing subjects and their perceptions.

The intended distinction between these "primary" qualities and such "secondary" qualities as colour is enough to give appropriate sense to the idea that colour is something subjective in a way those other properties are not. Truths about the colours of things are said to depend on perceivers in a way that truths about the shapes and other "primary" qualities of objects do not.

I do not mean to suggest that adopting this view of colours *requires* that one take a contrasting view about shapes, sizes, motions, and so on. It is, of course, possible to hold that the truth or falsity of everything we can think or believe about objects is dependent on possible human perceptions. That would be a completely general form of idealism or phenomenalism. It says, in effect, that nothing is fully independent of human perceivers and their responses; there is no completely independent reality at all. That theory faces great difficulties of its own, which are well worth going into. I am not going into them here. Such a completely general subjectivist theory is not part of the metaphysical project we are considering.

We are pursuing the project of distinguishing, among all the things we believe, between those which represent the world as it is independently of anything that is true about us, and those which in one way or another depend on us or our reactions. The view of colour we are now considering is an attempt to place colour and the colours of things on what I think there is good reason to call the "subjective" side of that dividing line, while leaving a considerable body of truth on the other side of the line to represent the world as it is fully independently of us. The goal is to preserve a rich world of independent fact in which the colours of things, but not all the properties of things, are shown to depend on the effects those things would produce in human subjects. The basis and prospects of some such metaphysical distinction are what is at stake. The question is whether and how this view of colour can be defended without holding that everything else is subjective as well.

Whether this view of colour can advance that project depends in large part on what an "analysis" of the colour of an object along these lines is supposed to be. How is it to be shown that the biconditional about yellow things tells us what it is for an object to be yellow, or what we believe when we believe that an object is yellow, or what 'x is yellow' means when said of an object? What would such a biconditional have to be like in order to do that? The first thing to notice is that it would not be enough for the biconditional simply to be true. When filled in with the appropriate specifications, the biconditional about yellow things probably is, in fact, true. What it says is that if there is a yellow object in a certain relation to normal human perceivers in certain kinds of perceptual circumstances, then those humans will get perceptions of yellow; and, in the other direction, if normal human perceivers get perceptions of yellow when they are in that relation to a certain object in those circumstances, then that object is yellow.

That is probably true, as a matter of fact. That seems to me, roughly speaking, just the way things are. But that truth does not reveal anything we could call the "subjectivity" of the yellow of an object or the dependence of its colour on the kinds of perceptions it would produce. If it did, it would also be true that being ovoid or being rectangular or having other so-called primary qualities is subjective or dependent on perceptions in the same way. A biconditional of that same form is true when 'ovoid' or 'rectangular' is substituted for 'yellow'. As things are, if there is an ovoid object in a certain relation to normal human perceivers in certain kinds of perceptual circumstances, then those perceivers will get perceptions of something ovoid, and if normal human perceivers get perceptions of something ovoid when they are in that relation to a certain object in those circumstances, then that object is ovoid. The truth of such biconditionals therefore cannot be taken as sufficient to "analyze" what being yellow or being ovoid is or consists in or amounts to. Their truth alone does not support any distinction between the "primary" and "secondary" qualities of objects.

As they stand, biconditionals like this simply state a relation between certain kinds of objects and normal humans' perceptions in certain kinds of circumstances: a relation between yellow things and human perceptions of yellow in the one case, and between ovoid things and human perceptions of something ovoid in the other. And it is the same relation in each case. There are comparable truths about a great many other observable matters of fact. If x is an elephant, for example, then normal human perceivers in a certain relation to x in certain kinds of perceptual circumstances will get perceptions of an elephant; and if normal human perceivers get perceptions of an elephant when they are in that relation to an object x in those circumstances, then x is an elephant. But that alone does not show that what it is to be an elephant is nothing more than being disposed to produce perceptions of certain kinds in human perceivers, or that being an elephant is in any way subjective or depends on the possible occurrence of human perceptions of certain kinds. Only a completely general idealism or phenomenalism would imply that. That is not to say that objects do not have the dispositions expressed in all such biconditionals. They do, if the biconditionals are true. The point is that their truth alone is not enough to express a subjectivist view of the property mentioned on the left-hand side of such biconditionals.

How then must the biconditional about yellow things be understood, or what must be added to it, to imply that an object's being yellow is dispositional and accordingly subjective in a way that its being ovoid or its being an elephant is not? It is not enough for it to tell us only what is, in fact, true of yellow objects. It should reveal what in some sense *must* be true of yellow objects. It is meant to tell us (as it is sometimes expressed) "what it is" for an object to be yellow, or what is "essential" to its being yellow, or what a thing's being yellow "consists in", in the sense of what 'x is yellow' means when said of an object or what we believe when we believe that an object is yellow.

These different expressions of the point of the "analysis" are perhaps not all equivalent, but each is to be understood as involving some claim of necessity between the colour of an object and its disposition. Although ovoid objects and human perceptions of something ovoid are perhaps, in fact, related as stated in the biconditional about ovoid things, the world presumably could have been otherwise in that case. The same is true of elephants. With our thoughts about the colours of things, by contrast, the idea is that there is some kind of *necessary* connection between an object's being coloured and human perceptions of colour.

To evaluate this suggestion, we have to ask whether, or in what way, the relation specified in the biconditional about yellow things holds necessarily. Even if it is, in fact, true as it stands, *could* things have been otherwise? The question is difficult and complex. For one thing, it is not easy to determine whether something that is true is necessarily true. When it is not a matter of demonstrative proof, the best we can do is to get as clear an understanding of the truth in question as we can and then try to determine whether, on that understanding, its opposite is really impossible. There is again no foolproof method for doing that.

Furthermore, to understand the proposal in this case, we need some understanding of what perceptions of yellow are. They might be understood as simply "sensations" with a certain distinctive character, or as "intentional" perceptions of certain properties, but not properties of physical objects. On either understanding, we need some way to identify the perceptions in question. That requires some way either to identify the distinctive kind of "sensation" or to identify the distinctive property that is seen. This is a necessary condition of success for this kind of view. It turns out to be difficult to fulfill it in a way that supports the unreality or the subjectivity of the colours of things.[1] Only with some such independent identification of the relevant perceptions will we have specified the conditions mentioned on the right-hand side of the biconditional in such a way as to evaluate whether it holds necessarily and expresses a subjectivist view of an object's colour. Whether it does depends as well on how the relevant perceivers, conditions, and

---

1. I argue in chapter 7 that the condition cannot be fulfilled, so an "error" theory of the unreality of colour cannot consistently be reached. If that is correct, dispositional theories also fail, since they, too, require independent specification of the relevant perceptions. For most of this chapter, I proceed on the assumption that the condition can be met.

circumstances are specified. There are many different possibilities, with different consequences in each case.

Nonetheless, keeping all these reservations and qualifications in mind, I think the question of the necessity of the biconditional about yellow things can be answered about as firmly as any such questions about possibility and necessity can ever be answered. I think we can see that there is no biconditional of this kind in the offing that is both necessarily true and expresses an appropriately subjectivist view of colour. Understanding perceptions of yellow in either way, but in either case as independently identifiable, as a dispositionalist view is constrained to understand them, it is not necessarily true that perceptions of yellow would occur, or would occur only, in the presence of yellow objects. It is possible for things to have been otherwise.

To conceive of the possibilities I have in mind, think first of all the yellow objects there have ever been, or even all the ripe lemons. Keeping your mind fixed on those yellow lemons, think of things that are not true now but could have been true in the world at large, or could have been true of human beings, which would have had no effect on those lemons but would have meant that normal human beings would not get perceptions of yellow when they stood to them in the relations stated in the biconditional. Suppose that lemons had been just as they are now—they grow and get ripe and turn yellow in the sun—but human beings and their perceptual mechanisms had been different in ways that are independent of the colour of those lemons.

To begin to get a feel for the possibilities I have in mind, suppose first that human beings had been just as they are now except for never having developed eyes. Then whatever normal human perceivers were like in other ways, they would not get perceptions of yellow when they stood in the specified relations to those yellow lemons. Now suppose normal human beings had eyes that were so constructed that perceivers normally got only perceptions of blue from those yellow lemons, and perceptions of yellow only from objects that are blue. Human perceivers who are normal in those circumstances would obviously be different from the normal human perceivers now on earth. But in conceiving of them and their differences from us, we do not have to suppose that those ripe lemons would be anything but yellow. We can also conceive of human perceivers with perceptual mechanisms in every way just as ours are now who live in a world with different laws of nature from ours. There could be such perceivers who, when standing in the specified relations to yellow lemons, would get perceptions of blue and who would get perceptions of yellow in the presence of things that are blue. None of this is true in the world as it is, but if any of it is even so much as possible, as it seems to be, it is not *necessarily* true that an object is yellow if and only if normal human perceivers standing in the stated relation to that object in the specified kinds of perceptual circumstances would get perceptions of yellow. We recognize that things could have been otherwise.

The contingency of the relation between yellow objects and perceptions of yellow seems unavoidable if perceptions of yellow are understood as a dispositionalist view is constrained to understand them. They must be identifiable independently of ascribing colour to any physical objects. Understanding perceptions of colour as "sensations" with a certain distinctive character, on the model of the traditional understanding of pains, would require that a "sensation's" having a certain character, or being of a certain type, is to be determined fully independently of its origin or surroundings. It would be a question simply of the character of the "sensation". That is one thing that we saw makes it difficult to understand what "sensations" of colour are, or whether there are any. It is doubtful that we understand even pains in the way that the traditional view understands them. But if we do, we must concede that it could have been true that a human being feels no pain when a pin is stuck into a finger, and that what we now in fact feel under those conditions is felt instead when a feather is drawn slowly along the skin of the upper arm. If feelings of pain can, in conception if not in fact, be separated from their usual causes and conditions in this way, so, too, can perceptions of yellow, thought of on this model of sensations of pain.

That is what leaves it always possible for sensations identified only as possessing a certain distinctive character to have occurred in human beings in circumstances different from those in which they, in fact, occur now. So perceptions of yellow, understood in that way, are the sort of thing that *could* have occurred in normal human beings standing in the stated relations to blue objects—or, for that matter, in the presence of no objects at all. And the perceptions normal perceivers standardly got in the presence of yellow objects could have been perceptions of blue, understood simply as "sensations" of a different kind. But in conceiving of perceivers' "sensations" having been different in those ways, we can continue to conceive of all the ripe lemons in that world as yellow. If the "sensations" that normal perceivers standardly got in the presence of them were not perceptions of yellow, then the biconditional that holds of yellow things in this world would not be true under those circumstances. It is at best contingently, and not necessarily, true.

Thinking of perceptions of colour as "sensations" with a certain distinctive character is not the only way to render the biconditional about yellow things contingent, and not necessarily true. On an "intentional" view that distinguishes perceptions of yellow from perceptions of other kinds only in terms of what they are perceptions of, the biconditional is also contingent, as long as it assumes what I have called an indirect connection between the objects of perception and of thought. On that assumption, what is seen in a perception of yellow is not what is ascribed to a physical object in the thought that it is yellow. If we suppose further, as a dispositional theory must, that the property seen in a perception of yellow is identified independently of specifying the colour of any physical objects that typically produce such perceptions, then it will be *possible* for perceptions of that property to be produced under the specified conditions by objects that are not yellow.

The dispositional view requires that the perceptions of yellow it speaks about be independently identified, even if the perceptions are understood as having certain "intentional" objects or contents. But if we did manage to identify a class of perceptions of yellow in that way, we could recognize that it is possible for them to be produced in normal perceivers by objects other than the kinds of objects that actually produce perceptions of that kind as things are now. There could be normal human perceivers with perceptual mechanisms different from ours in certain ways who would get perceptions of that kind from objects that are blue and would get perceptions of a different seen colour from objects that are yellow. And if the laws of nature had been different in certain ways, there could be normal human perceivers physiologically just like us who would get those perceptions identified as perceptions of yellow from objects that are blue. If that is possible, then perceptions of yellow, understood as "intentional", but as identifiable as such independently of specifying the colour of any physical object, *could* have standardly arisen in normal human perceivers standing in the stated relations to objects that are not yellow. If that is so in general, there is no necessary connection between the property seen in perceptions of colour, so understood, and the colours of the physical objects that produce them.

That might not be so on certain other ways of understanding perceptions of colour. For instance, if perceptions of yellow are identified only as perceptions of whatever colour normal perceivers perceive in the specified circumstances in the presence of an object that is yellow, the biconditional about yellow things would appear to be necessarily true. Even on the view of perceptions of yellow as "sensations" with a certain distinctive character, the biconditional would appear to be necessarily true if the distinctive character of the "sensations" in question is that they would be produced in the specified circumstances by objects that are yellow.[2] On either way of understanding perceptions of colour, the connection between perceptions or "sensations" of a certain colour and the colour of the objects that produce them could not then come apart.

Although this might serve to secure the necessity of the biconditional about yellow things, it would provide no defence of a subjectivist or dispositionalist view of the colours of objects. When the biconditional is shown in this way to be necessarily true, our acceptance of that necessity depends on a prior understanding of an object's being yellow. It does not explain an object's being yellow as its being disposed to produce perceptions of certain kinds; it explains what kinds of colour perceptions an object is disposed to produce by reference to the object's colour. That seems to me, in fact, much closer to the way we actually understand and identify perceptions of colour—or perceptions in general, for that matter. But it does not help explain what it is for an object to be coloured in the way the original dispositional suggestion was meant to do.

This shows that a subjectivist or dispositionalist view of the colours of objects is not established simply by finding some biconditional or other of this kind that is necessarily true. It depends on how that necessity is to be secured, or explained. For instance, normal human perceivers might be identified as those who would get perceptions of yellow in the specified conditions from objects that are yellow. That would make the biconditional about yellow things necessarily true. Another way in which the connection between perceptions of yellow and yellow objects could not break down is if the optimal conditions and circumstances for perceiving the colours of things were specified as those in which perceivers independently identified as normal would get perceptions of yellow from objects that are yellow. But neither of those ways of securing the necessity of the biconditional would show that the colours of objects depend on what kinds of perceptions would be produced in certain specified perceivers under specified conditions. They would not explain what it is for an object to be coloured in terms of the kinds of perceptions it is disposed to produce.

---

2. Strictly speaking, even this would be too weak as it stands, since yellow objects would produce many different kinds of "sensations", even perhaps other visual "sensations", in the specified circumstances, for example, "sensations" of shape. It would have to be added that the "sensations" in question are *colour* "sensations". That again raises the problem of how colour can be a property of a "sensation", understood non-"intentionally".

A defence of a subjectivist view of the contents of our thoughts about an object's colour requires that the conditions under which the right-hand side of the biconditional is true must be specified independently of any understanding of the left-hand side. The content of 'x is yellow', said of an object, is what is to be explained. And it can be explained in accordance with this kind of theory only by a prior and so independent specification of the object's disposition to produce perceptions of certain kinds in certain kinds of perceivers.

This is one thing that the success of a subjectivist or dispositional view of an object's colour turns on. To express the dependence of an object's colour on the kinds of perceptions it would produce under certain conditions, the relevant perceptions must be identifiable as such, and normal human perceivers and the optimal conditions of perception must be specifiable as such, independently of any appeal to the colours of objects. Assuming an indirect connection between the objects of perceptions of colour and of thoughts about the colours of objects, as we have been doing, is what makes it seem possible to fulfill those conditions. But in identifying perceptions of yellow in that way, whether we think of them as "sensations" or as "intentional" perceptions of a certain perceivable property, I think we find the biconditional about yellow things always to be at best contingently, but not necessarily, true. Once perceptions of yellow are identified or fixed independently of any appeal to the colour of an object, we will always be able to conceive of an object that is yellow, and a way the world could have been, such that, if the world were that way, that yellow object would not be disposed to produce perceptions of the kind identified as perceptions of yellow in normal human perceivers under the specified conditions. How the world could have been with respect to an object's disposition to produce perceptions of that kind would not be decisive for what colour that object is.

That is the way it is with the shape of an object. Even if a corresponding biconditional about ovoid objects is true as things are, we understand an object's being ovoid so that if in some possible circumstances normal human perceivers would not get perceptions of something ovoid when standing in the stated relation to an object, the object could still be ovoid. And if they standardly got perceptions of something ovoid in the stated relation to certain kinds of objects, those objects could still fail to be ovoid. The same holds for elephants. We do not regard the biconditionals as necessarily true in those cases. Our judgement of their contingency amounts to rejection of a dispositional or subjectivist view of an object's being ovoid, or of its being an elephant, even granting the biconditionals' truth.

I think it is the same with colours. Our understanding of the colours of objects tolerates the possibility of an object's being a certain colour even though it would not produce perceptions of that colour in human perceivers if the world were different in certain ways. How the world could have been with respect to objects' dispositions to produce perceptions of certain kinds in certain kinds of conditions is not decisive for what colours those objects are. That seems undeniable when the colour perceptions in question are identified independently of specifying the color of any physical object. Objects which in certain circumstances are disposed to produce a certain kind of colour perception in suitably placed human perceivers could be any one of many different colours.

I think the same is true even with perceptions of colour identified as I think we do, in fact, identify them—in terms of the colours of the objects that they are perceptions of. We know what property perceptions of yellow are perceptions of. If we then consider perceptions of yellow, and keep that kind of perception fixed, we have a definite class of perceptions in mind. If we then ask whether there are any possible circumstances in which perceptions of that kind would be standardly produced in normal human perceivers standing in the specified relations to objects that are not yellow, I think we must concede that there are such possible circumstances.

This concession might seem not to threaten a subjectivist dispositional view of the colours of things because of a suggested parallel between 'yellow' and certain obviously dispositional terms. In judging that a certain instrument is painful, we recognize that it might not cause pain to beings who differ from us in certain ways, or to beings just like us who live in very different circumstances. And objects that cause no pain at all to human beings as they are might be very painful to differently constituted humans, or to beings just like us in very different circumstances. The same holds for many other dispositional terms true of objects in our world, such as 'poisonous', 'nutritious', and 'dangerous'. Something that is poisonous to human beings as things are now might not be poisonous to rats as things are now, and not poisonous to humans with a different digestive system from ours or to beings like us in a world very different from ours. There is a certain relativity in the meaning of such terms. They refer to an object's disposition to produce effects only on certain things and only in certain possible circumstances, not all.

This can encourage the idea that, in conceiving of circumstances in which human perceivers of a certain kind would get perceptions of yellow from objects we think of as not yellow, we are simply conceiving of circumstances in which those objects would be, as we might say, "yellow to those other people" but "not yellow to us". And objects we think of as yellow that would not give other normal perceivers in other circumstances perceptions of yellow might accordingly be described as "not yellow to them" but "yellow to us". The same parochialism or relativity to us that is present in some dispositional terms might seem to be present in the colour terms we apply to objects.

I do not think this parallel holds. It is true that there is a hidden relativity in terms like 'poisonous', 'nutritious', and 'dangerous', but this talk of "yellow to us" and "not yellow to those others" does not function in the same way. And to understand the relativity on the assumption that perceptions of colour are identified as such independently of specifying the colour of any physical object would undermine, rather than support, a subjectivist dispositional view of an object's colour.

Saying that certain objects are "yellow to us" but "not yellow to them" could mean several different things. It might mean that we believe the objects are yellow and those other humans do not. But that shows no relativity in what we believe or in what those others do not believe. We believe the objects are yellow; those others do not believe it. On that reading, there is no parallel with 'painful' or 'poisonous'. 'Painful (or poisonous) to us but not them' does not mean 'believed by us but not by them to be painful (or poisonous)'. It is *what* is believed that is supposed to carry the implicit relativity: painful or poisonous to whom?

Someone who says that certain objects are "yellow to us but not yellow to them" is more likely to mean that the objects *look* yellow to us but do not *look* yellow to those other perceivers. If 'looks' here means that we are inclined to believe that the objects are yellow but those others are not, once again there is no relativity in the content of the belief. But if "looks yellow to us but not to them" is taken to refer to perceptual experience, as it seems most plausible to do, it would mean that the same objects give us but not those other perceivers perceptions of yellow. That would be genuine relativity, but it does not support a subjectivist dispositional theory of the colours of things.

This kind of relativity is precisely what I claimed is possible with respect to yellow objects and perceptions of yellow, if those perceptions are identified as such independently of specifying the colour of any physical object. Human perceivers different from us in certain ways, or beings just like us in a world with different laws of nature, could fail to get perceptions of yellow, so understood, from objects that are yellow. If they did not get perceptions of yellow from them, those objects presumably would not look yellow to those perceivers in those circumstances. The objects would be in that sense "not yellow to those humans", but they would still be yellow. That is at least a possibility. But if that is possible, the biconditional about yellow things is, at best, contingently, not necessarily, true.

It is perhaps tempting to put aside all these possibilities of different perceivers and different perceptions and try to secure the relativity of the colours of things to us as we are right now. With perceptions of colour thought of either as "sensations" or as "intentional" perceptions of certain seen properties, we could fix the right-hand side of a true biconditional about yellow things and say that yellow objects are all those objects which, as things are now, in fact produce the identified perceptions of yellow in the specified circumstances in normal human perceivers as now constituted. On the assumption that the perceptions in question can be identified, that would pick out yellow objects by appeal to the kinds of perceptions those objects are in fact disposed to produce as things are, with no concern for what kinds of perceptions they would produce under other conditions. It would tell us what objects are yellow, and so to that extent what yellow is, and it would do so by appeal only to what is true of normal human perceivers as we are right now.[3]

This would tie the identification of yellow objects to us as we are, and in thinking of yellow objects in this way, we could grant all the possibilities I have mentioned without regarding them as any threat. I have argued that, with perceptions of yellow identified independently, it is possible for an object that is yellow not to produce perceptions of that kind in normal perceivers standing in the specified relations to it. That is what counts against the necessity of some forms of the biconditional about yellow things, and so counts against any dispositional view that says that the colour of an object depends on what kinds of perceptions it would produce in normal perceivers in the specified

---

3. Saul Kripke puts forward a view of this kind expressed in terms of properties: "The reference of 'yellowness' is fixed by the description 'that (manifest) property of objects which causes them, under normal circumstances, to be seen as yellow (i.e., to be sensed by certain visual impressions)'" (*Naming and Necessity*, Cambridge, Mass., 1980, p. 140n). I take "normal circumstances" here to refer to the way things actually are. He points out that on this view yellowness is not a dispositional property. The specification alone leaves it open what property actually has that causal role. For all this view says, it could be the property yellow, or the property of being yellow.

Kripke's identification of the property appears to rely on a prior identification of "certain visual impressions" as impressions of yellow, or as seeing something as yellow. It is not clear from what he says how he thinks that prior identification is secured, or whether he thinks different kinds of "visual impressions" are identifiable as such simply by some distinctive character they possess, independently of their content, or of what they are impressions *of*.

relations to it. But those possibilities do not conflict with the present suggestion. The possibility of an object's not producing perceptions of yellow in normal perceivers different from us, or in perceivers like us in a world with different laws of nature, does not mean that that object would not give us as we are in the world as it is perceptions of yellow. And on the present suggestion, any object of which that is true is yellow.

It is true that this kind of specification does not imply that the colours of things depend on what kinds of perceptions they would produce in other sorts of beings, or in other sorts of circumstances. But that is because it does not imply that the colours of objects depend on what kinds of perceptions they would produce at all. The kind of perceptions objects are in fact disposed to produce in us as things are now is what serves to identify yellow objects, and in that sense to tell us what yellow is. But that property yellow—whatever it is—is something that objects retain even in circumstances in which they are not disposed to produce the kinds of colour perceptions they are disposed to produce as things are. So the suggestion does not reveal any relativity to us in the colours of objects. Nor does it support a subjectivist or dispositional view of an object's colour. It does not support the idea that an object's being yellow depends on its being disposed to produce certain specified kinds of perceptions in certain perceivers in certain circumstances.

Ovoid objects could also be picked out as those objects that are, in fact, disposed to produce perceptions of something ovoid in normal human perceivers standing in the specified relations to them as things actually are. That identifies the ovoid objects and to that extent tells us what being ovoid is, but it does not show that an object's being ovoid depends on what kind of perceptions normal human perceivers would actually get from it. It does not show that being ovoid is a disposition the specification of which makes essential reference to perceptions produced in certain kinds of perceivers. The right-hand side of a true biconditional of this kind about elephants could also be used to tell us what elephants are: they are those objects which, as things are, are disposed to produce perceptions of elephants in perceivers like us in the specified conditions. But that does not show that something's being an elephant is somehow dependent on, or relative to, what kinds of perceptions it is disposed to produce in beings like us.

On the present suggestion, being yellow would be the same in that respect. If the biconditionals are true, the objects in question, of course, have such dispositions. But being ovoid or being an elephant or being yellow does not depend on having them. If the kinds of perceptions in question are identified independently of the properties of the objects that produce them, it will be *possible* for normal human perceivers not to get perceptions of something ovoid, so understood, from objects that are, in fact, ovoid. And on the same assumption, it would be possible for us not to get perceptions of something yellow from objects that are, in fact, yellow.

A subjectivist dispositional view of an object's colour denies this. It implies that the possibilities I have in mind are not really possibilities. When we claim to conceive of circumstances in which normal perceivers would not standardly get perceptions of yellow from certain objects, the subjectivist view implies that we cannot consistently suppose that those objects are nevertheless yellow. What perceptions perceivers would get in the stated relations to those objects is precisely what determines what colour the objects in question are, on the subjectivist view. It says there is nothing else for us to think of in addition to those possible perceptions in thinking of the colour of objects.

Another tempting parallel with the painfulness of an instrument might seem to support this view. In thinking of an instrument as a painful instrument, there is nothing else to think of in addition to its propensity to cause pain. That is just "what it is" to be a painful instrument. It could even be said to be necessarily true that any instrument which normally causes pain is a painful instrument. But that does not imply that a thumbscrew, which is a painful instrument, causes pain in all conceivable circumstances. It means only that, if the world were different and thumbscrews did not cause pain, they would not be painful instruments. It makes no sense to suppose that a thumbscrew remains a painful instrument even if it would never cause pain to anyone to whom it is applied.

I think this is right about painful instruments. But the parallel would hold only if the subjectivist view of an object's colour were correct. I am asking whether it is correct, or what reasons there are to accept it in the first place. The idea is that the biconditionals in question are to hold somehow necessarily. But I think we can see that the biconditionals needed to express a subjectivist view do not hold necessarily, and those that hold necessarily do not support the subjectivist view. To object that the relevant biconditionals will be seen to hold necessarily if we have adopted the subjectivist view is to no avail. To assess that view, we need an independent judgement of whether the relevant biconditionals are necessarily true. We cannot simply insist on the necessity of a candidate biconditional to rule out what look like possibilities that show that it is not necessarily true.

It is important to see precisely which possibilities I have in mind as counting against the subjectivist theory, and not to mistake them for others which have no such implication. I am not saying merely that there could have been objects that would not produce perceptions of yellow in normal human perceivers in certain circumstances, or would not produce them in some circumstances in human perceivers just like us. That is obviously true. Most objects in the world right now do not standardly produce perceptions of yellow in normal human perceivers, and that is no objection to subjectivism. Nor am I saying only that certain objects that are disposed to produce perceptions of yellow in normal human perceivers in the world as it is now would not be so disposed if things had been different in certain ways. That, too, is true, and no subjectivist account of colour denies it.

I am not even saying only that there are possible circumstances in which ripe lemons are not disposed to produce perceptions of yellow in normal human perceivers standing in the stated relations to them. That, too, is something the subjectivist view of colour does not deny. It implies that in such circumstances ripe lemons would not be yellow. I, too, do not deny that ripe lemons could have failed to produce perceptions of yellow, but not for that reason. I think ripe lemons could have been a different colour from what they are now.

What I think we must deny is that ripe lemons would simply *have to* have been a different colour if human perceptual mechanisms, or the laws of nature affecting the human perception of ripe lemons, had been different in certain ways. The possibility I am specifying is the possibility of ripe lemons that are *yellow*, or simply *yellow objects*, not being disposed to produce perceptions of yellow in normal human perceivers under certain conditions. I think that possibility is consistent, given that perceptions of colour, understood either as "sensations" with a certain distinctive character or as "intentional" perceptions of certain perceivable properties, are identified as such independently of specifying the colour of any physical objects.

With an indirect connection between perceptions of colour and thoughts about the colours of objects, there always remains a possibility of objects being yellow but not being disposed to produce perceptions of yellow in the specified circumstances. If so, a subjectivist dispositional view of the colour of an object cannot be correct, not because yellow objects do not have the dispositions the subjectivist thinks they have but because that view requires that the biconditional about yellow things be more than contingently true. It requires that in attributing such a disposition to an object you must necessarily be saying or implying what colour the object is. But I do not think that is so.

This is an instance of a quite general point about possibilities. Which possibility is under consideration is fully determined by the stipulation given. If you raise the possibility of there having been something round on the table yesterday, for example, that is all that is involved in the possibility you specify. You say nothing about the size of the imagined object, for instance, or its colour. For all you have said, there could have been something there that is at least a foot in diameter, or it could have been less, and it could have been yellow, blue, or some other colour. Those are all further distinct possibilities; the possibility you specified does not imply one or the other, so it does not select among them.

Does that mean that you have not fully specified the possibility you have in mind? No. The original possibility is fully specified. It includes, in the sense of being compatible with, any of those distinct further possibilities and many more besides. Does it mean that you have failed to specify a fully determinate "possible world"? Perhaps. You have failed to specify all the further features of the possibility you have specified. But that is a "failure" you cannot possibly avoid. A specification that was "fully determinate" in that sense would specify *everything* that is true of a world in which there was something round on the table yesterday. And no specification you make, however rich, could be fully determinate in that sense, and not just because it is only a possibility. Even specifying an actual state of affairs always leaves indefinitely many features unspecified.

When you specify only what kinds of colour perceptions a certain class of objects are disposed to produce in perceivers and circumstances of certain kinds, you leave many other things about those objects unspecified. You say nothing about their shapes or sizes or weight, for instance. And on the views of perceptions of colour that dispositionalism is committed to, I think you have also left the colour of those objects unspecified. For all you have said, objects with those dispositions *could* be any colour whatever. Their being this, that, or the other colour all remain further, distinct possibilities. That is why the colour of objects can be conceived to remain fixed while the kinds of independently specified colour perceptions they are disposed to produce are imagined to change, or can be conceived of as different while the identified perceptions they are disposed to produce are imagined to remain the same. The truth of 'x is ovoid' or 'x is an elephant' is independent of (even conditional) facts of human perception in that way. And if the possibilities I have specified are really possible, then in that respect an object's being yellow is like an object's being ovoid or an elephant, and not like an instrument's being a painful instrument.

At this point, it perhaps begins to look more promising to return to the fork in the road and take up the first of the two alternative strategies

I distinguished.[4] The difficulty we have been facing seems to lie in the idea of what I have called an indirect connection between the objects of perception and of thought about the colours of things. That makes it tempting to abandon that idea and accept a direct connection. On that view, what we see in a perception of colour is an instance of that very property, or of an object's having that very property, that we also ascribe to an object in the thought that it is coloured. The word 'yellow' denotes the same property in each of our sample sentences.

I think that "intentional" view of perceptions of colour is the much more promising view. Whether we can accept it and still arrive at the unreality or subjectivity of the colours of things remains to be seen. It faces different but equally serious obstacles of its own. But what I think we cannot do is accept a direct connection between the intentional objects of perception and of thought and combine it with a dispositional theory of the colours of objects. Such a hybrid is unstable and unsatisfactory, however attractive each of its separate ingredients might appear. It cannot explain the content of our thoughts about the colours of objects in a way that supports a subjectivist dispositional theory. Any such theory requires an indirect connection between perceived colour and the colour thought to belong to physical objects.

On an "intentional" understanding of perceptions of colour which sees a direct connection between perception and thought, the property we see, or see an object to have, when we see something to be yellow is the same property that we also think of an object as having when we think of it as being yellow. A dispositional theory of the colours of objects is meant to tell us what property an object's being yellow is, and so what property we think of an object as having when we think of it as yellow. With a direct connection, this would imply that the property we see when we see yellow, or the property we see an object to have when we see it to be yellow, is the property that the dispositional theory says we attribute to yellow objects in the thought that they are yellow. That is the property of being disposed to produce perceptions of something yellow in normal human perceivers in the specified circumstances. Some objects do have that disposition; that is not in question. The question for this hybrid theory is whether an object's having that disposition is what we see the object to have when we see it to be yellow. I think it cannot be.

One reason that might be given for saying that cannot be what we see is that we cannot see an object's dispositional properties or see an ob-

---

4. See chapter 5, pp. 116–117.

ject to have a dispositional property. It can be conceded that we see particular exercises of an object's disposition or capacities (we can see an
object dissolving, for example), but it might be denied that we can see
the object's disposition—its solubility—or can see that it has such a disposition. If that were so, it would be fatal to this hybrid view. If we
could not see things to have dispositional properties, and being yellow
is a dispositional property, then we could not see things to be yellow.

But I do not think the objection is correct. I think a reasonably informed person who watches what goes on in a teacup can see a lump
of sugar to be soluble, or see that it is soluble. Of course, having such
a perception involves much more than simply having a visual "sensation" with a certain distinctive character. And it is not a perception you
could have if you were confined to perceiving only properties of things
seen, not including physical objects. But the hybrid theory is not so restricted. It acknowledges a direct connection between the objects of perception and of thought, so it allows that we can perceive objects to have
the same properties that we also think or believe them to have. So it
can allow that we can see objects to have dispositional properties, or
see that they have them.

I think it is right that we can see objects to have dispositional properties. And just as with the disposition to dissolve, I think that in looking at a lemon we can see that it has a disposition to produce perceptions of something yellow in suitably placed perceivers. The difficulty
for the hybrid theory is not whether that is something we can perceive.
The real question is whether that dispositional property that we can see
an object to have is the same property that the dispositional theory identifies as the object's being yellow.

I think the answer is "No". The dispositional theory describes a yellow object as being disposed to produce perceptions of something's being yellow. That still leaves an unexplained occurrence of the word 'yellow' in the specification of the content of those perceptions. On an
indirect connection between the objects of perception and of thought,
that creates no difficulty, since the perceptions in question are to be
identified independently of predicating 'yellow' of a physical object.
But with a direct connection between the objects of perception and of
thought, the word 'yellow' in that perceptual context stands for the same
property that the dispositional theory says we ascribe to an object in
the thought that it is yellow. 'Yellow' is supposed to have the same
meaning on both sides of the dispositionalist biconditional. That means
that what the word 'yellow' is said to mean when said of a physical
object on the left-hand side must be substituted into its occurrence on
the right-hand side in order to give the content of the perceptions in

question. So a perception of something's being yellow would then be explained as a perception of something's being disposed to produce perceptions of something's being yellow. That still contains an unexplained occurrence of the word 'yellow'.

To expand that occurrence in turn by inserting into it what 'yellow' is said to mean when said of a physical object would mean that a perception of something's being yellow would then be explained as a perception of something's being disposed to produce perceptions of something's being disposed to produce perceptions of something's being yellow. And so on, into the night. There could be no end to specifying what property it is that the object has a disposition to produce perceptions of, and hence no specification of what perceptions of yellow are. But without a way of identifying the relevant kinds of perceptions, there would be no adequate specification of the disposition that an object's being yellow is supposed to be identified with.

This is fatal to this hybrid combination. A dispositional theory needs to identify the disposition in question, and that requires some way, other than through the disposition itself, to specify the effects that objects with that disposition are disposed to produce. We can specify the effects in question for the dispositional term 'painful' said of an object or instrument; they are sensations of pain. We can do it for the term 'soluble'; the effect in question is the object's dissolving. For a nourishing object, it is nourishment in the consumer. For a yellow object, on the dispositional theory, the effects in question are said to be perceivers' perceiving something yellow. Those perceptions must therefore be understood or identified as perceptions of something other than the presence of that very disposition. But on a direct connection between the objects of perception and of thought, there is no difference between the property ascribed to the object in thought and the property we see in a perception. It is one and the same property. If the only way to specify what is perceived in perceptions of colour is to say that it is the object's being disposed to produce those very perceptions, we cannot appeal to those perceptions to give an independent specification of the disposition. And without a specification of the disposition, we will have no specification of the colour of the object in terms of a disposition.

This, of course, is not to deny that some objects do have dispositions to produce certain kinds of perceptions in certain kinds of perceivers under certain circumstances. And I have granted that we can see objects to have such dispositions. So there is nothing wrong with saying that we can see an object to have the disposition to produce those very perceptions we get when we look at it. That is just what we would expect of such a disposition. The point is rather that such a disposition cannot be what we ascribe to an object in the thought that it is yellow. What we ascribe to an object in the thought that it is yellow is a different property from what we ascribe to it in the thought that it is blue. But objects we think of as yellow and objects we think of as blue are alike in having, and in being capable of being seen to have, a disposition to produce those very perceptions that we get when we look at them. Some further specification is therefore needed in each case to distinguish yellow objects from blue objects.[5]

The hybrid theory tries to combine a dispositional theory with a direct connection. It cannot succeed. A dispositional theory therefore can succeed only if it assumes an indirect connection between the objects of perception and of thought. This is the source of another defect in a dispositional theory. It cannot give a satisfactory account of the familiar fact of predicational seeing—of seeing a lemon to be yellow by seeing yellow, and seeing it to be the yellow of a lemon.

I tried to show that understanding perceptions of colour as "sensations" with a certain distinctive character cannot make the right kind of sense of this kind of perception.[6] The property we see, and see to belong to the lemon, is just the property we think it has in the thought that it is yellow. But on the "sensation" view, perceptions of colour are not "intentional". They do not have "objects" or contents that can be shared with other psychological attitudes. So on that view, we cannot both see a certain property and see that property to belong to a physical object.

The difficulty of accounting for predicational perception is not confined to the view of perceptions as "sensations" with a certain distinctive character. Even on an "intentional" view that accepts an indirect connection between what is perceived and what is thought about the colours of objects, the same problem arises. A dispositional theory cannot say that what is seen in seeing yellow is that property that the dispositional theory says is *thought* to belong to an object in the thought that it is yellow.[7] But if what is seen in seeing yellow is some other property, or a property of something else, then what is seen is not the property that is thought to belong to an object in the thought that it is yellow. But predicational perception involves the perception of a

---

5. This makes it tempting to identify the kinds of perceptions (and so the dispositions) in each case *demonstratively*. I take up this idea in chapter 7, pp. 164–166.
   6. See chapter 5, pp. 112–113.
   7. Again, this is not to deny that we can see an object to have such a dispositional property. I mean only that the dispositional property we see the object to have is not the yellow that we see.

property, and perception of an object to have that same property, where the property in question is the property that is also thought to belong to an object in the thought that it has that property.

If Jones thinks there is a yellow lemon on the table and then sees a lemon on the table to be yellow, she sees the lemon to have the same property she thinks it has. That requires a direct connection between the object of perception and the object of thought. The most that the idea of an indirect connection between them would allow is that when we see a lemon to be yellow we *see* a certain property but *think* a certain other property to belong to the lemon. But that would be to deny that we ever see a lemon to be yellow at all. On an indirect connection, there would be no such thing as predicational perception of the colours of things.

A dispositional theory requires that perceptions of yellow be understood as perceptions of a different property from the property ascribed to an object in the thought that it is yellow. And it requires that perceptions of yellow be identifiable as such independently of any appeal to the colours of any objects. But however perceptions of colour are understood—either as "sensations" with a certain distinctive character or as "intentional" perceptions of properties of things seen, not including physical objects—that requirement is just what leaves it always *possible* for an object that is disposed to produce perceptions of that identified kind in normal human perceivers in the specified conditions not to be yellow. That means that when perceptions of yellow are identified in that way, the biconditional about yellow things is not necessarily true. But a dispositional theory requires a necessary connection.

The dispositional theory therefore cannot account for our thoughts and beliefs about the colours of physical objects or for our perceptions of the colours of objects. But the metaphysical project must grant that we have such beliefs and perceptions in order to have something to explain. I conclude that we cannot reach the unmasking metaphysical conclusion on the assumption of an indirect connection between the objects of perception and the objects of thought. It is time to consider the alternative of a direct connection. It has many merits, not least of which is that in adopting it we abandon all dispositional theories of an object's colour.

7

Perception, Judgement, and Error

I think the facts of perception and belief involving colour are best understood by taking perceptions of colour to be "intentional" perceptions *of* something. What I am calling a direct connection between the objects of perception and of thought makes better sense of the relation between perceptions and beliefs than the indirect connection we considered. On the direct view, perception of colour and thought involving the colours of things are intelligibly linked, and predicational seeing is unproblematic. What we believe to be so when we believe an object is yellow is what we see to be so when we see it to be yellow. And when we see an object to be yellow, we see it to have that very property we see when we see yellow. 'Yellow' has the same meaning in each of our sample sentences.

What are the prospects of arriving at an unmasking conclusion about the colours of things if we accept this straightforward conception of perception and belief? The unmasking project cannot deny that we perceive many different colours or that we believe physical objects to be coloured. Those are some of the facts to be explained. But if what we believe when we believe that an object is yellow is ever true, there will be at least one yellow object, so some object will be coloured. To reach the conclusion that nothing in reality is coloured, then, we will have to show that no such belief is ever true. But since on a direct view what we believe to be true of an object when we believe it is yellow is just what we can see to be true of it when we see it to be yellow, we will have to conclude that what we see to be true of coloured objects is not, in fact, true of them. All our perceptions of the colours of objects must be illusory in that way. But we cannot deny that we perceive many different colours. Nor can we deny that we see colours to belong to physical objects, or perhaps even that we cannot help believing that they do. The metaphysical conclusion will say that no physical objects have any of the colours that we see, or any of the colours we see them or believe them to have.

The project has to start with our full, rich conception of the world, as embodied in everything we believe. It will successfully expose those everyday perceptions of and beliefs about the colours of things as illusory only if the conception of the world it appeals to in explaining them does not contain anything that says or implies that any physical object is coloured in a way that is independent of all facts about human perceivers. In carrying out the project, we must therefore understand human beings to believe many things about the colours of objects without ourselves holding any beliefs about the colours of things in that sense. That is how those beliefs are to be exposed as false. And we must acknowledge that people have perceptions of colour, and of objects' being coloured, without ourselves believing or implying that any physical object has any colour. That is how those perceptions are to be exposed as illusory, or "mere appearance".

This raises the question whether we could find people to have such beliefs and perceptions if we were barred from the outset from believing that anything in the world is coloured. This is a more complicated question than it might seem. It can look as if there is no real difficulty, since we often do acknowledge the presence of perceptions we know to be illusory and thoughts and beliefs we know to be false. We recognize that people have thoughts or beliefs and sometimes even perceptions of such things as unicorns or dragons or golden mountains, for example, although we know that no such things exist. Something similar can occur in the case of colour. Shine a blue light on a ripe lemon and anyone looking at it will see green. We know that there is no green object there, but we understand how and why the person sees green, even sees the lemon to be green. We attribute such a perception to the person and can explain why it occurs, without ourselves attributing green to anything that is there. If the perceiver does not know about the blue light, he might even believe that the lemon is green, but we know that belief is false and can explain why he holds it.

There is no doubt that there are a great many cases like this, but they do not show that there is no difficulty for the explanatory project. It is true that our understanding and attributing to people thoughts of unicorns or dragons do not require us to believe the world contains the things those thoughts are about. We can concede that people who can think of such nonexistent things might even have perceptions of them. One traditional explanation of how such thoughts and perceptions are possible was that they are "complex". Thoughts of unicorns and dragons are made up of thoughts of things that we believe do exist, like horses, horns, wings, claws, and fire. Even if we accept the appeal to "complexity" in cases like these, the same kind of story is not plausible for the colours of things. Some particular colours or shades can be understood to be combinations of other colours or shades, so we can perhaps think of green as a combination of yellow and blue. But there do not seem to be properties that are not colours at all which we could somehow put together to give us the thought of colour in general. It seems that our understanding and recognition of the colours of things cannot be built up out of noncolour building blocks in the way we can perhaps build up a thought of a unicorn from thoughts of a horselike body and a well-placed horn.

In the example of seeing green because of blue light on a yellow lemon, we appeal to the known effects of mixing yellow and blue. We explain the perception of a colour that is not there in terms of colours that are there. But that illusion is not an instance of what the unmasking metaphysical project requires in general. It is only an example of our understanding someone to perceive something as having a certain colour when we know that the thing has a different colour. The question for the metaphysical project is whether we can acknowledge someone's perceiving a certain colour if we do not hold that anything anywhere has any colour at all. This kind of example does not show that we can. If we generalized it and tried to think of the world in general as we think of it in that particular case, we would still not be conceiving of a colourless world. We would be thinking of a world of objects with different colours from the colours they are seen to have.

It is possible to imagine more extreme cases in which a person perceives a certain colour, although nothing with any colour at all is present, or not in the appropriate place. There are fewer good examples than you might think; it is more common to think of seeing a different colour from the one that is there. One good instance of the more extreme possibility is seeing a rainbow; another, perhaps, is seeing the blue of the sky. In the case of the rainbow, light strikes transparent drops of water in the transparent air and is reflected and refracted so that anyone looking in a certain direction sees many of the colours of the spectrum. Nothing in the vicinity has those colours, yet everyone sees them. In fact, nothing that seems relevant to what is seen has any colour at all. But still we know that everyone in the right place at the right time gets perceptions of colour. Also, in the experimental study of the physiology of perception, our seeing the colours we do appears to be explained by appeal only to physical processes occurring between the object and the eye and brain. The colours of objects do not seem to come into the story at all.

Since there obviously are successful explanations of these kinds, there is apparently a strong temptation to generalize and to think it must therefore be possible for us to understand ourselves in general as perceiving colours and as believing that things are coloured, while holding that nothing anywhere has those features that we perceive and believe things to have. But I think there is a real question whether we can coherently generalize in that way. We have learned (I hope) to be suspicious of that kind of inference in other areas of philosophy—in philosophical discussions of knowledge that appear to lead to scepticism, for instance. It is obviously possible for someone to be wrong on a particular occasion and fail to know what is so, right before his eyes. Could that be the way things are in general, so that nobody ever knows anything about the world around us? Certainly, it does not follow immediately. It is an inference that requires the closest scrutiny.

Whatever hesitation one feels in that case should be extended to the attempt to reach a metaphysical conclusion about the unreality or subjectivity of colour from familiar everyday illusions or mistakes about the colours of things. Even the experimental study of perception is understood to take place in a world we think of as containing coloured objects and human beings with perceptions of colour. We cannot simply assume that by generalizing from explanations invoking only physical processes and events we could reach a completely global conception of the kind needed for the unmasking philosophical project. That project will succeed only if we can be sure that *all* appeal to the colours of things has been eliminated from everything we must accept in order to undertake and carry out the project.

This brings out in another way the extreme generality of the enterprise. We have seen that it involves our asking how psychological facts of perception and belief are best understood, in general. That is part of the staggeringly general question that the unmasking explanatory strategy inevitably raises: what are psychological facts, and what is "added" to our conception of the world when we think of it as containing such facts? Anyone seriously engaged in the metaphysical project needs some idea of an answer to that question, but it is not the only question. We also have to ask what makes it possible for us to think of the world in those ways. What do we have to do, think, or know to understand and acknowledge the psychological facts that we accept? This is a different question, but it equally demands an answer.

This new question is at least equally general, and equally daunting. It is not easy to determine, with any assurance of completeness, exactly what is and is not required for us to understand one another in all the ways we do. But the unmasking project can succeed only if in carrying it out we do not presuppose any of the things we claim to unmask. We must admit perceptions and beliefs about the colours of things in the world for there to be something for the unmasking explanation to explain. But in acknowledging those psychological facts, we must fulfill all the conditions of acknowledging them. And if those conditions of acknowledgement and attribution include our holding some beliefs about the colours of things, the conception of the world that we would have to hold, even to admit all the psychological facts that need to be explained, would be too rich to enable us to find that the colours of things had been unmasked. Eliminating the colours of things entirely from our conception of the world, which is a condition of success of the project, would leave us incapable of acknowledging the very facts that the unmasking explanation is supposed to explain. If that were so, we could never achieve by this explanatory route a conception of a world in which there are perceptions and beliefs about the colours of things but no coloured objects.

This is one version of the completely general suspicion voiced earlier.[1] The quest for reality asks whether things really are as our beliefs represent them to be, so it appears to require a certain detachment from all beliefs about the colours of things. But if acknowledging the psychological facts that are supposed to be explained requires beliefs in the colours of objects, the metaphysical project would require both detachment from and engagement with the very same beliefs, and at the same time.

This dilemma would be fatal to the attempt to reach the unmasking metaphysical conclusion by the explanatory route. I think there is reason to think the dilemma is real. The contents of all our perceptions of and beliefs about the colours of things make up such a large, pervasive, and irreducible portion of all the things we take to be true of the world that they cannot be sliced off that conception while leaving intact our understanding of ourselves as perceiving and believing all the things we now do. It is probably too much to expect to prove such a thing, once and for all. But some very general considerations about the acknowledgement of psychological facts suggest that it is true. And when applied to beliefs about the colours of things in particular, they make what I think is a very strong case.

---

1. Chapter 2, p. 28.

The conception of the world from which any unmasking project begins must contain both psychological and nonpsychological facts. That is to say, some of the things we believe are expressed in sentences with a psychological main verb attributing thoughts, beliefs, perceptions, feelings, or other attitudes to someone, and others contain no such verbs and ascribe no such attitudes to anyone. Nonpsychological statements say nothing that implies the existence of any thinking, perceiving, feeling subjects at all. But we typically use what we take to be nonpsychological facts in understanding and specifying the psychological facts we accept. We identify what different people think, believe, and perceive in ways that are as rich and complex as our conception of the nonpsychological world onto which those thoughts, beliefs, and perceptions are directed. That is to be expected if—as we are now supposing—there is a direct connection between the intentional objects of perception and of thought. We believe that many people perceive and believe that there are yellow, ovoid lemons, large grey elephants, and countless other physical things, for example, and we also believe such nonpsychological facts as that there are yellow, ovoid lemons, large grey elephants, and countless other physical things. The suspicion I want to explore is that that is no accident, in general. Perhaps we can have beliefs of the one kind only because we have some beliefs of the other kind.

The best reason to think that might be so is to be found in an important idea that helps us understand ourselves better as beings with minds, and makes better sense of our understanding of psychological facts, than any philosophical theories that ignore or deny it have been able to do.[2] It involves taking seriously the conditions that must be fulfilled for the successful ascription to human beings of perceptions, beliefs, or other attitudes with specific contents. Those contents are typically specified in terms which mention only circumstances that do or could hold in the nonpsychological world. That will be no accident, in general, if we who inhabit the world can understand someone in that world as believing something or as perceiving something only if we can somehow connect the possession of the psychological states we attribute to the person with facts and events in the surrounding world that we

---

2. The idea is at the heart of Wittgenstein's treatment of psychological concepts in his *Philosophical Investigations* (Oxford, 1953). Donald Davidson has stressed its importance in another way in what he calls "radical interpretation". See his "Radical Interpretation" and "Belief and the Basis of Meaning" in his *Inquiries into Truth and Interpretation*, Oxford, 1984; "A Coherence Theory of Truth and Knowledge", in D. Henrich (ed.), *Kant oder Hegel?* Stuttgart, 1983; and "Three Varieties of Knowledge", in A. Phillips Griffiths (ed.), *A. J. Ayer: Memorial Essays*, Cambridge, 1991.

take the beliefs and perceptions to be about. We understand one another to be parts of, and engaged in, a common world we all share. If we ourselves had no beliefs at all about what is happening in the environment or what another person is most likely to be paying attention to, we would be in no position to attribute any beliefs or perceptions to that person at all. So it looks as if we interpreters and ascribers of beliefs and other psychological states must be engaged in the world, in the sense of taking certain nonpsychological things to be true of it, if we are ever going to attribute beliefs or perceptions to anyone.

In identifying the contents of the attitudes we ascribe, we must inevitably start with what we already know or believe, or can find out, so we have no choice but to attribute to others, at least in general, beliefs in and perceptions of the very things we ourselves take to be true or to exist in the world. We cannot make sense of someone as believing something we know to be false unless we can identify what he believes and can offer some explanation of how he comes to get it wrong. That involves attributing to the person many other beliefs, the possession of which helps make his particular divergence intelligible. And those further beliefs will typically include many that we share. Those we do not share will, in turn, be attributed only if we can understand how a person inhabiting and reacting to the world we all live in nonetheless came to have them.

These very general observations perhaps go some way towards explaining why our understanding of psychological facts should be expected to be connected with our understanding of the nonpsychological world. They make intelligible what is a striking and important feature of psychological facts: that they typically have what might be called both a psychological and a nonpsychological aspect. There is an attitude or state of a certain kind, on the one hand, and the object or content of that state on the other, which is typically specified in nonpsychological terms. Putting it in terms of the sentences we use to express them, what psychological fact a sentence states depends both on the verb specifying the psychological attitude or state of the person and on the complement of that verb specifying the object of that attitude or state. Of course, people differ, so it depends on the subject of the sentence as well. One person can have a certain thought or perception or feeling without anyone else having that same thought or that same kind of perception or feeling. Psychological attitudes or states also differ, so there can be different psychological facts with the same person and the same object or content. 'Jones wonders whether there is a yellow lemon on the table' states a different fact from 'Jones hopes that there is a yellow lemon on the table'. One could be true without the other.

But it is equally true, and striking, that even with the same person and the same attitude there can be different psychological facts. Only what follows the psychological verb is what serves in such cases to distinguish the one fact from the other, if the sentences are true. We understand and recognize differences between psychological facts where the only differences are in the nonpsychological specifications of the objects or contents of the attitudes. This is clearest with attitudes that take propositional objects. 'Jones believes that it is snowing in Buffalo' states a different psychological fact from 'Jones believes that it is raining in Budapest', even with the same Jones in each case. The first sentence could be true without the second being true, and vice versa. But the sentences differ only in what comes after 'Jones believes that . . .', and those parts of the sentences state or imply nothing psychological. Our understanding of nonpsychological sentences and facts is inextricably involved in our understanding of psychological sentences and facts.

That is not to deny that attitudes like perception and belief can also take psychological states of affairs as their objects. 'Smith believes that Jones believes it is raining in Budapest' attributes to Smith a belief with a psychological propositional content. An attitude with nonpsychological content is typically involved at some point as well, as in this case, but that is not always so. 'Smith believes that Jones feels pain' involves no attitude with a nonpsychological object. Nor does 'Smith sees that Jones feels pain'. But still the specification of the object of the attitude expressed in the main verb is what is needed to specify the psychological state or condition the person is said to be in.

When the object of the attitude is not propositional, the specification of the object can also be all that serves to distinguish one psychological fact from another. 'Jones wants a ball' differs from 'Jones wants a brick' only in the difference between the objects Jones is said to want. We understand the difference between those two psychological facts because we know the difference between a ball and a brick. And a ball or a brick is nothing psychological. It is not that the sentences imply that there is an actual ball and an actual brick which are different objects. The point is only that the difference we recognize between those psychological facts is identified only in terms of the difference between the kinds of things wanted. 'Jones is thinking of a unicorn' states a different fact from 'Jones is thinking of a dragon' because unicorns are different from dragons, even though there are no such things anywhere. If we did not know what unicorns and dragons are, and that they are different, we would not understand those sentences and so would not know what psychological facts they state and that they are different facts.

This is equally true of perception. It is because we know the difference between a ball and a brick that we know that seeing a ball is different from seeing a brick. If we did not know the difference between
those objects, we would not understand the difference between those
perceptions, and we would be in no position to attribute them to anyone. We would not know whether we ourselves were having such perceptions either, even if we were. Knowing that I am having a perception of a certain kind is a matter of knowingly ascribing a perception
of that kind to myself. But without knowing what a ball or a brick is, I
could not ascribe perceptions of such things to anyone.

The same is true of predicational perception of an object, such as
seeing a red ball or seeing a yellow lemon. We recognize that seeing
such things is different from seeing a green lemon, but only because we
know what balls and lemons are and we know the difference between
an object's being red or yellow and its being green. The thoughts required for ascribing such perceptions are predicational thoughts; we
must be able to think of a certain object as having a certain property. If
we could not think of a yellow lemon, we could make no sense of predicational perception of a yellow lemon, since we could make no sense
of what it is a perception of. We could not then intelligibly ascribe such
perceptions to others or to ourselves.

In thinking of a yellow lemon, the predication is part of the content
of the thought; it is not simply a thought of a lemon which, in fact, happens to be yellow. But what is thought of in such a predicational thought
is just what is thought of as being so in a propositional thought to the
effect that a certain lemon is yellow. Thought of an object with a certain property is connected in that way with the possibility of propositional thought. Only insofar as propositional thoughts in which properties are ascribed to objects are intelligible to us are we capable of
thinking of objects with certain properties.[3] We can think of coloured
objects, and so think of ourselves as seeing such things, only because
we can make sense of propositional thoughts in which colours are predicated of physical objects.

---

3. This connection was stressed by Frege, who held that "we cannot recognize a
property of a thing without at the same time finding the thought *this thing has this
property* to be true. So with every property of a thing there is tied up a property of
a thought, namely truth," ("Thoughts", in his *Logical Investigations*, Oxford, 1977,
pp. 5–6). What is true or false is a full propositional thought. In speaking of "recognizing a property of a thing", Frege appears to have in mind recognizing *that* the
thing has the property. But even in "grasping" such a thought, without judging it to
be true, we show that we already have the idea of truth, in the sense that we "grasp"
a propositional thought that is either true or false.

Understanding or making sense of a propositional thought does not require that we accept it or judge it to be true. We can understand or, in Frege's word, "grasp" the propositional thought that a certain thing has a certain property, even if we have no idea at the moment whether it is true or not. But its being true must be intelligible to us. So to think of a yellow lemon, in the sense of thinking of it as yellow, is at least to understand, if not necessarily to assert, the propositional thought: this lemon is yellow. But to understand or "grasp" a propositional thought is to know what would be so if it were true. And that is to know under what conditions it would be correct to judge or assert it to be true. In this way, understanding propositional thought involves a capacity for judgement or assertion. That capacity is exercised by someone who believes that a certain physical object is coloured. But someone who only thinks of a coloured object, in the sense of thinking of it as coloured, must at least possess a capacity for such a judgement, even if he does not believe the corresponding proposition or judge it to be true.

The attribution of *propositional* perceptions involving the colours of things requires not only a capacity for judgement but also the actual making of a colour judgement. To assert that Jones sees that there is a yellow lemon on the table is to accept or endorse the fact that there is a yellow lemon on the table. That same judgement is also made in having such a propositional perception oneself, not only in attributing it to someone else. Jones sees that there is a yellow lemon on the table only if she accepts or endorses the proposition that there is a yellow lemon there. The attribution of *predicational* perceptions of the colours of things does not require making such judgements, but it does require a capacity for it, since it requires that the thought of an object's having a colour be intelligible to the attributor. And the intelligibility of such thoughts, and so the same capacity for judgement, is also required for having predicational perceptions of the colours of things, not just for attributing them. Someone who lacked a capacity for judging that an object has a certain property could not have predicational perceptions of an object with that property.

Being incapable of predicational thought of a yellow lemon would leave us incapable of seeing a yellow lemon, in the sense of seeing it to be yellow. We might see a lemon that is yellow, but that is no great achievement. Even a creature without colour vision can see a lemon that is in fact yellow. Without being capable of objectual predicational thought, we might also see yellow; the yellow of something might be what draws our attention to it visually. But that would not necessarily be to see something to be yellow either. We might even simultaneously see a lemon and see yellow, but if we lacked the capacity for predicational thought, that would not be to see a lemon to be yellow. Seeing several properties together in one perception is not the same as seeing something to have all or any of those properties. For that, we need the thought of an object's having properties. We need a capacity for predicational thought. But if understanding predicational thought involves, in turn, a capacity for propositional thought, and hence for judgement, then anyone who sees a lemon to be yellow must be capable of judging that a lemon is yellow.

Locke, Berkeley, Hume, and others spoke of our perceiving objects with properties, like yellow lemons and red cherries, but in accounting for such predicational perceptions they were faced with a difficulty they did not fully recognize. For them, perception was prior to thought. They took nonpropositional seeing as basic, and officially regarded it as restricted to direct acquaintance with its "proper objects"[4]—colours and shapes and perhaps a few other properties. But even on an "intentional" understanding of perception, with properties as the "objects" of perception, the possibility of predicational perception is left problematic. Seeing properties is not the same as seeing something to have properties.

What I think those philosophers missed is that predicational perception of an object with properties requires that the thought of an object with properties be intelligible to the perceiver. And that, in turn, requires the possibility of propositional thought and judgement. Judgement involves endorsing or putting forward as true a complete thought with a truth value. And that is possible only where there is predication, or when two different aspects or elements of the proposition are combined in a special way. One part of an expression of a propositional thought—a predicate, or what Frege called an "unsaturated" expression—must carry within it an empty place for a term referring to an object. And only when the right kind of term is inserted do we have an expression of the full thought that the object referred to has a certain property. That expression will be a sentence with a truth value, not just a list of names referring to objects. Even if one or more of the objects named by a list of names is a property, the list still does not amount to a sentence that says that some object has that property.

Hume at least saw the importance of the problem of belief or assertion or putting forward something as true, as opposed to merely thinking about it. He thought no one before him had even noticed the

---

4. See G. Berkeley, *An Essay towards a New Theory of Vision*, section 156; *Principles* I, 44; in Berkeley, *Berkeley: Philosophical Works* (ed. M. Ayers), London, 1975, pp. 54, 89.

problem, or its difficulty. But he did not recognize its connection with perception or with the possibility of predicational perception in particular. He took it for granted that we have "impressions" of such things as a round, red apple and went on to say that we think about such objects by having "ideas" that copy those "impressions" and differ from them only in the degree of "force" or "vivacity" with which they are present in the mind. But he could find no satisfactory account of the difference between having an "idea" of a red apple in the next room and believing that there is a red apple in the next room. He found it "impossible to explain perfectly" the notion of belief.[5] What he was right about, and insisted upon, was that what we believe can be the very same as what we imagine or merely conceive of; only the "manner" in which that common content is "in the mind" differs from one kind of attitude to another.

When that important idea—of the same content or intentional object being shared by different psychological states or attitudes—is extended to perception as well, it makes possible what I have called a direct connection between the objects of perception and of thought and belief. That makes predicational perception of an object possible for any perceiver to whom predicational thoughts of an object's having a certain property are intelligible. But those thoughts in turn require a capacity for propositional thought, and so for judgement. That makes a capacity for propositional judgement in which a certain property is predicated of an object a condition of having predicational perceptions of an object with that property. And that same capacity for judgement is required for the attribution of predicational perceptions to others.

Having a capacity does not imply that the capacity is ever exercised. Someone who attributes predicational perceptions of certain kinds to others, and so can make sense of the thought of things' having those perceivable properties, might not believe that any objects at all actually have the properties in question. Such a person could also attribute to others beliefs to the effect that certain objects have those properties, without having any such beliefs himself. But if that were true in general, for all perceivers and objects and properties, and no one had any beliefs about perceivable objects' having any perceivable properties at all, all connection between perception and thought would have been severed.[6] No one would have propositional perceptions involving per-

---

5. D. Hume, *A Treatise of Human Nature* (ed. L.A. Selby-Bigge), Oxford, 1958, p. 630.

6. I argue in chapter 5, pp. 113–114, that not all possible objects of perception can be excluded from the realm of possible objects of thought, on pain of disconnecting thought and perception completely.

ceivable properties either, since that, too, requires judgement or endorsement of the proposition in question. So no one would ever see that something he believes to be so is so.

If some connection between the objects of perception and of thought is to be preserved, then, there must be at least some perceivable properties that we both see and believe objects to have. Having and attributing perceptions of objects with those properties therefore require not only the capacity but also the actual exercise of judgement attributing those properties to perceived objects. There must be some perceivable properties that we believe perceived objects actually have.

That is still a completely general observation. Even if it is correct, it does not say which properties those are. It does not show, in particular, that anyone who has perceptions of coloured objects and attributes such perceptions and beliefs about the colours of things to others must himself believe that some objects are coloured. The question is whether the colours of things are like unicorns, dragons, golden mountains, and other myths and illusions that we can acknowledge that people believe in and perhaps even perceive, without ourselves accepting their existence. The completely general fact that we must believe some things about the nonpsychological world in order to ascribe perceptions and beliefs does not show anything one way or the other about colours in particular.

Is it a necessary condition of our acknowledging the presence in the world of perceptions of and beliefs about the colours of things that we believe that some objects are coloured? It is not easy to answer the question. A conclusive proof one way or the other is difficult to envisage. The best way to settle the question is probably to try it out. Try to start with no beliefs about the colours of objects, make no use of any such beliefs anywhere, and see if you could ascribe to anyone perceptions of or beliefs about the colour of something. The difficulty would be to be sure you are not relying at any point on any beliefs about the colours of things. That is not something it is easy to be certain of, especially if it remains unclear how such beliefs are or are not implicated in our acknowledgement of all the psychological facts we recognize. Perhaps the best we can do is to explore what we can see to be the consequences of explicitly excluding all such beliefs.

The question is not simply what perceptions and beliefs we would have if we held no beliefs about the colours of objects; it is a question of what perceptions and beliefs we could then understand human beings to have. First, it is clear that we could find no circumstances in which to attribute to someone any beliefs about the colours of things which we ourselves agree with and hold to be true. Nor could we attribute to others propositional perceptions involving the colours of things. 'Jones sees that there is a yellow lemon on the table' implies that there is a yellow lemon on the table. But nothing that implies that objects are coloured could be part of a metaphysical unmasker's conception of the world.

This means that we could not ascribe nonpropositional perceptions of coloured objects either, if those attributions contain even what we might call a "transparent" predication of colour. If I say that Jones sees a yellow lemon because I believe that what she sees is, in fact, a yellow lemon, my own belief about the colour of an object is essential to that attribution. That is true even if I think she does not see it to be a lemon or see it to be yellow. Attributions of predicational perceptions carry a similar commitment if the colour of the seen object is specified "transparently". 'Jones sees a yellow lemon on the table to be green' implies that what Jones sees is a yellow lemon. The same is true even of the veridical ascription 'Jones sees a yellow lemon to be yellow', understood "transparently". In fact, the same is true of every statement about a person and any object described as coloured. 'Jones ate a yellow lemon' and 'Jones stepped on a yellow lemon' both imply that objects are coloured. We could believe no such things about anyone if we had no beliefs about the colours of things.

With no beliefs about the colours of any objects, we could find other people to have beliefs to that effect only if we regarded them all as at best false. We could not share those beliefs. But could we even find or identify the beliefs in question? If Jones utters the sentence "There is a yellow lemon on the table" about the table right before us, what belief could we recognize her to be expressing? What property could we understand her to be predicating of a lemon on the table? It could not be a property that we find to belong to any physical object. If she said, "There is an ovoid lemon on the table", we could presumably identify the property in question because we know that 'ovoid' stands for a property that we believe and can often see to belong to physical objects. In perceptions and beliefs about ovoid things, we exercise our capacity to judge, of an object, that it is ovoid. But we would not be in the same position for identifying what Jones means by 'yellow'.

If she goes on to say, "I see yellow, and I see a lemon on the table to be yellow", she would seem to be predicating of the lemon we all see some property that she sees, and sees the lemon to have. We might think that the property she believes the lemon to have is the same property she sees it to have. But that still would not enable us to identify the property in question and so attribute to her a particular, determinate belief.

In saying what she does in this last utterance, she would seem to be attributing to herself a predicational perception, but a would-be unmasker must regard all predicational perception of the colours of physical objects as at best illusory. Even if we could somehow identify the property Jones has in mind, we could not take her to be seeing a property that the object actually has. We could perhaps understand her to be seeing an object, and seeing an instance of some property, while *thinking* of that property as a property of the seen object.[7] That thought, if its content involves a colour, we would have to regard as false. It predicates of an object a property that we could not find physical objects to have. The most we could allow to be, strictly speaking, *seen* would be a physical object and a property of something, but not a property that belongs to physical objects.

I argued earlier that to extend this verdict about colour to all predicational perception would mean that objects have no perceivable properties at all. Nothing that we believe to be true of physical objects could ever be perceived to be true of them. The public world we believe in would be cut off from everything we can perceive. An unmasker of the colours of things therefore has every reason not to deny the possibility of veridical predicational perception in general. He can allow that we see shapes and see objects to have certain shapes, for example, as well as other "primary" qualities of objects. But for colours, he would have to understand them at best as properties perceived, but not properties of any physical objects we perceive.

But would even that much be intelligible? With no beliefs about the colours of objects, what sense could an unmasking interpreter make of the property Jones apparently says she sees when she says, "I see yellow" and "I see that there is a yellow lemon on the table"? To ascribe perceptions of a certain kind, we have to have some idea of what such perceptions are perceptions of and how having one kind of perception differs from having another. There is a question whether a would-be unmasker could be in a position to recognize perceptions of colour at all.

Of course, we can distinguish among different perceptions of colour without difficulty as things are. We do so in terms of differences among the colours of objects that they are perceptions of. We ascribe a perception of yellow to someone whom we believe to be a competent perceiver, facing with eyes open in good light what we know to be a

---

7. It would be too strong to infer that the perceiver *believes* that the object has the property she sees. It is possible to see an object to be yellow without believing that it is.

yellow lemon, and a perception of red to someone face to face with a red tomato. We do not always require such direct grounds. If Jones, whom I know well, calls out from the next room, "I see a yellow lemon here; what a beautiful yellow!" I would believe that she sees yellow, even though I have no independent knowledge of the colour of anything in that room. I do not have to withdraw that attribution if I discover that there is, in fact, nothing yellow there. But still it is because I understand what Jones says, and know what perceptions of yellow are, that I attribute a perception of yellow to her in those circumstances. And I know what perceptions of yellow are because I know what yellow is. It is the colour of yellow objects. I believe that many objects are yellow.

As metaphysical unmaskers, we could not identify perceptions of yellow in that way. We would acknowledge no yellow objects in the world. Nor could we identify perceptions of yellow as perceptions of that property that people *believe* to belong to objects that are yellow. We would admit no objects that are yellow. It would get us no further to say that perceptions of yellow are perceptions of that property that people believe to belong to objects that they believe to be yellow. That specification is not unique. There are many properties that people believe to belong to objects they believe to be yellow. Even to say that perceptions of yellow are perceptions of that property that people believe to belong to an object in believing that it is yellow would be no help. That is true, but it serves to identify perceptions of yellow only if the content of the belief that an object is yellow can be specified independently.

A belief that an object is yellow involves the same property that is seen in a perception of yellow. That is a consequence of there being a direct connection between the intentional objects of perception and of thought about the colours of things. But that direct connection alone provides no independent specification of the content of either the perception or the belief. A belief that an object is green also involves the same property that is seen in a perception of green, which is a perception of that very property believed to belong to an object in the belief that it is green. But none of this tells us what perceptions of green or perceptions of yellow are, or how they differ from one another.

We are not confined to such a circle as things are, because we know what colour certain objects are, and we can exhibit objects with the colour properties in question. Perceptions of yellow are perceptions of the colour that yellow objects have. Perceptions understood as "intentional" perceptions *of* something are identified and distinguished from one another only in terms of what they are perceptions of. As would-be unmaskers, we could not understand perceptions of colour to be perceptions of properties that any physical objects actually have. To understand them as perceptions of properties at all, then, we would have to take them to be perceptions of properties of other things, not physical objects. Or perhaps as properties, but not properties of anything at all.[8]

Some philosophers have held that we see, or "directly" see, only colours and shapes or only variously coloured regions or patches of a visual field or perceptual array with which we are presented. Without going as far as accepting any such general philosophical thesis, I think it must be admitted that we can and sometimes do see patches or regions of colour. A would-be unmasker might then hold that those are the only things we see in seeing the colours of things. The colours we see could be said to be properties of the shapes or patches or regions that we see. "That rectangular patch I see is yellow" predicates yellow of a seen patch; it ascribes to it the yellow that is seen. Seen colours would then be properties of seen objects. This would mean that the colours we see could not be said to be properties of nothing at all. As long as they come in some shape or other, the colours we see would be properties of something, and seeing a patch or region of a certain colour would be veridical predicational perception of the colour of something—namely, that very patch or region. Even seeing a formless expanse of blue would be seeing something—that expanse—to be blue.

Of course, this would be congenial to the unmasking project only if the patches or regions we see are not patches on clothing or expanses of pigment on canvas. Those things are physical objects, and so could not be allowed to be coloured. For an unmasker to acknowledge veridical predicational perception of the colour of something, then, the things he thinks we see to be coloured would have to be shapes or patches or regions that exist only insofar as they are seen. They could not be public physical objects. On this view, we could not understand two or more perceivers to see colour and to see the same thing to be coloured. The things veridically seen to be coloured could not be shared between different perceivers. I might see a patch of a certain colour, and you might see a patch of that same colour, but your patch and my patch could not be one and the same thing. Yours could go away while mine remains, or vice versa, by one of us simply closing his eyes.

---

8. B. Maund describes colours as "virtual properties"; they are properties, but there is, in fact, nothing that they are properties of. The most he explicitly argues is that colours are not properties of any physical objects (*Colours: Their Nature and Representation*, Cambridge, 1995, pp. 34–38).

On this view, attributing perceptions of colour to someone would require that one start from one's own perceptions of colour. If a would-
be unmasker could identify the contents of his own perceptions of
colour, and he could recognize the circumstances in which they typically arise, he might form the hypothesis that other perceivers are probably affected in the same ways and so learn to attribute similar perceptions to others whom he knows to be in similar circumstances. That
might also enable him to attribute to others beliefs about the colours of
objects, by taking them to be beliefs to the effect that objects have those
properties that are perceived in perceptions of colour. This would be
fully in the spirit of the unmasking strategy, since the attributor would
not have to share those beliefs in order to attribute them in that way to
others. But to understand the contents of those beliefs in this way, he
would have to be able to identify what is seen in a perception of colour
and understand how it differs from what is seen in a perception of a
different colour. He would also have to be able to recognize the circumstances in which people get perceptions of those different kinds.
And he would have to gain both kinds of information by starting from
his own perceptions of colour.

All this might seem to present no problem for the unmasking project. It might even seem to be the way we actually attribute perceptions
and beliefs. But it is not. In the simplest and most basic cases, we can
attribute perceptions of colour to others on the basis of what we know
to be the colours of the objects they see. Even if it were true that anyone who is confronted with his eyes open in good light by a yellow,
ovoid lemon will see a yellow elliptical patch in his visual field,[9] that
would be of no use to a would-be unmasker who has no beliefs about
the colours of objects. He could not recognize that a yellow lemon was
present. The most he could rely on in attributing perceptions of colour
to other people would be certain noncolour facts that he could recognize to be correlated with perceptions of patches of certain kinds. And
he could directly observe such correlations only in his own case.

Finding the required correlations would not always be easy. With no
information about the colours of the relevant objects, he would have to
make do with whatever other information was available. It could not
be the yellowness of lemons that he finds to be correlated with perceptions of a yellow patch, since he could find no yellow lemons. Perhaps he could find that the ripeness of seen lemons is what is so cor-

---

9. This is (almost) the view of C. Peacocke. He speaks only of having, or there
being, a patch in one's visual field, not of one's *seeing* it there, and of the patch's being yellow', not yellow. Peacocke, *Sense and Content*, Oxford, 1983, pp. 20–21.

related, and he could test for ripeness by feel, taste, or smell. He might then attribute perceptions of yellow patches to anyone he knows to stand in the appropriate relation to a lemon that is ripe. That would not work for kinds of objects whose members can differ in colour while being otherwise alike, like billiard balls, tulips, shirts, and automobiles of the same make and model. There is no distinctive feel, taste, or smell of those billiard balls that produce perceptions of yellow, or any particular feel, taste, or smell of those 1995 Honda Accords that produce perceptions of red. No doubt there are minute physical features that distinguish them, but few of us know what those features are, and we typically make no use of them in attributing perceptions of colour to ourselves or to others.

But if the relevant correlations could be found, then by assuming a similarity between other people's perceptual mechanisms and his own, an unmasker could perhaps hold that others get perceptions of the same kind as he gets from a certain kind of object. This assumption of similarity among different perceivers might seem unjustified and so problematic. How can one person be so sure that others get the same kinds of perceptions as he gets in the same circumstances? This has been a standard objection to all attempts to arrive at conclusions about the minds of others by starting only "from one's own case". But the objection concedes too much or starts too late. The difficulty for a would-be unmasker of the colours of things is not simply that of reaching a conclusion about other people's perceptions on the basis of what he can recognize to be true of himself and his own perceptions. The question is what he would be in a position to recognize about himself and his own perceptions.

To attribute perceptions to others on the basis of what happens in his own case, he must know what happens in his own case. He could attribute to others perceptions with determinate contents only if he knew what kinds of perceptions he himself gets from the kind of object he sees them to be perceiving. To attribute to them perceptions of the same kind as he gets, he needs some conception of the kind of perception he gets from objects of that kind.

To attribute perceptions of colour in particular, he must know or believe that he gets perceptions of colour under certain circumstances. It would not be enough for him simply to get a perception of yellow, or to see an elliptical patch of yellow, whenever he is appropriately related to a ripe lemon. He has to recognize that that is true of him. To do that, he has to understand what a yellow patch of colour is and understand what he is predicating of a patch when he sees it or thinks of it as yellow. He also has to recognize that he sees patches of that kind, and recognize the circumstances under which he sees them. The question is whether a would-be unmasker of the colours of things could do all that. What property could he recognize himself to see, and see his patch to have?

We know that it could not be a property he thinks of as a property of physical objects; he could regard it only as a feature of patches that are seen. But what feature? How is he to identify the property he sees, and so identify the kinds of perceptions he is prepared to attribute to anyone who sees a ripe lemon? This is not a question about the conditions of someone's seeing a yellow patch; it is about the conditions of someone's thinking of himself as seeing a yellow patch. What property could he think of himself as seeing?

He could not identify the property by definite description as simply that property that he sees to belong to his elliptical patch in the presence of a ripe lemon. That specification is not unique. There are many such properties. One property he can see to belong to such an elliptical patch is its shape; he can see it to be elliptical. But perceptions of shape are not what is in question. Nor could he specify the property by elimination, saying only that it is that property *other than its shape* that he sees to belong to his elliptical patch. That is still not a unique specification. He can also see the patch to appear in the presence of a ripe lemon, to be in the middle of his visual field, or perhaps to appear to the left of a rectangular patch next to it, and so on. Each of those properties of the patch is something other than its shape, but not the property yellow.

It might seem easier for him to specify the property in question directly, by a kind of ostension or demonstration. But similar obstacles arise. Suppose he concentrates his attention on a yellow patch he sees in the presence of a ripe lemon and says, "This" or "This that I now see". That alone does not determine what he perceives or takes himself to perceive. He could be referring to the patch, to the area surrounding the patch, to the event of his seeing the patch, or to something else. Even if he makes it clear that he means a property of the patch and explicitly says, "This property" or "This property that I see this patch to have", it is left indeterminate which property he means, or whether he has succeeded in identifying a property at all. There are many different properties that he can see the patch to have when he says or thinks, "This property".

This might seem to be no difficulty since the property in question will be whatever property he concentrates his attention on when he says, "This property". But what property is that? And how does he concentrate his attention on it? It is no good saying that *he* knows which property he is attending to or concentrating on, even if we don't know. The question is what he knows, and how he knows it. He knows what he is concentrating on only if he has some way of thinking of himself *as* concentrating on a certain property or some way of thinking of *what* he is attending to when the patch is present. What property he has in mind, and hence what he can be said to be concentrating on for the purpose of identifying it, depends on how he regards that property—what sorts of things he thinks can have the property, how it differs from other properties such things can have, and under what conditions he is prepared to ascribe the property to something.

If he has a word for the property, and he explains the meaning of that word by concentrating his attention on the property when it is present to him, what he means or understands by the word depends on how he is prepared to use it in sentences to say something that is true or false.[10] He must understand what he is predicating of a thing in

---

10. Wittgenstein draws attention to this feature of "ostensive definition" in his *Philosophical Investigations*, §§ 28–35. It is perhaps best summed up in:

So one might say: the ostensive definition explains the use—the meaning—of the word when the overall role of the word in language is clear. Thus if I know that someone means to explain a colour-word to me the ostensive definition "That is called 'sepia'" will help me to understand the word. (§ 30)

The point is later applied to sensations:

When one says "He gave a name to his sensation" one forgets that a great deal of stage-setting in the language is presupposed if the mere act of naming is to make sense. And when we speak of someone's having given a name to pain, what is presupposed is the existence of the grammar of the word "pain"; it shews the post where the new word is stationed. (§ 257)

An early expression of the same idea appears in *Philosophical Grammar*, Oxford, 1974, I, I, 24:

It may seem to us as if the other grammatical rules for a word had to follow from its ostensive definition; since after all an ostenstive definition, e.g. "that is called 'red'" determines the meaning of the word "red". But this definition is only those words plus pointing to a red object, e.g. a red piece of paper. And is this definition really unambiguous? Couldn't I have used the very same one to give the word "red" the meaning of the word "paper", or "square", or "shiny", or "light", or "thin" etc. etc.?

However, suppose that instead of saying "that is called 'red'" I had phrased my definition "that colour is called 'red'". That certainly is unambiguous, but only because the expression "colour" settles the grammar of the word "red" up to this last point. . . . Definitions might be given like this: the colour of this patch is called "red", its shape "ellipse".

I might say: one must already understand a great deal of a language in order to understand that definition. Someone who understands that definition must already know where the words ("red", "ellipse") are being put, where they belong in language.

applying that word to it and so understand the conditions under which such a predication would be true. He must to that extent be capable of making judgements in which that term is predicated of something. Merely being presented with a patch that is, in fact, yellow—or even repeatedly seeing such things—is not enough to give him that competence or capacity. But without it, saying, "This property" or "I call this property 'yellow'" whenever a yellow patch is present to him, would be nothing but an empty ritual. It would give no determinate meaning to the word and do nothing to identify a property that he recognizes to belong to his patch.

We cannot understand what such a would-be unmasker would be in a position to recognize about his own perceptions until we know what property he sees his elliptical patch to have, or what he means by the word he uses to pick it out. If there were some determinate property that he understands himself to perceive when a yellow, elliptical patch appears to him in the presence of a ripe lemon, then perhaps he could attribute perceptions of that same property to others whom he knows to be related in the same way to ripe lemons. We have found no such property and so cannot make sense of the kind of perceptions we have been trying to imagine he might understand himself to have. So we have made no sense of the kinds of perceptions he might make use of in attributing perceptions to others.

But we can conclude at least this much: if there were any such perceptions, or any such property that he could understand himself to see instances of in the imagined circumstances, it could not be a colour. The use that he is prepared to make of a term standing for whatever property he might have in mind is not the use of colour words. Any property he could have in mind would be something that belongs only to seen patches. So even if he were able to attribute some perceptions to other people in certain circumstances, and they were just like the perceptions he himself gets in those circumstances, the perceptions he could attribute to them would not be perceptions of colour.

For those who are competent in the use of colour terms, the property they take themselves to see in a perception of colour is the same property that they believe a physical object to have, in the belief that it is coloured. That is just the assumption on which this whole discussion of the "error" version of the unmasking strategy rests—that there is a direct connection between the objects of perception and of thought about the colours of things. Whatever property a would-be unmasker could understand himself to have perceptions of when a yellow, elliptical patch appears to him in the presence of a ripe lemon, it could not be the same property that others *believe* to belong to objects in believing them to be yellow. The property that others believe to belong to objects in the thought that they are yellow is the same property that those other people also see when they have perceptions of yellow. They take themselves to have veridical predicational perceptions of yellow objects. So even a would-be unmasker's attribution to others of perceptions of some property that he takes himself to perceive would not be the attribution to others of perceptions of yellow. Since the unmasker could not understand himself to have perceptions of yellow, he could not attribute perceptions of yellow to others on the basis of what he can recognize in his own case.

This would theoretically leave it open for a would-be unmasker to recognize that other people have perceptions of some property that he has perceptions of. He might even be able to recognize that others also *believe* that physical objects have a certain other property which they call "yellow". Whether such an unmasker could understand what those others mean by 'yellow' in those beliefs is what I have just been questioning. The present point is that if he could understand them as having any such beliefs at all, he would have to acknowledge that the property they attribute to a physical object in the *belief* that it is yellow is a different property from the property that he can understand them to *perceive* in any perceptions he can attribute to them on the basis of their similarity to the perceptions he understands himself to get in the presence of a ripe lemon.

But to acknowledge that two different properties play those two different roles would be to accept at best an indirect connection between the objects of perception and of thought about the colours of things. An indirect connection encourages a subjectivist account of the colours of objects. And we have seen that the equivalences needed to sustain any such account are not forthcoming. That is what I argued in chapter 6. It is a requirement on any successful dispositional theory that the kind of perceptions that objects of a certain colour are disposed to produce must be identifiable as such independently of the attribution of colour to any physical objects. That is what leaves the dispositionalist's biconditional about the colours of objects always contingent and not necessarily true, and so is fatal to subjectivist dispositional theories. If the present argument is correct, there is not even a suitably independent way to identify a class of perceptions as perceptions of colour in the first place. So a further necessary condition of success of subjectivist theories will remain forever unfulfilled. It does not serve the unmasking project to adopt an indirect connection between the objects of perception and of thought.

It would be an even greater step backwards to think of the property that a would-be unmasker can understand himself to have perceptions of as simply a certain distinctive feature of certain "sensations"—something he can be directly acquainted with or aware of, as one can feel the painfulness of certain sensations. That would be to abandon the "intentional" conception of colour perception altogether and return us to all those difficulties in the "sensation" view canvassed in chapters 5 and 6. Even if it were possible on that view to identify a class of perceptions as colour "sensations" or as "sensations" of yellow—as I believe it is not—it would leave unexplained how our beliefs about the colours of objects are related to perceptions of colour, so understood. The conditions of successful attribution of beliefs about the colours of things would still not be fulfilled.

The difficulties we have found for any would-be unmasker who takes the conditions of success of the unmasking project fully seriously strongly suggest that no one could abandon all beliefs about the colours of things and still understand the colour terms essentially involved in ascribing perceptions and beliefs about the colours of things. If that is so, no one competent to understand and acknowledge the perceptions and beliefs he hopes to unmask could free himself completely from all commitment to a world of coloured things. So no one could succeed in unmasking all those perceptions and beliefs as giving us only "appearance", not "reality". And someone who started out with no beliefs at all about the colours of things would be unable even to find the relevant perceptions or beliefs in the first place, so he would have nothing to unmask. That would mean that no one could consistently reject *all* truths about the colours of objects while retaining the capacity to understand the colour vocabulary we need to attribute perceptions and beliefs about colour to ourselves and our fellow human beings.

This huge question probably cannot be settled once and for all by abstract general argument. I have tried to draw attention to the severely impoverished position that the jettisoning of all beliefs about the colours of things would leave us in and so make as strong a case as I can for the negative side. I conclude that we cannot consistently reach the unmasking metaphysical conclusion and defend an "error" theory of our beliefs about the colours of things by the explanatory route we have been exploring. In accepting a direct connection between the "intentional objects" of perception and of thought about the colours of things, we can find no general reason for abandoning or questioning our belief in a world of coloured objects.

8

Discomforts and Distortions
of Metaphysical Theory

Starting with all our beliefs about the world and trying to reach the metaphysical conclusion that the colours of things are unreal is filled with difficulty. I have concluded that it cannot be done by following the unmasking explanatory strategy.

If that is so, it is in part because of the conditions of our acknowledging certain psychological facts as part of the world. We must admit some such facts to carry out the unmasking strategy. But if we cannot attribute perceptions of and beliefs about the colours of things to anyone without ourselves having beliefs about the colours of objects, then the psychological facts that the project of unmasking the colours of things needs to explain cannot be acknowledged without our also accepting some nonpsychological truths about the colours of things that the project means to deny. Accepting the relevant *explananda* violates a necessary condition of the project's success. Fulfilling that condition would render the relevant *explananda* unavailable. Either way, the project cannot succeed.

I now want to take up the question of where this leaves us, if it is correct. I think it should leave us just where we were at the beginning, before we even considered the metaphysical project. We found ourselves then in a world of coloured objects that we see and form beliefs about, as well as a world of physical facts and physical goings-on as described in the physical sciences. We also found ourselves in a world of social and psychological and economic facts, and of countless other kinds of facts as well.

Those different "worlds" can be seen as just different parts or aspects of the totality of what we take to be so. Granting, as I have, that among all the physical or physical-scientific facts there are no facts of the colours of things does not create a conflict among all the things we believe. What is asserted in one description of the world and goes unmentioned in another is not thereby denied. Only if the physical and other noncolour facts are said to be the *only* facts there are will the colours of things be excluded from the world, and the problem of accommodating them somehow within the facts already accepted then become pressing.

That is the position we would be in if the metaphysical project had succeeded. But without the pressure created by that project, we can continue to think of the world in many different ways and to move among them as our purposes and our interests change. The very objects we think of at one time and for certain reasons only in the most austere scientific terms, we can think of at other times and for other reasons as coloured and as having many other nonphysical properties.

The metaphysical enterprise presses the question of which of those different ways of thinking of things represents them as they really are. The question would have some purchase if the physical-scientific description of objects could be seen to be in conflict with our everyday beliefs about yellow lemons, red tomatoes, and green grass. We could not then comfortably continue to hold both sets of beliefs. But I find no such conflict.

This might seem to fly in the face of well-known facts. Colours are obviously very different from other properties we naturally and unreflectively take to be part of the way things are. And it is apparently easy to think that those differences show colour to be dispensable, or less fundamental to the world's being the way it is, than, say, the shapes, sizes, and motions of bodies and the forces under which they move and interact. Colour can seem more closely tied to perception and so find no intelligible place in what goes on whether it is perceived or not. The unique features of the colours of things as we understand them in everyday life are widely thought to be enough in themselves to exclude colours from any world in which the physical-scientific account of things that we accept is correct. The only way of accommodating them would then be by accepting either a subjectivist or an "error" account.

The reflections that are supposed to lead to one or the other of those metaphysical conclusions are what I have been investigating. My doubts do not imply that there is nothing special or different about colour.

There is no question that colour is different from other properties of things in the world, such as shape and size and motion. Shape is different from size, too, and size differs from motion. Each is a different kind of property from the others. In fact, every property is different from every other property. Everything is what it is and not another thing. The question is not whether there are differences but what exactly the differences are, and whether they support the idea of a conflict between an object's being coloured as we ordinarily understand it and its having the physical-scientific properties that we also ascribe to objects.

To reach the conclusion that the colours of things are not really part of the independent world or, if they are, that they are dependent on the responses of perceivers, it is not enough to find that colour is different—even very different—from other properties. It is not even enough for statements about the colours of things to have no place in a purely physical or physical-scientific description of the world. That is something we have been taking for granted throughout. Simply to describe, without metaphysical preconceptions, all the ways in which the colours of things are unique among all other properties of things would lead only to a greater appreciation of colour's special character. To bring the metaphysical status of colour into question, something more than those differences is needed. But if what it takes is the promise of explaining away all our perceptions of and beliefs about the colours of things without supposing that anything in the world is coloured, we have found that no such threat has been raised.

If what I have argued so far is right, colour is not unmaskable by explanations in terms only of the quantifiable physical properties of things. So it does not differ in that respect from the shape, size, or motion of an object. They are not unmaskable in that way either. But to deny that colour differs in that way from so-called primary features of the world is not to deny that colour is different—in fact, unique. Nor is it to deny that from certain points of view colour can even be felt to be in some ways less "fundamental" or somehow less fully integrated into the rest of what goes on. It is only to deny that any or all of colour's differences are reason to conclude that objects' being coloured conflicts with their having the physical-scientific properties we believe in, and that therefore either objects are not coloured or their having the colours they do is somehow dependent on the kinds of perceptions they would produce.

One difference between the colour of an object and its shape or size or state of motion or rest is that colour is perceivable only by sight, while those other properties can be perceived by both sight and touch. That is an important difference, but in itself it does not bring the colours

of objects into question as part of the world or suggest that they somehow depend on what kinds of perceptions the object would produce. It
is simply a fact about colour and perception. It does not even extend
to belief or knowledge. Someone can believe or know that an object is
a certain colour without having seen that object, or even without anyone's having seen it. One can even believe or know that an object is a
certain colour without anyone's ever having seen that particular colour.
Think of Hume's missing shade of blue.[1] And conversely, although the
shape, size, and motion of a great many objects can be perceived by
both seeing and touching the object, that is not always enough for knowing or coming to believe something about its shape, size, or state of motion or rest. The object has to be the right size for that. We can see and
feel the earth, for example, but we do not thereby come to know its size
or shape or motion. And the shapes, sizes, and motions of many very
small things are not perceived by sight or touch at all.

Colour, perception, knowledge, and belief are related in another way.
There probably would be no knowledge of, or even beliefs about, the
colours of anything if no one had ever seen any colours. But that alone
should not suggest that the colours of things are somehow less real or
less robust than other properties of things, or that they depend in some
way on what kinds of perceptions people would get from objects that
have them. Knowledge of the colour of a thing does not require perception of that thing or of its colour. It does not even require the power
of sight. I think many blind people know that lemons are yellow, tomatoes are red, and grass is green. Of course, they would not know such
things if none of the rest of us had ever seen colours, but given that we
have, the blind can know what we know.

To know that lemons are yellow, you have to understand what property you are ascribing to lemons in that thought. That is something the
blind can understand to the extent they understand the rest of us when
we speak of the colours of things. They are in that way dependent on
us for their understanding and their knowledge, just as each of us is
probably dependent on others for our understanding and knowledge of
many of the things we know.

The blind who have never seen colour certainly lack something that
the rest of us have, but I do not think what they lack is knowledge of
the colours of things. It is perhaps tempting to say that they lack knowl-

---

1. D. Hume, *A Treatise of Human Nature* (ed. L. A. Selby-Bigge), Oxford, 1958,
p. 6.

edge of what yellow lemons or red tomatoes look like. But that does not seem to be right. A blind person who knows that lemons are yellow could know that they look yellow. Someone who has the idea of a distinction in general between 'seems' and 'is', and knows, for example, that smooth things feel smooth in normal circumstances could know that yellow things look yellow in normal circumstances. Even to say that the blind still could not know what things that look yellow look like seems to me to go too far. They could know that they look yellow. What the cogenitally blind do not have and we do have is perceptions of colour. They never see what we see every minute. But you do not have to see an object, or see an instance of a property, to know that the object has the property, or even to know that it looks to most people as if it does.

I think it must be conceded that colour is different from some other properties in that total ignorance about the colours of things would be much less a handicap in understanding and getting along in the world than would ignorance of the shapes, sizes, and motions of bodies and of how bodies interact. Colour can, in that sense, be thought to be less "fundamental" than those other properties. If all human beings had been blind from birth, but circumstances had been otherwise favourable, they might well have known a great deal about the world without knowing anything about the colours of things.

That shows something about how the colours of things figure in our conception of the world, but it does not suggest that colour is therefore somehow less real than those other properties or dependent on being perceived in a way they are not. Europeans once knew a great deal about the world without knowing anything about America. With expanded capacities, they found it. Even those who never visited it came to know a lot about it; it came to be part of their acknowledged world. We who can see know a great deal about the colours of things which no one would know at all if sighted perceivers had never come along. Our capacities enable us to find what those without those capacities could never have found. The blind are dependent on the rest of us, just as stay-at-home Europeans had to depend on reports of the more adventurous. But that does not show that colour is dependent on being perceivable by us, any more than America is dependent on being perceivable. Nor does it show that someone who could not see it could not possibly know anything about it.

One thing that appears to encourage the idea that the colours of things depend on what kinds of perceptions they would produce is the great variation there is said to be among different people's perceptions of the colour of an object, or among one person's perceptions of it at different times, depending on the state of the perceiver's body and the circumstances in which the thing is viewed. This is a familiar refrain in philosophical discussions of perception, but as an observation on what actually goes on, it does not seem to be true.

Most people see yellow when they see a ripe lemon in good light and red when they see a ripe tomato. It is at best an extreme exaggeration to say that there are great variations in the colours people see, especially if the colours in question are identified by words as tolerant as 'yellow' and 'red'. What colour you see when you see an object on a particular occasion does, of course, depend on the condition you are in and the circumstances in which you find yourself. The colour you see under abnormal conditions might be very different from what you would normally see. But that is true of the perception of all properties. Whether you get a perception of something ovoid from an ovoid object or a perception of an elephant from an elephant equally depends on your current state and the perceptual conditions. Alleged facts of "perceptual relativity" do not support a distinction between colours and certain "primary" or "real" properties which objects are said to have on their own, independently of all human perception.

Philosophers sometimes appeal to the "relativity" of perception to show that *everything* we perceive exists only insofar as it is perceived. Berkeley held that whatever we perceive we perceive immediately or directly, and for immediate objects of perception, *esse* is *percipi*: the things we perceive are nothing more than, or are "essentially", objects of perception. Whatever one makes of the arguments for this, it is a completely general conclusion which draws no distinction between colours and other kinds of perceivable properties.

What would be needed to separate colour from certain "primary" qualities on the basis of such facts is the further idea that variations in perception are much greater—or perhaps that we are much more susceptible to what we take to be error or illusion—in the case of colour than in the perception of certain "primary" qualities. But that is simply not so. We are as easily or as often misled in the perception of the shape or size or motion of a thing as in the perception of its colour.

Many philosophers who now acknowledge this fact nonetheless continue to attribute the mistaken observation to defenders of what they call "traditional arguments" for a distinction between "primary" and "secondary" qualities. The unfortunate Locke is most maligned in this respect. He is continually saddled with the manifestly false idea that there is greater variation, or that we are more often wrong, in our perceptions of "secondary" qualities than in our perceptions of "primary" qualities.[2] Not only does Locke not base his distinction between "primary" and "secondary" qualities on that alleged fact; he never even mentions it or asserts it as a fact. The relativity of perception to perceptual conditions is well known to hold for all qualities—for extension as well as for colour, as Berkeley put it. But, as he was not alone in pointing out, even that does not establish that extension and colour are not really in the object or that they depend on the responses of perceivers. It shows at most that we cannot tell from a single perception the true extension or colour of an object.[3]

The security or reality of the colours of things has even been thought to be threatened, and so the subjectivity of colour thought to be supported, not by the fact of illusions or disagreements in our perceptions of colour, which after all are rare, but on the contrary by the very fact of consensus. Jonathan Bennett puts the thought this way:

> The occasional failures of agreement bring home to us how dependent our public secondary-quality terminology is upon the fact that we usually *do* agree in our secondary-quality discriminations—the failures help us to realize that our notion of two things' having the same colour, say, is only as secure as our ability to muster an overwhelming majority who see them as having the same colour.[4]

There seems to me no question that we are largely in agreement about the colours of most things, and that is a very important fact for the "security" of our beliefs. But I do not see how this can "bring home to us" or "help us to realize" the unreality or subjectivity of colour. We are largely in agreement about the shapes and sizes of most things, too.

If there is something in our ordinary understanding of the colours of things that suggests that two things' having the same colour depends on a majority's seeing them to be the same colour, is there something comparable in the case of shape or size? If the dependence in the case of colour is taken to mean that, necessarily, two objects have the same colour if and only if normal human perceivers in standard perceptual circumstances would get the same kinds of perceptions of colour from them, then that looks like nothing more than a dispositional theory of an object's colour, or of two objects' having the same colour. Far from

---

2. Among those who have attributed this line of argument to Locke are R. Aaron, *John Locke*, Oxford, 1937, p. 110; G. Warnock, *Berkeley*, London, 1953, p. 94; J. Bennett, *Locke, Berkeley, Hume: Central Themes*, Oxford, 1971, p. 95; I. Tipton, *Berkeley: The Philosophy of Immaterialism*, London, 1974; and B. Williams, *Descartes: The Project of Pure Enquiry*, Harmondsworth, 1978, p. 238.

3. G. Berkeley, *A Treatise concerning the Principles of Human Knowledge*, Part I, Section 15, in *Berkeley: Philosophical Works* (ed. M. Ayers), London, 1975, p. 81.

4. Bennett, *Locke, Berkeley, Hume*, p. 96.

being supported by our everyday understanding of the colours of things, we have found that it fails as an account of what we believe.

This is not to deny that agreement in our colour judgements is important. It is probably true that if we did not largely agree about the colours of things we would have no firm or secure beliefs about the colours of things at all. But the same is true of beliefs about the shapes and sizes and motions of things, and of everything else we believe. Without general agreement, we could not say or understand or believe anything. But that does not mean that what we all believe when we agree about something is only that we all agree. The point is not that what we believe when we believe that an object is yellow or ovoid is that a majority of our fellow human beings agree with us in our belief. That would leave the belief with no determinate content. What we all believe, or agree about, is that the object is yellow or ovoid. But if we did not largely agree in the application of those concepts and in many of the judgements we make with them, we would have no such concepts and could make no such judgements at all.

Considered on their own, then, independently of the pressures of the metaphysical project, I think the ways in which the colours of things differ from the properties mentioned in the physical-scientific account of the world do not show that objects' being coloured is in conflict with their having those other properties, or that their being coloured depends on what kinds of perceptions they would produce in a way that their having those other properties does not. But there remains a widespread feeling that colours are still less robust or more dispensable than those physical properties and that they are in a way even superfluous to an adequate account of what goes on in the world. J. L. Mackie perhaps gives expression to this idea in his appeal to "economy of postulation" as a way of eliminating colour from the world. As we saw in chapter 4, it is difficult to make that idea both fairly definite and plausible, if it is not taken as simply expressing the conclusion of a metaphysical unmasking of the kind I have argued cannot succeed. But there is perhaps something behind it.

Colour, for instance, is said to be causally inert; it does not *do* anything in the world. The idea is that if it is there at all, it is completely idle and plays no role in what goes on. Billiard balls behave the same way whatever their colour. The effects that different-coloured objects have on one another can be explained without mentioning their colour. That is true of the physical goings-on on the billiards table, but it is not true that colour plays no role in what goes in the world if part of "what goes on" is that people see lemons to be yellow, tomatoes to be red, and so on. Jones sees a lemon on the table and sees it to be yellow, in part because there is a yellow lemon there. If an object of that colour had not been there, she would not have seen the colour she saw. We appeal to facts about the colours of things to explain many of the familiar occurrences we acknowledge and rely on every day.

It will be replied that the *colour* of the lemon is not really what explains Jones' perceiving yellow. All that happens is that light reflected from the lemon strikes Jones' eyes and has a certain effect on her brain. There need be no mention of colour anywhere in the whole story of her interaction with the lemon. So to explain her perceiving what she does, we need only the physical-scientific story.

This is the position of someone who has already reached the metaphysical conclusion of a colourless world. It is true that the physical-scientific story is enough to explain Jones' physical interaction with the lemon. But what is to be explained in a case like this is the fact that Jones sees yellow and sees the lemon to be yellow. Since those psychological facts are not equivalent to anything expressed in purely physical-scientific terms, an austerely scientific explanation of the state of Jones' brain in the presence of the lemon does not explain why she sees yellow there. It explains only something expressible in purely physical-scientific terms. This is a consequence of the assumption that there are no psychological and no colour terms in the vocabulary of the physical sciences, combined with the idea that explanations explain facts, not objects.

Not only do such physical-scientific facts alone not explain psychological facts. I have argued that restricting ourselves to physical-scientific facts alone would prevent us from even acknowledging any psychological facts of the kind we want to explain in this case. The presence of a yellow object does help explain that fact. It makes intelligible to us Jones' seeing something yellow on that occasion, not something red or green.

But even if it were true that colour is causally inefficacious and "does nothing" in the physical interactions in the world, it would not follow, without additional metaphysical support, that colour is not part of the way things are. There are many properties, some of them expressible exclusively in the vocabulary of the physical sciences, whose presence does not "do" anything in the physical world in that sense but which nonetheless belong to objects in the world and are undeniably part of the way things are.

The length of an object sometimes makes a difference to its causal powers—to what it can do. But an object's having a length in centimetres that is an odd number is not likely to be relevant to its interactions with other objects.[5] That is a perfectly real property of some objects in the independent world; they have it whether anyone knows or thinks of them as having it. Also, some billiard balls are made from material that comes from Africa; some are not. The origin of the material from which they are made is irrelevant to their causal powers if they are uniformly made from the same kind of material. But a billiard ball's coming from Africa rather than from some other place is something true of that ball and is part of the way things are, even if its coming from Africa is causally inert. Colour could be equally secure, even if it were causally inefficacious.

Suspicions about the metaphysical status of colour cannot be simply read off the differences between colour and other properties. For that, a metaphysical standard, or project, or question, is needed. If the promise of a thorough unmasking is what is needed as the standard or project against which colour's prospects are to be measured, I think a negative conclusion, or even a serious challenge to the colours of things, cannot be reached. But being unable to arrive at an appropriate metaphysical verdict, or even to raise the metaphysical question in the right way, can be disappointing and frustrating. It leaves us without something we feel we want and should be able to get. This makes it tempting to try to get what we want in some other way.

One way would be to dismiss or ignore all the difficulties I have drawn attention to in previous chapters and simply opt for a theory that would answer the metaphysical question. That would avoid the frustration of having no metaphysical position, but it would be no real solution. It would bring with it dissatisfactions and disappointments of its own. What present themselves as obstacles on the way to reaching a satisfactory theory by the explanatory route reappear in another form as difficulties in accommodating any such theory to what we already know or believe. The view that the colours of things are unreal appears to conflict with many facts that demand a place in one's conception of the world. It is the negative or exclusionary implications of the metaphysical theory that cause the trouble.

The metaphysical theory is exclusionary in the sense that it does not simply leave the colours of things unmentioned. It takes a stand that appears to have direct implications for the truth or meaning of what we believe when we believe that objects are coloured. If it did not, it would be hard to see how it could promise to reveal what is really so with re-

---

5. See D. Hilbert, *Color and Color Perception*, Stanford, 1987, p. 10.

spect to the colours of things. Could we then simply opt for an "error" theory that says that all our beliefs about the colours of physical objects are false? That might sound easy to do, like putting your money on a horse in a race or joining a political party and resolving to defend it against all opposition. But accepting that metaphysical theory would require at the very least that we adjust our acceptance of many other things we take to be so. Not all of our previous attitudes could remain unchanged.

The theory says that no objects are coloured, so if we simply acquiesced without comment in our familiar beliefs that lemons are yellow, tomatoes are red, and so on, it would be as if we had not really accepted the theory after all. We would be paying lip service to it while still believing what it says we should not believe. Of course, we might then try to purge ourselves of all beliefs about the colours of things. That would not be easy to do, to put it mildly, but if what I have argued is correct, it would require that we also stop thinking of other people as having beliefs about the colours of things as well. That would not be easy to do either. But to succeed in those tasks would not be to hold a metaphysical "error" theory of the colours of things. It would be to have arrived at a conception of the world which includes no coloured things and no beliefs about the colours of things. The metaphysical error theory acknowledges such beliefs while at the same time holding that they are all false. The beliefs must be recognized for their contents to be denied.

Even if we could somehow manage to repudiate all beliefs about the colours of things, we still would be faced with the facts of perception. We presumably could not deny that we see colours or even that we see coloured objects, at least in the sense that we typically see the objects around us to be coloured. That is what would make it so difficult for us to give up our belief in coloured things. They stare us in the face virtually every time we open our eyes. Seeing objects to be coloured is what I have called predicational seeing, and even if that kind of seeing is not strictly speaking believing, it is the kind of seeing that makes it difficult to avoid believing.

One way to resist the pressure from perception would be to shut our eyes forever and so get no more perceptions of colour. Whatever satisfactions such self-denial might bring, it would not leave us with a metaphysical theory of the colours of things either, but only with perversely restricted perceptual access to the world. If we kept our eyes open, and so continued to get perceptions of colour and of coloured objects while thinking of objects in the ways we do, we could not avoid getting beliefs about the colours of things. But those beliefs would confict with the theory we had officially accepted, so we would be thrown into conflict. We would not have a stable, intellectually satisfying position.

The metaphysical theory implies that those beliefs are false, so it encourages rejection of the colours of things. But the beliefs we could not help getting about the colours of things imply that the metaphysical theory is false, so they encourage rejection of that theory. It would seem like a complete stand-off. We would not have a consistent, fully satisfying conception of the world.

The metaphysical theory might appear to be in a superior position, since it acknowledges the presence of the beliefs that appear to challenge it, and it negates the challenge by holding that those beliefs are not true. That everyone *believes* that objects are coloured does not conflict with the metaphysical theory; in fact, it is part of it. What conflicts with the theory is the truth of those beliefs, and that is what the theory denies. This might seem to give the metaphysical theory the edge if it could explain why people believe that objects are coloured even though they are not.

I have argued that that cannot be done. But even if it could, it would yield no stable resolution on its own. Starting from everything we think we know about the world, including our everyday colour beliefs, we might equally explain why many people accept the metaphysical error theory even though objects are, in fact, coloured. That would return the conflict to at least a stand-off. It might even tip the scales in favour of our everyday colour beliefs, since everything we perceive supports them, and we could explain why some people deny them without ourselves having to deny anything we perceive or believe to be so. If that explanation were better than the unmasking explanation offered by the error theory, the metaphysical unreality of colour is what would then have been unmasked as an illusion.

It is perfectly consistent with the metaphysical error theory that human beings will inevitably come to believe that objects are coloured, given their perceptions and the thoughts they cannot help having about them. But on that theory, the inevitability would indicate only something about us, and nothing about objects' being coloured. We could admit that we cannot help believing that objects are coloured, but we would have to insist that that unavoidable belief is not true.

This would leave us in a position that is unsatisfactory or disappointing in a different way. Finding that a belief is not true, or that our acceptance of it can be explained independently of whether it is true, is usually an excellent reason for abandoning or at the very least reexamining that belief. But if we simply could not help believing that objects are coloured, we would see that we had excellent reasons for rejecting something that we would also see we cannot help believing. This would bring home to us with respect to our colour beliefs something like what Hume called "the whimsical condition of mankind, who must act and reason and believe; though they are not able, by their most diligent enquiry, to satisfy themselves concerning the foundations of those operations, or to remove the objections, which may be raised against them."[6] This is not a happy intellectual position. We would be unable to resist believing what the theory we accept says is not true. 'Whimsical' is an understatement.

Acceptance of the metaphysical error theory is what would put us in this uncomfortable position. There is nothing in itself disconcerting in admitting that we simply cannot help getting certain beliefs on certain kinds of occasions. It is often the best indication that the beliefs in question are true. With our eyes open in good light in the presence of a perceivable object, being unable to avoid believing that it is there and has a certain property is all it takes for us to discover that the object is there and has that property. When the obvious truth of what we perceive and believe to be so is what makes us unable to believe otherwise, our inability is not seen as a failing. On the contrary, it is a mark of our openness or unproblematic access to the way the world is. The metaphysical theory puts us in the position of seeing it as a failing, something we are apparently stuck with.

Our chagrin at that unavoidable failing might be somewhat reduced if we could at least see ourselves as right about perception. But the error theory requires that if we take colours to be properties of some things that we see, they cannot be properties of any physical objects that we see. And to think of them as properties of coloured patches or regions of our visual field—something each of us sees but does not share with other perceivers—would leave mysterious the application of a shared set of terms like 'yellow', 'red', 'green', and so on to such objects. We could not understand them as colour terms. We probably could not even understand the terms other people apparently use to speak of their so-called patches. This would create pressure towards denying that what we think of as colour is properly understood as a property of anything we see, and so as properly an object of perception at all. Taking the error theory seriously in this way could lead us to regard colour as nothing more than a quality or feature that is inevitably present in our experience whenever we see physical objects, much as a feeling of sadness can accompany one's perception of one's long-unvisited childhood

6. D. Hume, *Enquiries concerning the Human Understanding and concerning the Principles of Morals*, (ed. L.A. Selby-Bigge), Oxford, 1966, p. 160.

home. This leads away from the idea of perceptions of colour as having intentional contents at all and towards the view that they are like sensations with a certain distinctive character.

That is what I believe happened in the seventeenth century. Prior acceptance of the exclusively scientific story of the physical world is what encouraged the idea of perceptions of colour as nothing more than "sensations". There was nothing in that restricted physical world for them to be perceptions of. A similarly distorted understanding of perceptions of colour is still with us today, and for similar reasons.

It is in these ways that the difficulties we saw earlier would continue to destabilize acceptance of the metaphysical error theory. I have tried to show how thinking of perceptions of colour in any of those ways makes it impossible to understand the contents of our perceptions of and beliefs about the colours of things in the right way. Some of the facts the metaphysical theory is meant to account for are thereby distorted or even denied. To the extent we succeeded in regarding the colours we see as not properties of any objects, we would tend to lose our grasp of the beliefs the theory is supposed to account for. Understanding those beliefs without distortion would lead us to think of perceptions of colour as perceptions of properties of the objects we see. But then perceiving the colours of objects would tend to confirm our beliefs about the colours of things, and we would be thrown back into conflict with the metaphysical theory that denies them. No stable, satisfying understanding of ourselves would be available.

To say that the course of our everyday experience inevitably leads us to believe that objects are coloured is not to say that we cannot think of physical objects without thinking of them in colour terms. We do that whenever we think of things in certain ways without mentioning their colours. That is what happens in the physical sciences, if, as I have been assuming, those sciences make no use of colour terms. We change our ways of thinking of the world at different times and for different purposes. If there is no conflict between the different ways of thinking, there is no intellectual discomfort in accepting all of them.

The possibility of shifting from one point of view to another in this way might encourage the thought that we could avoid the difficulties that arise from accepting the metaphysical error theory by a similar kind of manouevre. The verdict that objects are not really coloured is a conclusion arrived at (if at all) only when we are concerned with the metaphysical status of the colours of things. When we are not concerned with that question, as in the normal activities of everyday life, we might continue to acquiesce in our familiar judgements about yellow lemons, red tomatoes, and the like. From within that everyday standpoint, those judgements will be perfectly acceptable. Just as we can operate within the austere scientific story and then shift to the richer conception of a world of coloured things as our interests change, so, the suggestion is, we can move back and forth without discomfort between the metaphysical error theory and that richer everyday conception of coloured objects. If there is no need to force a choice between the metaphysical theory and the everyday conception, we can accept them both without discomfort or dissatisfaction. The difficulties our everyday beliefs might seem to create for accepting that theory will then prove to have been illusory.

This suggestion will have these encouraging consequences only if we can find a way of not being forced to choose between the metaphysical error theory and our everyday conception of a coloured world. As they stand, the two conceptions certainly seem incompatible. It is difficult to see how both could be true. That is what creates the difficulty of accommodating that theory to what we all believe about the world. The encouraging suggestion is to eliminate the incompatibility by finding each set of beliefs in its own way acceptable and so denying the inevitability of intellectual dissatisfaction or disappointment in accepting them both.

P. F. Strawson has put forward a suggestion of this kind.[7] It is not just the thought that there is no explicit conflict between an austere scientific account of the world and richer conceptions which acknowledge the colours and other "phenomenal" qualities of objects. That would be only to grant that no colour or other "phenomenal" terms are used in a strictly physical science. But Strawson thinks he sees a way to go further and avoid any disturbing conflict between our everyday conception of a coloured world and what he calls the philosophical or metaphysical theory of "scientific or Lockean realism". That is the theory that physical objects "have no properties but those which figure in the physical theories of science".[8] Assuming that colour does not figure in the physical theories of science, that implies that physical objects are not coloured and that "no such phenomenal properties really belong to physical objects at all".[9] The metaphysical theory Strawson considers is exclusionary in that sense. Nonetheless, he thinks there is a way to accept that theory and also to retain our everyday judgements about the colours of things, as we do most of the time.

---

7. See P. F. Strawson, "Perception and Its Objects" in G. F. Macdonald (ed.), *Perception and Identity*, Ithaca, N.Y., 1979, and his *Skepticism and Naturalism: Some Varieties*, London, 1985.

8. Strawson, "Perception and Its Objects", p. 58.

9. Strawson, *Skepticism and Naturalism*, p. 42.

He does not mean simply that we cannot help believing most of the time that objects are coloured, or that our accepting the metaphysical theory can never, in fact, lead us to give up those everyday beliefs. That would leave us only in the unsatisfactory intellectual position of being stuck with our shameful inability to avoid believing what we had "discovered" to be false. Rather, Strawson means to suggest that there is no conflict involved in accepting both the everyday and the metaphysical beliefs. Our everyday judgements of the colours of things are not threatened by "scientific or Lockean realism". Although there is a "radical difference in the standpoint from which what are in a sense identical objects or events or phenomena may be viewed",[10] he thinks there is a way of acknowledging what he calls the "metaphysical acceptability"[11] of both standpoints. We can have our colours and deny them, too.

The key to this accommodating resolution is a certain relativity in what is claimed from each of those standpoints, and so "a certain ultimate relativity in our conception of the real":

> Relative to the human perceptual standpoint, commonplace physical objects really are . . . bearers of phenomenal visual and tactile properties. Relative to the standpoint of physical science (which is also a human standpoint) they really have no properties but those recognized, or to be recognized, in physical theory.[12] . . . Once the relativity of these "really"s to different standpoints, to different standards of the "real" is acknowledged, the appearance of contradiction between these positions disappears; the same thing can both be, and not be, phenomenally propertied.[13]

It is difficult to see how the same thing "can both be, and not be, phenomenally propertied". One way of being what Strawson means by "phenomenally propertied" would be to be yellow. And it is difficult to see how a thing can both be and not be yellow. Of course, someone might believe that a certain thing is yellow when acquiescing in our everyday colour judgements, and deny that it is yellow when judging

---

10. Strawson, *Skepticism and Naturalism*, p. 35.

11. Strawson, *Skepticism and Naturalism*, p. 68.

12. I take Strawson to mean by "the standpoint of physical science" here what he elsewhere calls "scientific or Lockean realism". This latter position does imply that objects have no properties other than those recognized in physical theory. I do not think that physical theory alone has that implication. It does not mention any other properties, but that does not mean that it conflicts with our everyday judgements about the colours of things. The position Strawson hopes to accommodate with those everyday judgements does appear to conflict with them. It says that physical objects have no such properties.

13. Strawson, *Skepticism and Naturalism*, pp. 44–45.

things from the standpoint of metaphysical "scientific realism". But that would simply be vacillation, and—if the two standpoints do conflict—inconsistency. The thought that a thing cannot both be and not be yellow is precisely what forces the question of which of the things said from those two different standpoints is correct. That is the pressure that Strawson says should, and can, be resisted. But one would not manage to resist it and avoid the question of correctness simply by accepting "scientific realism" some of the time—in philosophical moments—and believing in the colours of things the rest of the time. Strawson thinks the idea that at most one of the two views is correct can be resisted; there is only "the appearance of contradiction" between them.[14] "It is mistaken to think of these views of the world as genuinely incompatible".[15]

The thought that the views are incompatible is a "mistake" because it fails to recognize the availablity of a certain "relativizing move"[16] that can erase the apparent conflict. As Strawson explains it, this appears to involve understanding the statements of the apparently opposed positions as elliptical, or as containing an implicit reference to a standpoint or set of standards which the statements in question express. The "relativizing move" would then be a matter of making those references explicit and thereby revealing what lies hidden in the briefer statements taken on their own.

This is a familiar idea in other contexts. We can remove the appearance of inconsistency from the statement 'Mickey is large and Babar is small and Babar is larger than Mickey' by making it explicit that Mickey is large for a mouse and Babar is small for an elephant. We reveal the hidden relativity in the terms 'large' and 'small'. Applying a similar idea to the present case, we might try to remove the apparent inconsistency from 'Lemons are yellow and lemons have only those properties recognized in physical science and physical science does not recognize the colours of things' by making explicit the standpoints from which each of the apparently conflicting things is said. It is from the everyday human perceptual standpoint that lemons are said to be yellow, and from the standpoint of metaphysical "scientific realism" that they are said not to be. To make the relativity explicit, we might say, "From (or according to) the human perceptual standpoint, lemons are yellow" and "From (or according to) the standpoint of scientific realism, lemons have only those properties recognized in physical theory".

14. Strawson, *Skepticism and Naturalism*, p. 45.
15. Strawson, *Skepticism and Naturalism*, p. 50.
16. Strawson, *Skepticism and Naturalism*, pp. 42, 50.

There is no inconsistency between those two expanded statements. They can both be correct, and there is no pressure to force a choice between them. In fact, I believe both are true. It is one of our everyday beliefs about the colours of things that lemons are yellow. That is something we take to be true from "the human perceptual standpoint". And, as the second expanded statement says, it is part of metaphysical "scientific realism" that no physical objects are coloured, so none is yellow. But if expansion along those lines is what the "relativizing move" amounts to, it does not provide a satisfactory resolution of the original conflict. The originally felt conflict is between two opposed conceptions of what is so, or what the world is like. And this move does not give us the promised satisfaction on that issue. It is true that the two expanded statements do not conflict. But in believing both of those expanded statements, we do not thereby hold any belief as to whether objects are coloured. It was in answering that question in two apparently incompatible ways that the conflict arose.

It is also true, for example, that from (or according to) the Christian standpoint, there is a God and humans enjoy eternal life, and from (or according to) the atheistic standpoint there is no God and no eternal life. There is no confict between those two observations; both of them are true. But their compatibility does nothing to ease the discomfort of someone who wonders what to believe or which standpoint to accept. In believing each of those expanded statements, we do not thereby answer that question. The question we want answered is not simply what does each of the different positions say or what is so according to each of them. It is a question of what is so or of what to believe. If the two positions conflict, that is equivalent to the question of which one, if either, is correct.

Of course, we could accept the expanded statements and still express categorical beliefs about whether objects are coloured. We could simply add to one of the expanded statements the further assertion that the mentioned standpoint is correct. We could say, "From (or according to) the metaphysical scientific realist standpoint, objects have no colour, and that standpoint is correct" as a way of saying that objects are not coloured. But we could also make a similar assertion to the opposite effect about the correctness of the "human perceptual standpoint". Which statement to make is just the original question of which standpoint is correct. That is the conflict that the "relativizing move" was supposed to enable us to avoid.

Even if the "relativizing move" so understood did resolve the conflict—as I think it does not—there would still be the question of whether it is right to make it. It seems to rest on nothing more than a general recommendation to expand whatever we believe when we believe something from a particular standpoint into something that mentions or refers to that very standpoint. But if every belief were expanded in that way, we would be left with no determinate beliefs about the world at all.

A "standpoint" or position from which we believe something appears so far to be nothing more than a set of terms or assumptions within which a particular belief is expressed. If that is so, then every time we believe something, we believe it from some standpoint or other. This suggests that in believing that p from a particular standpoint, S1, what we believe is more fully expressed as 'From (or according to) standpoint S1, p'. If that were so in general, we could never simply believe that p, for anything that might be put in for the 'p'. It would not even be possible to believe what the first application of this general idea says we believe when we believe that p from some particular standpoint; that is, 'From (or according to) standpoint S1, p'. To have that expanded belief, we presumably must have it from some standpoint or other in turn, either the same as or different from the standpoint from which we are said to believe that p. Call that newly mentioned standpoint S2. Then in believing, from S2, 'From (or according to) S1, p', we would really be believing 'From (or according to) S2, from (or according to) S1, p'. But that belief, in turn, must be held from some standpoint or other, given the general idea. So the move must be applied again. And so on forever. Even if each of the mentioned standpoints is one and the same standpoint, it would not help. The content of any belief held from a standpoint would have to include a specification of the standpoint from which it is held, so the content of any belief could never be fully specified.

This shows that if we hold any determinate beliefs at all, we must hold some beliefs to which no such further specification of standpoint has to be added. But if our beliefs about the colours of objects and our acceptance of the metaphysical error theory are both beliefs whose contents are determinate in that way, then we are faced once again with the original conflict. We would not avoid it by applying a "relativizing move" that would leave us with no determinate belief. It is because we seek beliefs with determinate categorical content that the conflict arises. We are interested in how things are, not only in how certain standpoints or sets of beliefs say things are.

The relativity thought to be present in the acceptance of both the metaphysical theory and the everyday view that things are coloured might seem to be analogous to a certain relativity many find to be implicit even in our everyday colour judgements themselves. Strawson holds, for example, that our everyday colour judgements contain an implicit reference to certain conditions or standards which usually remain unmentioned unless they are thought to differ from what we regard as normal. We say that blood is red, but we acknowledge that, when seen under a microscope, it is mostly colourless. The two judgements appear to conflict, but they are made from different perceptual points of view. As Strawson puts it: "we are quite content to say, and can without contradiction say, both that blood is really uniformly bright red and also that it is mostly colorless".[17] Seen with the naked eye in the clear light of day, blood is really red; seen under the microscope, it is really mostly colourless. We shift our standard from one perceptual situation to another. "Such shifts do not convict us of volatility or condemn us to internal conflict. The appearance of both volatility and conflict vanishes when we acknowledge the relativity of our 'really's."[18] If there is a similar relativity when we say in everyday life that lemons are really yellow and say in philosophy that lemons are really without colour, it looks as if there would be no conflict or discomfort in accepting the metaphysical error theory while continuing to acquiesce in our everyday beliefs about the colours of things.

I do not think there is a parallel here that explains how the apparent conflict with the metaphysical theory can be avoided. That is partly because I do not think relativity to certain perceptual conditions or standards is part of the content of everyday beliefs about the colours of things. If 'It is red' and 'It is colourless' are said of the same thing, they do seem to me to conflict. Not both of them could be true. There is admittedly no conflict between 'Blood looks red when seen in normal circumstances with the naked eye' and 'Blood looks mainly colourless when seen under a microscope', but those statements say how blood looks under different perceptual conditions, not what colour it is under different perceptual conditions.

The question what colour a thing looks to be does require specification of the prevailing conditions and the state of the perceiver—looks to whom? and under what conditions? The same holds for the shape a thing looks to be or the size it looks to be. But saying what shape or what size a thing is does not make reference to perceivers or perceptual conditions, and I do not believe specification of a thing's colour does either. In fact, it does not seem to me true that blood is red under normal conditions and colourless when under a microscope. Blood does not change its colour simply by being moved about.

---

17. Strawson, *Skepticism and Naturalism*, p. 46.
18. Strawson, "Perception and Its Objects", p. 57.

Anyone who holds a subjectivist, dispositional theory of an object's colour will, of course, insist that specification of an object's colour does include reference to possible perceivers and perceptual conditions. That is perhaps what lies behind Strawson's defence of relativity in our everyday colour judgements on the grounds that "colours are visibilia or they are nothing".[19] If that means only that colours are the sorts of things that can be seen, it has no relativistic consequences. Nor does it have such consequences if it means only that colours can be perceived by visual perception alone. If it means rather that the colours of things are "essentially" visibilia in the sense that questions about the colours of things are questions about how they would look, or what kinds of perceptions they would produce, under certain conditions, then it does have relativistic implications. Further specification of the relevant perceptions and conditions would be needed. It makes no sense to say simply what kinds of perceptions a thing would produce without specifying the kinds of perceivers in whom, and the kinds of conditions under which, those perceptions would occur. But I have argued that no subjectivist dispositional account along such lines captures the content of our everyday beliefs about the colours of things. That is another way of saying that those everyday beliefs do not contain an implicit relativity to perceivers and perceptual conditions of the kind that the dispositional theory implies.

Even if the dispositional theory had succeeded in capturing the content of those beliefs, it could not be pressed into service to free the metaphysical error theory from a conflict it is otherwise unable to overcome. It would simply introduce a different, but equally troubling, conflict, since a dispositional theory and an error theory of an object's colour cannot both be correct. Or rather, they cannot both be correct if some objects in the world would, in fact, produce perceptions of a certain colour in normal human perceivers in standard perceptual circumstances. A dispositional theory says that all such objects are coloured. The error theory says there are no coloured objects. If there are some objects that would have such effects on perceivers, and a dispositional theory is correct, the error theory is wrong. We cannot accept both theories and find intellectual satisfaction.

Acceptance of the metaphysical error theory seems to lead to inescapable conflict. It denies what our everyday colour judgements assert, and vice versa. We say of certain objects in everyday life that they are yellow and of others that they are red; if we accept the metaphysical error theory, we say of those same objects that they have no colour

---

19. Strawson, "Perception and Its Objects", p. 56.

at all. The fact that we say what we do in each case from different "standpoints", or from within different "worlds", makes no difference if the things we say from each of those standpoints cannot all be true together. In the physical sciences, with no metaphysical pretensions, we say only that objects have those properties with which those sciences are concerned. In economics, we speak only of their economic features. If there is no conflict among the different things we say from those different standpoints, no "relativizing move" is needed to reconcile them. But if some of the different things we say are incompatible—as they are if we accept the metaphysical error theory—no "relativizing move" will succeed in removing the conflict while leaving us with categorical, ground-floor beliefs about the world.

I believe this unavoidable conflict is one of the things that can make a dispositional theory of an object's colour look appealing. It retains basically the same metaphysical picture of the world as the error theory does, but it tries to avoid conflict by taking a different view of the contents of our beliefs about the colours of things. There is a semantic and not primarily metaphysical disagreement between the two philosophical theories. It is not strictly true on either theory that physical objects have *only* those properties attributed to them in the physical sciences. Both theories agree that physical objects have the capacity to produce perceptions of colour in appropriately qualified perceivers under certain circumstances, and that is not something expressible in the austere terms of the physical sciences alone. So both theories agree that objects in the world have more than purely physical properties.

Where the difference between an error theory and a dispositional theory lies is not in the conception of what is "really" true of physical objects in the world, but in a semantic or psychological thesis about what we mean or what we think when we say or think that an object is coloured. If we say or think only what the dispositional theory of an object's colour says we do, there is no conflict between the scientifically based metaphysical picture of the world and our everyday beliefs about the colours of things. By opting for a dispositional theory, we would then appear to avoid the paradoxical or unacceptable consequences of the error theory, with no felt loss of anything that is metaphysically or "really" so in the world as it is independently of us.

It is true that the dispositional theory does not deny that physical objects are coloured, and in that respect it enjoys an advantage over the error theory. But I have argued that it distorts and to that extent denies what we believe in everyday life when we believe that objects are coloured. Even if we could identify perceptions of colour in the way that theory requires—which I have argued we cannot do—the theory cannot give the right account of how our perceiving what we do is related to our believing what we do about the colours of things.

For anyone committed to the scientifically based metaphysical conception of reality, that will not seem to be so. What I am claiming is distortion of our everyday beliefs will appear in the light of that conception to be the only possible contents our beliefs about the colours of things could have. Possessing a disposition to produce perceptions of certain kinds under certain kinds of circumstances will be all that an object's being coloured could possibly be, on that conception of reality. There would be nothing else in reality that could serve to express the conditions under which what we believe is true. Anyone who thinks otherwise will be dismissed as wrong about the contents of our assertions and thoughts about the colours of things. He will be thought to be demonstrably in error about what our everyday conception of the world amounts to, just as our everyday conception itself is accused of error by the metaphysical error theory.

It is in these ways that I think the metaphysical quest for reality distorts and so leads us away from our everyday conception of the world, and so away from an accurate understanding of ourselves.

9

Engagement, Invulnerability, and Dissatisfaction

In saying that the failure of the unmasking project leaves us back in the everyday world from which we began, I mean only that and no more. The point is worth stressing because once the metaphysical project's failure to reveal the unreality or subjectivity of colour is admitted (if it is), I think there is a temptation to conclude that objects really are coloured after all. If the austere conception of an objectively colourless world cannot be reached, and the colours of things cannot be shown to be unreal or subjective, we are inclined to think that they must be real and objective.

This temptation is well worth examining—and resisting. To yield to it would be to accept what looks like a metaphysical account on the same level as—but in direct opposition to—the view of reality as completely colourless. It would be a reassuring, positive answer to the same metaphysical question to which the subjectivist and the unmasker hoped to give one or another kind of negative answer: do our perceptions and beliefs involving the colours of things represent anything that is part of the world independently of us?

There are good reasons for not inferring from what has gone before that the answer to this question is 'Yes'. For one thing, giving a positive answer would seem to require just what giving a negative answer required or presupposed—that we can get ourselves into a position to ask the question in the right way in the first place. We would have to be able to consider all human perceptions and beliefs concerning the colours of things, on the one hand, and the world as it is independently of us, on the other, and manage to ask a still-open question about the relation between them. If we cannot do that in a way that leads to a negative answer—because even to acknowledge the relevant psychological facts we must also have some beliefs about the colours of objects—then we cannot get any closer to the detached position we would have to be in to give a reassuringly positive answer either. If asking a certain question imposes conflicting demands on anyone who would answer it, answering it positively should not be any easier than answering it negatively. In trying to raise the question, we cannot rid ourselves of a conception of the world as filled with coloured objects, so we can never achieve the kind of detachment from our beliefs that the metaphysical question seems to require.

Another reason to resist drawing a reassuringly positive metaphysical conclusion about the colours of things is that nothing follows about them from anything we have found. The most we have found is that the metaphysical conception of a completely colourless reality cannot be reached by the explanatory route. If that is correct, and if it is correct because one needs beliefs about the colours of things even to acknowledge the relevant facts of perception and belief, it does not follow that the world is, in fact, coloured. As far as I can see, the impossibility of a successful unmasking explanation implies nothing one way or the other about what the nonpsychological world is like with respect to colour. Given that we competently attribute to one another perceptions and beliefs about the colours of things, and given that that, in turn, requires that we also believe that the world contains many coloured objects, no necessary links have thereby been established or proposed between the presence of such beliefs and their truth. The most we can conclude is that we cannot carry out a certain intellectual project.

If we cannot carry off the feat of unmasking all the relevant beliefs and perceptions, we will have found in the attempted quest for reality no reason to abandon our everyday judgements about the colours of things in the world. Lemons are yellow, tomatoes are red, grass is green, and so on. Even if we cannot abandon all those beliefs and still find that human beings perceive colours and believe that objects are coloured, that does not imply that anyone's beliefs about the colours of things are true.

I do not mean to suggest that perhaps those beliefs are not true or that there is reason to doubt them. If what I have argued is right, the everyday judgements about the colours of things with which we began are left completely untouched by the unmasking metaphysical project as we have been able to understand it. But to conclude from that failure that our beliefs about the colours of things must therefore be largely true would be to draw a nonpsychological conclusion about the world around us from certain psychological facts of belief. It would be to say that statements about the colours of things would have to be true if psychological statements attributing perceptions and beliefs about the colours of things to people were true. The two kinds of facts could not come apart in general.

Sometimes it is possible to draw conclusions about the colours of things directly from certain kinds of psychological facts. What I am calling a psychological fact is whatever is stated by a true sentence with a main psychological verb attributing a thought, perception, feeling, or other "attitude" to a human subject. So the fact that someone sees that there is a yellow lemon on the table is a psychological fact in that sense. And from that psychological fact it follows that there is a yellow lemon on the table, just as it also follows from the fact that someone knows that there is a yellow lemon on the table. But those are not the kinds of psychological facts that someone who engages in the metaphysical project with unmasking aspirations will acknowledge. Nothing that directly implies that objects are coloured could be part of the conception of the world from which a would-be unmasker begins. It is a more difficult question whether psychological facts of the kinds that even an unmasker must admit imply that the world contains many coloured things. If they do, the view an unmasker aspires to could not possibly be true. Necessarily, any world containing the psychological facts he must start from would be a world of coloured things.

A necessary connection between our beliefs and a world of coloured objects would confer on our beliefs about the colours of things a very special status. They would not just be beliefs that we hold and cannot give up if we are to acknowledge all the psychological facts of perception and belief. The truth of all or most or some of our beliefs about the colours of objects would be guaranteed by the psychological fact that humans perceive and believe what they do. That would mean that beliefs about the colours of things could not all be false if there are beliefs of that kind that people hold to be true. Nothing more than the conditions of admitting certain beliefs into the world would be enough to guarantee the truth of those beliefs. That would be a remarkable result.

A further reason for not drawing such a strong conclusion is that some explanation would then be needed of how and why that remarkable necessary connection holds. A philosophical theory would be called for, and a theory that does the job in the right way is not easily come by. It is precisely the demand for such a theory that I think tends to distort or even to deny the familiar psychological facts that any such theory starts out trying to account for.

To draw that reassuring conclusion about the colours of things would put us in a position that is structurally similar to the position Kant thought he could prove we are in in general. He looked for some of the necessary conditions of our thinking and experiencing the world in the ways we do, and he found that some of those conditions are not simply further psychological facts about us, but apparently nonpsychological facts of the way things are. He held, for instance, that if we think of the world as containing events that happen in space and time independently of us and our reactions, then not only must we think of those events as linked to one another in accordance with general laws, but those events *are* (or even must be) linked to one another in accordance with general laws. That events in the world are or are not so linked appears to carry no implication as to whether or how anyone thinks or experiences anything. If it is a fact, it looks like a nonpsychological fact. But for Kant, it is to be "deduced" as a necessary condition of our thinking and experiencing the world in certain ways.

If psychological facts of perception and belief have some such nonpsychological necessary conditions, then certain nonpsychological things must be true of the world if anyone has certain kinds of experiences or beliefs. Kant's transcendental philosophy was an attempt to identify and establish the necessary conditions of thought and experience in general. The necessity in question was not merely causal or nomological. It was a kind of necessity that is knowable *a priori*. The conclusions of Kant's "deductions" would thereby be shown to have a very special status in our conception of the world. They would have to be true if we have any beliefs or experiences of a world at all. They could not be false if anyone thinks or experiences anything. Even to think that they are false or to doubt or wonder about their truth would guarantee that they are, indeed, true. Doubts about them could be allayed simply by the demonstration that they are necessary conditions of thought and experience.

This would be one way of showing that, at least in general, the world we understand and believe in cannot fail to match up to our beliefs and perceptions of it. There might be much room for error in particular cases, but with respect to basic general "principles" which must hold of any world we can think about or experience, we must be getting things right, given that we think and experience as we do. That would be to say that the nonpsychological world must be a certain way if certain psychological facts hold in it.

What is most distinctive of Kant's transcendental philosophy is that he thought this was something he could prove, and in a special way. He thought the "deductions" he offered are what it takes to put metaphysics on the secure path of a science and so avoid otherwise endless "dogmatic" disputes about the nature of reality. But to achieve that result, the proofs of those conclusions about the world would have to be truly impressive. They would have to take us by necessary steps from facts about how we think and experience the world to conclusions which appear to say how things are independently of all human thought and experience. And those apparently nonpsychological conclusions were to be reachable *a priori*, by nothing more than reflection on the conditions of our thinking and experiencing things as we do. To carry out such proofs would be to proceed by necessity from how we think to how things are. Kant saw that some explanation would certainly be needed of how such momentous discoveries are possible *a priori*.

His explanation was a form of idealism: transcendental idealism. The world of which such "principles" as 'Every event is linked to another in accordance with a general law' are true is not a world that is in every sense fully independent of all human thought and experience. Such principles hold only of the "phenomenal" world which is somehow "constituted by" the possibility of our thought and experience of it. Events and states of affairs in that world are, in general, empirically or contingently independent of each of us and our responses to them, but "transcendentally" speaking, that world depends on or is "constituted" by the possibility of our thinking and experiencing it. That is a form of idealism. It is "transcendental" because that idealism is the only explanation of our *a priori* knowledge of those necessary features of the world. Any world we could know about in that way must somehow be dependent on features of the rational beings who know it. "Reason has insight only into that which it produces after a plan of its own".[1]

It is not easy to accept, or even to understand, this philosophical theory. Accepting it presumably means believing that the sun and the planets and the mountains on earth and everything else that has been here so much longer than we have are nonetheless in some way or other dependent on the possibility of human thought and experience. What we thought was an independent world would turn out on this view not to be fully independent after all. It is difficult, to say the least, to understand a way in which that could be true. But it is easier to understand the felt need for some such theory. Kant thought that without it a certain necessary connection, and the possibility of our discovering that

---

1. I. Kant, *Critique of Pure Reason* (tr. N. K. Smith), London, 1953, Bxiii (p. 20).

connection, would remain unexplained and unsupported. A philosophical theory was needed to make intelligible to ourselves how we could proceed *a priori*, by necessary steps, from our thinking of the world in certain ways to the truth of the basic general principles of that world. Only then would we understand how the way we think things are and the way things are could not possibly come apart, in general.

Kant's theory was completely general. He did not apply it in particular to the restricted class of judgements about the colours of things. But an equally convincing explanation would be needed in that case of how and why the world's being coloured in many different ways could not come apart in general from our perceiving and believing it to be coloured in just those ways. To show that such a connection holds, we would have to explain how we can proceed by necessity from the admitted psychological facts of perception and belief involving the colours of things to the conclusion that the world contains many coloured objects. That would be a truly impressive "deduction".

Kant's proofs of his completely general conclusions turned on the necessary conditions of our having any thoughts or experiences at all, which he thought required that we be able to think of and experience a world that is independent of us. So the concepts he focussed on, he claimed, were indispensable to any possible thought and experience of an objective world. Colour does not seem to be indispensable in that way. It seems that people who could not see, and hence had no conception of colour at all, could still have a pretty rich conception of a world that endures as it is independently of them. So if a necessary connection could be demonstrated to hold between our perceiving and believing what we do about the colours of things and the world's containing coloured objects of the kinds we believe in, it could not appeal as Kant does to the indispensability of those beliefs for any conception at all of an independent world.

The dispositional theory of an object's colour promised in its own way to provide just such a connection. It is a theory of colour concepts. It does not say that such concepts are indispensable to any possible thought of an independent world. It aims only to give an account of what we think when we think objects are coloured. If what it means to say that there are coloured objects were fully expressible in terms only of (possibly very complicated) facts of actual or possible human perceptions of colour, then there would have to be coloured objects in any world in which those complicated psychological facts held. It would be impossible for the two to come apart because there would not really be two different kinds of facts after all. This would be a form of phenomenalism or reductionism of the colours of things, and if there were psychological facts of the kinds it appeals to, it would refute an "error" theory that says that all our beliefs about the colours of things are false. It would show on the contrary that most of those beliefs are true, given the psychological facts. And the psychological facts in question would be facts that any would-be unmasker has to admit.

A dispositional theory, if it were correct, would therefore provide a kind of explanation of a necessary connection between our perceptions and beliefs about the colours of things and the truth of those beliefs. Given the perceptions we do or would get, and the conditions under which we do or would get them, it would have to be true that objects are coloured. But the theory would explain that necessary connection in the disappointing way that any form of idealism would explain it: by making the world of coloured things dependent on the possibility of our getting the kinds of perceptions we do. It is in that sense a "subjectivist" view of an object's colour. It is more intelligible, and so easier to assess, than completely general idealism, since it restricts itself to the meaning or content of statements about the colours of things. But insofar as we were able to find it intelligible, we saw why that reductionist view cannot succeed.

The dispositional theory requires what I have called an indirect connection between the "objects" of perception and of thought about the colours of things, and for that reason it cannot adequately account for what we believe when we believe that objects are coloured. The trouble is that the truth or falsity of our everyday colour beliefs is recognizably independent of the psychological facts of perception understood in that way, and that is something the theory cannot accommodate. But that independence is precisely what makes a necessary connection between the relevant psychological facts and the truth of our beliefs about the colours of things so hard to establish.

Donald Davidson has argued on completely general grounds that most of our beliefs must be true. Belief, he says, "is in its nature veridical".[2] He thinks that can be seen by considering "what determines the existence and contents of a belief",[3] which, in turn, can be understood by investigating the conditions of correct attribution of beliefs and other propositional attitudes.

Davidson's position does not turn on the indispensability of certain concepts for any possible thought or for any possible conception of an

---

2. D. Davidson, "A Coherence Theory of Truth and Knowledge", in D. Henrich (ed.), *Kant oder Hegel?* Stuttgart, 1983, p. 432.

3. Davidson, "A Coherence Theory of Truth and Knowledge", p. 432.

independent world. His argument is that any large, reasonably comprehensive set of beliefs must be largely true. Of course, he does not deny that there are certain concepts that anyone would have to have in order to think about an independent world at all—of enduring objects in space and time, for instance, or of other persons with thoughts and beliefs, and so on—but he does not focus on the apparent indispensability of any such concepts. He concentrates on the conditions of the successful attribution of any perceptions and beliefs at all, and on the quite general observation that we can understand someone as perceiving or believing something with determinate content only if we can connect that person's possessing those states with some facts or events in the surrounding world that we take them to be about. We must to that extent be engaged in the world and take certain nonpsychological things to be true of it if we are to find such psychological facts as that someone perceives or believes something that we can identify and understand. We will therefore typically share a great many beliefs with any human beings we can interpret as holding recognizable propositional attitudes with content.

These are just the very general ideas about belief attribution that I have relied on in finding that a would-be unmasker must have some beliefs about the colours of objects in the world if he is to find his fellow human beings to perceive colours and believe that objects are coloured. Davidson does not apply his theory directly to that class of beliefs in particular. Nor can his view be applied indiscriminately to any fairly large subclass of a person's or a community's beliefs to yield the conclusion that those beliefs are true. There are many sets of interrelated beliefs that we can recognize our fellow human beings to have without ourselves regarding any of them as true, let alone without their being true.

But I have argued that in the particular case of colour beliefs it is plausible to draw conclusions parallel to those warranted by the general conditions of belief attribution. Beliefs about the colours of things are pervasive in our conception of the world, and it is impossible to define or explain their contents in completely noncolour terms. Our grasp of them in general is not something we could build up from simpler ingredients. It is sufficiently self-contained and *sui generis* to appear to be an indivisible package deal. That is crucial to the argument that without beliefs about the colours of things we could not recognize the presence in the world of perceptions of and beliefs about the colours of things, and that if we do think that people have such perceptions and beliefs, we must believe that objects are coloured.

The conclusion Davidson draws about beliefs in general appears to be stronger than that. He says that most of our beliefs must be true. If we applied that verdict to the case of colours in particular, it would yield the conclusion that most of our beliefs about the colours of things are true. It would be to say that those beliefs must be true, in general, since we do have a large set of irreducible beliefs about the colours of things, and (even for beliefs about the colours of things) "belief is in its nature veridical". That would seem to assert a necessary connection between the psychological facts a would-be unmasker must admit, on the one hand, and nonpsychological facts of the colours of things, on the other. The two could not come apart in general, since the presence of the beliefs would require their (for the most part) truth. The view a would-be unmasker aspires to—a conception of the world in which there are many people with beliefs about the colours of things, but no coloured objects—would therefore represent an impossibility. It could not possibly be the way things are in any world. From the fact that people have the beliefs they do, we could infer, with necessity, that the world contains many coloured objects.

That would confer on our beliefs about the colours of things a certain special status. It would be a necessary condition of our having any such beliefs that all or most of them are true. That special status, and how we know that our colour beliefs enjoy it, would then have to be explained and justified. It could not be justified, as in Kant, by arguing that the beliefs are indispensable to any possible conception of an independent world. And to preserve the independence of the world that idealism denies, the explanation should not imply that truths about the colours of things depend in some way on certain psychological facts. They should not be thought of as "constituted" or "made true" by our believing them or by our having the kinds of perceptions of colour that we do. Preserving that independence while showing that truths about the world are nonetheless a necessary condition of certain psychological facts of perception and belief seems to me a pretty tall order. And it looks as if any explanation that fulfilled that condition would be a positive answer to the metaphysical question of the reality or objectivity of the colours of things.

I have given reasons to doubt that we can even get ourselves into a position to ask that metaphysical question in the right way. They are therefore equally reasons against drawing any conclusion about the nonpsychological world from what we have discovered about the metaphysical project. But in expressing such doubts and reservations, I do not mean to doubt either that the world contains coloured things or that many people believe that the world contains coloured things. Both of those everyday beliefs of mine remain unaffected by anything we have found to be true of the metaphysical project. I say only that I do not think the content of my belief that things are coloured follows from the content of my belief that people believe that things are coloured. Or, more to the present point, I do not think that what we have found so far implies that the first must be true if the second is. What we have found (or concluded) so far concerns only the conditions of our understanding human beings as having beliefs about the colours of things: to recognize and attribute such beliefs, one must hold some beliefs about the colours of things oneself. That says something about what one must do or think in order to do or think something else. One must have a certain capacity in order to have or exercise a certain other capacity. But that does not say that the thoughts involved in the exercise of either of those capacities are or must be true.

If the conditions of the attribution of beliefs about the colours of things guarantee that any attributor of such beliefs must believe that some objects are coloured, then no would-be unmasker could ever find that the view he aspires to is true. If he finds the beliefs he would seek to unmask, he believes there are coloured things, so he cannot reach the view that nothing is coloured. If he does not believe there are coloured things, he cannot find beliefs to the effect that there are coloured things, so he cannot reach the conclusion that people's beliefs about the colours of things are all false. But the impossibility of an attributor's discovering the truth of the unmasker's view does not imply that that view is contradictory or could not possibly be true. An unmasker's guaranteed failure does not imply that if people have beliefs about the colours of things, then the world contains coloured things.

Anyone who finds people with beliefs about the colours of things will find those people's beliefs to be largely true. Having ascribed the beliefs, he might well express his opinion by saying, "Most of their beliefs are true" or even "They must be true" or "It is impossible for most of them to be false". That is an understandable way for him to express what he has found, if finding all those beliefs to be false is inconsistent with his having found that people have them. It would be natural to say, "Given that they have got those beliefs, most of them have to be true". But in giving that verdict, an attributor would not be claiming to have discovered that the truth of most beliefs about the colours of things is a necessary condition of people having them. Anyone who has ascribed such beliefs will, of course, *regard* the beliefs as largely true. That is because he will find the beliefs he has ascribed to be largely in agreement with his own beliefs, and he regards all his own beliefs as true. Everyone regards as true whatever he fully believes. But it does not follow that what everyone believes is, in fact, true.

It must also be granted that the truth of most beliefs about the colours of things does follow from *what* someone who attributes such beliefs to people believes. An attributor believes that people believe that lemons are yellow, that they believe that tomatoes are red, that they believe that grass is green, and so on, and he can ascribe such beliefs to them only because he himself also believes such things as that lemons are yellow, tomatoes are red, grass is green, and so on. So from everything such an attributor believes, it follows that those people's beliefs about the colours of things are largely true. What such an attributor believes is:

(A) People believe that lemons are yellow. They believe that toma-
    toes are red. They believe that grass is green. . . .
(B) Lemons are yellow. Tomatoes are red. Grass is green. . . .

And it follows from (A) and (B) that the beliefs the attributor attributes to those people are true. But that is so, not because of a remarkable necessary connection between attributed beliefs and their truth, but because from any statement of what a person believes, together with the statement that he believes it, it follows that the beliefs in question are true. That does not show that the beliefs are, in fact, true. The implication holds even when the beliefs are false. The truth of the attributed beliefs follows from what such an attributor believes, not from his believing what he believes or from his having attributed the beliefs in question.

What I have concluded so far about the attribution of beliefs about the colours of things could be put by saying, not that such beliefs are in their nature (largely) true, but that attribution of such beliefs is in its nature (largely) truth-ascribing. An attributor of such beliefs must find the beliefs he attributes to be largely true. Davidson says that the truth of most of our beliefs is guaranteed by the nature of "correct interpretation".[4] If "correct" interpretation is belief attribution carried out by those whose beliefs about the world are true, then that is clearly right. And it applies to beliefs about the colours of things as well. The truth of beliefs about the colours of things that attributors attribute to others is guaranteed *if* belief attribution is in its nature (largely) truth-ascribing, *and* the attributors' beliefs about the colours of things are (largely) true. But again that does not imply that every large set of attributed beliefs about the colours of things must be largely true.

---

4. D. Davidson, "Three Varieties of Knowledge", in A. Phillips Griffiths (ed.), *A. J. Ayer: Memorial Essays*, Cambridge, 1991, p. 160.

There might be further considerations that could be brought forward to yield that stronger conclusion, with no commitment to subjectivism or idealism. I have my doubts, but I do not want to pursue the question further here. I am concerned with the prospects of carrying out the unmasking metaphysical project I have described, and with what can be concluded from what we have discovered about why it cannot succeed. I am not trying to establish by philosophical argument the truth or falsity of what we all believe about the colours of things. Those beliefs need no help from philosophy. They need no validation or support from a reassuringly positive metaphysical verdict, and if I am right that the metaphysical project cannot be carried out, those beliefs cannot be unmasked by metaphysics either. And I think the conditions of the attribution of beliefs about the colours of things are enough to demonstrate their invulnerability.

We believe such things as that lemons are yellow, tomatoes are red, grass is green, and so on. If we cannot arrive at the conclusion that although we have those beliefs they are all false, that unavailable view can represent no threat to those everyday beliefs. But to remove or disarm that potential threat, it is not necessary to show that the view in question is contradictory and could not possibly be true. That would certainly remove it from consideration. But I have argued that such a killing blow cannot be justified by the conditions of belief attribution alone, without additional, and dubious, metaphysical theorizing. I think no such step is needed; it would be a case of overkill. To eliminate from consideration the view that objects are not coloured even though we believe they are, it is not necessary to prove that objects must be coloured if we believe they are.

To say that the unmasking view can be eliminated from consideration because it cannot be reached, or that no one could find it to be true, is to say that no one can carry off a certain intellectual feat. That is not necessarily to say or imply anything about how things in the world are or must be. The outcome of a successful unmasking would be a view with two parts: (1) people have many beliefs about the colours of things, and (2) those beliefs are all false; things are not coloured. What we have concluded about the conditions of belief attribution is that anyone who finds the first conjunct to be true will believe that objects are coloured, so he cannot consistently believe the second conjunct to be true. Anyone who finds the second conjunct to be true, and so holds no beliefs about the colours of things, cannot find the first conjunct to be true. So he cannot find any relevant beliefs to unmask as false. Without beliefs about the colours of things, he would have no opinion one way or the other either about whether things are coloured, or about whether anyone believes that things are coloured. No one could consistently find both conjuncts of the unmasker's view to be true.

A would-be unmasker's position is therefore formally similar to a person's relation to the paradoxical sentence 'I believe that it is raining, and it is not raining'.[5] That expresses something that no one could consistently believe or assert to be true—but not because it could not possibly be true. It could be true that I believe that it is raining when it is not raining. The first conjunct does not imply that the second conjunct is false, and the second does not imply that the first is false. In that sense it expresses a genuine possibility. But no one could consistently believe or assert that both conjuncts are true. If I say that the first is true—that I believe that it is raining—I cannot consistently assert the second, that it is not raining. If I believe that the second is true, I cannot consistently say that I believe that it is raining. The "paradox" illustrates one way in which it can be impossible for anyone to consistently believe or assert a certain thing without that thing itself being impossible or inconsistent. The utterance of 'I am not speaking' gives another version of the point.[6]

It is the impossibility of anyone's consistently finding the unmasker's view to be true that I think follows from what we have concluded about the attribution of beliefs about the colours of things. The view itself does not have to be contradictory or inconsistent for that to be so. That many people believe there are coloured things would not have to imply that there are coloured things. But if the view could not consistently be found to be true, it can represent no threat to our beliefs about the colours of things, even if what it expresses remains in some sense a possibility.

Even if this is right as far as it goes, it can easily seem like too exclusively negative a result. It can leave us with a certain uneasiness or dissatisfaction. It does not establish that objects are, in fact, coloured, and even seems to leave open the possibility of their not being coloured even though we all believe that they are. It is easy to feel that if we all believe that objects are coloured, perhaps even cannot help believing it, it should be possible for us to show that it is true. So we want to go further and establish that the alleged possibility is not actual, that the would-be unmasker's view is false, and that objects really are coloured after all. That would get rid of that otherwise troubling possibility once and for all.

---

5. See, for example, G. E. Moore, "Russell's Theory of Descriptions", in P. A. Schilpp (ed.), *The Philosophy of Bertrand Russell*, New York, 1951, p. 204.
6. See chapter 3, p. 67.

I think there is a way in which we have done that already. We have found that lemons are yellow, tomatoes are red, grass is green, and so on. Our beliefs about the colours of things are about as well supported and secure, in general, as beliefs can be. We can confidently say that objects are coloured and that most of the particular beliefs we hold about the colours of things are true. We can even say that we know them to be true. But if we know that objects are coloured, we know it in the way we know many other things—by observing the world around us and doing the best we can to find out on that basis what is so. We do not know that objects are coloured by deducing it from the fact that we all believe that objects are coloured. We do not know it by having established that the would-be unmasker's view is contradictory. But we do know that objects are coloured. So we do know that the second conjunct of the view the unmasker aspires to is false.

We saw earlier that settling the question of the colours of things in this everyday way does not settle the metaphysical question about the reality of colour. Nor do the conditions of the attribution of beliefs about the colours of things establish that the metaphysical unmasker's view is contradictory. But our everyday colour beliefs can be invulnerable to unmasking even if that view is not contradictory. So in granting that it is not contradictory, and so in that sense that it is possible for objects not to be coloured, even though we all believe that they are, we admit or create no threat to our beliefs about the colours of things, or even to our knowledge of them. What I am calling the invulnerability of our beliefs to unmasking is not brought into question by these concessions.

Kant tried to prove that the thoughts or beliefs that he held were essential to any thought of an independent world—and so to any thought at all—had to be true of such a world. If his proofs were sound, the truth of such beliefs, and so the world's being the way they say it is, would be guaranteed by anyone's thinking anything. I have said that such a strong conclusion seems difficult to establish without the help of some form of idealism. Suppose such a conclusion cannot be established without that kind of help. Suppose the truth of the beliefs in question does not follow simply from the fact that people think at all or think of the world in the ways they do. Then in that sense we could say that, given the premisses of Kant's arguments, there remains a possibility of their conclusions' being false, of the world's not being as everyone believes it to be. It is possible for 'People believe that p, believe that q, believe that r, . . .' to be true even though it is not true that p or q or r. . . .

Even when the beliefs in question are indispensable for thought of any independent world at all, it is no threat to those beliefs to grant the

possibility of their falsity, given only premises to the effect that people believe them. If there are any beliefs that are indispensable to
thought, as Kant held that there are, they will still be invulnerable to
unmasking. None of them could be abandoned consistently with our
having a conception of an independent world. We must continue to
think of any world we can think about at all as being the way those indispensable beliefs say it is. To think of our fellow human beings in
that world as having a conception of, or beliefs about, an independent
world, we would have to think of them also as holding those indispensable beliefs. We could not think of them as thinking of an independent world without them. So we could not consistently find others
to have those indispensable beliefs without having them ourselves. We
therefore could not ascribe them to others without ourselves believing
them. So for indispensable beliefs, no one could ever consistently find
that people believe that p, believe that q, believe that r . . . but it is not
true that p or q or r. . . .

This shows that the indispensability of certain beliefs for any conception of an independent world implies their invulnerability to unmasking. The invulnerability does not require or depend on the truth
of the beliefs in question or on their truth following from the fact that
the beliefs are held. But there can also be invulnerability to unmasking
without indispensability. I have argued that our beliefs about the colours
of things are invulnerable to unmasking, although they are not indispensable to any possible conception of an independent world. And in
that case, too, if the beliefs are invulnerable to unmasking, it is not because they must be true if they are held or attributed. As with indispensable beliefs, if there are any, it is in that sense possible for them to
be false, even though everyone believes them to be true.

To grant that possibility is to grant no more than that 'People believe
that objects are coloured' does not imply 'Objects are coloured'. It is
only in that sense that the view to which an unmasker aspires is conceded to represent a possibility. But that possibility, understood in that
way, is no threat to our beliefs about the colours of things, to their being in general true, or even to our knowing them to be true. We can *see*
that objects are coloured, so we have excellent reason for believing that
they are. Given that we see that objects are coloured, it is *not* possible
that they are not coloured. 'We see that objects are coloured' implies
'Objects are coloured'. Given that we have found that objects are
coloured, then, we cannot grant that it is possible that objects are not
coloured. Given that something is so, it is not possible that it is not so.
But still, we can grant that, given only that we all *believe* that objects
are coloured, it is possible for them not to be. Belief alone does not

eliminate the possibility of falsity. The unmasker's view is not contra-dictory. We can grant the point even if we *know* that objects are coloured.

The mere possibility of there being no coloured objects, even though we all believe that there are, would threaten our knowledge that objects are coloured if the only way we could come to know that objects are coloured was by inferring it somehow from our believing it. If the in-ference in question had to be deductive to give us that knowledge, the possibility would mean that we could never know that objects are coloured; the deduction would be invalid. But the assumption that that is the only way we could come to know that objects are coloured is ab-surd. We know it, if we do, by seeing objects to be coloured and so com-ing to believe and to know that they are. The possibility in question is no threat to that.

That possibility shows only that our believing what we do about the colours of things carries no certification of truth. In believing alone, even in holding a large, interconnected set of beliefs for the strongest reasons, truth is not guaranteed. Nor do the conditions of belief attri-bution provide any such guarantee. I have concluded from those con-ditions that no would-be unmasker could arrive at the view that there are no coloured things. But that is not because there being coloured things is guaranteed by the fact that we believe that there are. It is be-cause the denial that objects are coloured cannot consistently be reached by the unmasking route.

The fact that we could not abandon our beliefs about the colours of things and still find the world to contain people who believe that ob-jects are coloured does not even assure us that we could not abandon our beliefs about the colours of things. It does mean that philosophers who claim that objects are not really coloured should in consistency also give up the idea that people believe that objects are coloured. Some philosophers seem willing to take that step.[7] As far as I can see, there is nothing inconsistent in such a conception. It says nothing one way or the other about the colours of things or about whether anyone be-lieves anything about the colours of things. It is simply silent on such matters. But then it is not a conception from which one could try to es-tablish by the explanatory unmasking strategy that nothing in the world is coloured. Without beliefs about the colours of things in the world, there would be nothing relevant to unmask.

---

7. For instance all those who would repudiate what they call "folk psychology" in favour of purely physical or nonintentional descriptions of human organisms and other physical objects.

That again does not mean that a denial that objects are coloured could never be reached. Whether it can is the question whether we have or ever could find good reasons to abandon our beliefs in the colours of things. I have conceded that we can always reflect on our beliefs and ask which of them are true. That is at least an intelligible question, even if we usually have no special reason to ask it and no grounds for doubting our current beliefs. So I think we can ask, in as critical or reflective a spirit as we can muster, whether we are right to believe that things are coloured, that lemons are yellow, tomatoes are red, and so on. The way to answer such a question is to do whatever is needed to confirm or disconfirm the beliefs in question, investigate matters further in relevant ways, and scrutinize our efforts as best we can. We can do no better than to put ourselves in the best position for getting the most accurate and reliable beliefs about whatever is in question and carefully drawing the best supported conclusions.

We have already done that with beliefs about the colours of things in general. But that is where the metaphysical project is supposed to begin, not where it ends. What set us off at the beginning was the idea that the metaphysical question about the reality of colour apparently remains unanswered, even when we have done our best in every ordinary way to find out what is so. It was not simply a question of the truth or acceptability of our beliefs. So the assurance we have in everyday life that objects are coloured does not assure us that the answer to the metaphysical question is "Yes. Objects are really coloured".

This can perhaps lead us to feel that our ordinary conviction that objects are coloured is not decisive and that we can no longer simply take for granted all the ways we settle questions about the colours of things in everyday life. If we re-examine our beliefs with the metaphysical question in mind, the obvious differences between colours and many of the other properties we unproblematically ascribe to objects around us can seem to take on special significance. I have argued that without that metaphysical question, the ways in which colours differ from other properties of objects can be appreciated as just that—differences. If our everyday beliefs about the colours of things can seem threatened or in need of reassessment only in the face of that question, and if the question can have that significance only if an unmasking explanation of all those beliefs is in the offing, then our beliefs that lemons are yellow, tomatoes are red, grass is green, and so on have not been put under threat.

But I think this still feels like a less than fully satisfying outcome. It leaves our everyday beliefs so far untouched, perhaps, but as a response to what looks like a grand metaphysical project it can seem too noncommittal, even complacent. It does not give us the kind of under-standing of our position in the world that we feel the metaphysical ques-tion seeks. It is disappointing, not because of what it positively tells us about ourselves and the world, but because we feel there is something it still does not tell us. It offers no detached or (as we want to put it) fully "objective" view of ourselves and the colours of things. If we find that our believing as we do in everyday life that things are coloured does not amount to such a fully satisfying view, and if we also find that we can never consistently reach the conclusion that colours are unreal or subjective, we are tempted to conclude, and so would like to be able to show, that they must therefore be real or "objective".

I think it is undeniable that we feel a strong urge to draw some such conclusion if we are convinced of the failure of the view that colours are unreal or subjective. The strength of that urge is a measure of the strength of a metaphysical desire I think we have to discover how we really stand to the independent world around us. I have been trying to identify more precisely what that desire amounts to and what it would take to satisfy it. What, exactly, do we seek? I think we are now in a position to see that if we do have such a desire concerning the colours of objects, it is a desire we can never satisfy. We cannot get into a po-sition to ask the metaphysical question about the reality of colour in the right way.

That leaves us dissatisfied. We think there must be such a position, and we think that by reflecting on ourselves and the world in the right way we can get ourselves into it. But when we look closely at the course such reflections would have to take, as I have been trying to do, the re-sults are disappointing in the presence of that metaphysical urge. I do not say it can be proved once and for all that such disappointment is inevitable in the quest for the reality of the colours of things. Any con-vincing proof of such a verdict would give us finality and so a kind of metaphysical satisfaction after all, and so it could not be sound. But even if each assault on the metaphysical nature of colour is found want-ing, and for very good reasons—as I have argued is likely—that will not put an end to the quest either. The most we will do, and continue to do, is keep trying.

10

Morals

If we cannot lift ourselves out of the everyday world and reach a reality that does not contain coloured things, what can be expected from the quest for reality elsewhere in philosophy? I think no general morals can be drawn directly from the metaphysically discouraging conclusion we have reached in this case. Even about colours, it has proved difficult to arrive at a final, unquestionable verdict. But if everything here were correct and had been conclusively established, we still could not immediately generalize to other applications of the same philosophical idea.

Even to draw conclusions about the rest of what have come to be called "secondary qualities" would be premature and unwarranted. Sounds, for example, which are usually thought to belong to that class and are accordingly regarded as subjective or not part of the world as it is independently of perceivers, are not, strictly speaking, *qualities* of things at all. They are particulars with definite temporal position, and not the sort of thing that gets predicated of objects as colours do. Colours are thought to be properties of physical objects, and our perceptions of them can have the same predicational contents as we can also think to be true of the world in our beliefs about the colours of things. But none of that would be directly relevant to the metaphysical quest for the reality of sounds, if they are not qualities of things at all. Each application of the philosophical idea of reality must be examined on its own.

But I think we have seen enough of how the quest for reality is supposed to work in this case to give us a good idea of what to look for in assessing its feasibility and validity elsewhere. I have concentrated on some conditions of success that are essential to the project in any form. Any investigation of the relation between our conception of the world and the world that conception purports to be about must start with the idea of our having a determinate conception of the world. This means that any philosophical investigator of that conception must identify the beliefs in question and so must acknowledge that the conditions of our having beliefs with just those contents, and the conditions of his recognizing us as having them, are fulfilled. The question is whether that can be done consistently with finding that the beliefs represent nothing that is or could be so in the independent world.

I have stressed the importance and the difficulty of this question. They are often overlooked. There is apparently a strong tendency to let a prior metaphysical conception of reality control one's understanding of the beliefs in question. If it is believed or thought to be known in advance that there simply could not be in the world anything like what a straightforward reading of certain ordinary beliefs seems to imply there is, those attitudes will be given some other reading. It will be held that, contrary to appearances, their contents do not really go beyond states of affairs that do or can hold in that more restricted reality after all. That is reductionism. Or if it cannot be denied that they go beyond what is available in that more restricted reality, they will be regarded as illusions, or not really beliefs at all. They will perhaps be seen as confusions or as projections of certain natural feelings or reactions, but in any case not as straightforwardly true of the world as it is independently of us.

I think this tendency is at work in philosophical accounts of colour. It makes unmasking or subjectivist views look easier to reach than they turn out to be. I have tried to show that when our everyday beliefs about the colours of things are understood independently of such metaphysical preconceptions, they cannot be unmasked or reduced in those ways. One moral I would draw is that the tendency should be resisted wherever it appears. If the project begins with a preconceived and metaphysically loaded conception of what is available for understanding the very things it must account for to succeed, it can hardly fail, but it will provide no illumination. And if it distorts or misconstrues those everyday attitudes, it can result only in undiscoverable philosophical illusion.

Keeping one's understanding of the scrutinized beliefs free of any prior conception of what is supposed to be available in reality gives the metaphysical project a chance of revealing something about the relation between those beliefs and reality, if it can be carried out. But it also makes it possible to resist the pressure towards reductionism or unmasking that any such prior conception carries with it. The beliefs in question can then be found to be intelligible and either true or false of the world, even though their contents are not reducible to any combination of ingredients of that more restricted conception. And if those irreducible beliefs are indispensable to our understanding of the world, or can be attributed to others only if one has some such beliefs oneself, they could not possibly be unmasked as nothing more than illusions or projections onto a world that contains nothing corresponding to them.

The unspoken assumption that reductionism or mere "fictions" or "projections" are the only alternatives available is widespread in philosophy. Thus Hume granted that we believe that one thing happens because another does, but he thought there was nothing in the independent world to make such thoughts true. There was a "necessary connection" to be taken into account,[1] but no necessary connections could be found between things in the world. Our everyday causal beliefs therefore had to be something other than judgements that are straightforwardly true or false of the world. "Necessity is something that exists in the mind, not in objects",[2] he said. He did not mean that there are necessary connections between things in the mind but not between objects in the outer world. He meant there are no necessary connections anywhere; we think there are only because of something that happens in our minds. Whatever is so in the world as it is independently of us, it is only what in fact happens to be so and could have been otherwise; it contains no necessity. The best that could be done for the idea of necessary connection was therefore to explain our possession of it and to see the "beliefs" we express with it as nothing more than "fictions" that we cannot avoid.

This same conception of reality as containing only what is, in fact, so but could have been otherwise is also what has made it so difficult to account for our thoughts of absolute—or what is sometimes called "logical" and sometimes called "metaphysical"—necessity. We appear to think that certain things just must be so, that there is no possibility at all of their being otherwise. But with such a conception of reality, it is impossible to find anything in the world that corresponds to the necessity or special modal force in such thoughts.

Reductionism is out of the question, since nothing contingent could be equivalent to something that holds necessarily. The only alternative is to seek the source of the idea of necessity in something that is in a

---

1. D. Hume, *A Treatise of Human Nature* (ed. L. A. Selby-Bigge), Oxford, 1958, p. 77.
2. Hume, *Treatise*, p. 165.

broad sense subjective—something on "our" side of the divide between what "we" contribute and what the world as it is independently of us contributes to our conception of what is so. Nothing on "our" side of that line could capture the full content of the idea; whatever is there is contingent and could have been otherwise. And even to account for our possession of the idea, some way must first be found to identify it. If it is an idea which could not apply to anything in reality, nothing intelligible that is allowed to be either true or false could be found to express its content. Nothing could be said without circularity about what it adds to our thoughts of what is so. The modal beliefs to be unmasked could not even be identified as such.

This quandary is avoided by accepting the irreducibility of the ideas of both causal and absolute necessity while insisting that they are intelligible ideas which we make essential use of to say things that are either true or false. That would not be to advocate a richer metaphysical conception that includes causal and absolute necessity as part of reality after all. That no more follows from the failure to reach a satisfactory unmasking view of necessity than the "objective reality" of the colours of things follows from the failure of the unmasking strategy in that case. It would serve only to remind us that our having an idea that is not reducible to any combination of ideas which do not themselves make use of it does not imply that we understand nothing by that idea, or that its application does not make a difference to the truth or falsity of what we say in using it.

In fact, it is only because we understand causation and necessity as we do that we recognize their irreducibility. We know that no statement of mere sequence could be equivalent to a causal statement, and nothing that holds necessarily could be equivalent to something that holds only contingently. The one could be true while the other is false. Our understanding of the thoughts in question is all we ever have to go on in resisting what we can recognize to be distortions of them, even where reductionism is not so obviously ruled out, as it has seemed to many it is not in the case of colours.

It is in the philosophical understanding of moral judgements, or of evaluative statements more generally, that the unspoken assumption seems to be most strongly held. Reducing them to something non-evaluative or unmasking them as "fictions", "projections", or some other "noncognitive" attitude have come to be seen as the only possible alternatives. With a prior conception of reality restricted to nonevaluative states of affairs, reductionist accounts of their contents will be ruled out on the grounds that no combination of nonevaluative statements could ever be equivalent to an evaluation of something. The conclusion seems inevitable that evaluations can be understood only as something other than holding something to be true.

Parallels are frequently drawn between colours and values. I think the parallel could be most profitably pursued by starting with what we have now found to be true of colours and asking whether similar difficulties arise in attempts to reach subjectivist or unmasking conclusions about evaluative judgements. That would be a huge task, at least as large as what I have begun here. But we should now have a better idea of what to look out for.

The main question is whether, aside from metaphysical preconceptions, there is good reason to force evaluative judgements onto one side or the other of the assumed dichotomy. That can only be decided by the extent to which either side does justice to the contents we independently understand such judgements to have. Some understanding or other of them is needed, even to attempt a reduction or an unmasking. But whether either of those strategies can succeed must be left an open question, at least at the beginning. A prior conception of an exclusively nonevaluative reality would close the question, just as an exclusively physical or otherwise noncolour reality would close it for the colours of things. But it will do so legitimately only if such a restricted conception of the world has already been consistently and legitimately reached. I think that cannot be done in the case of colours. Can it be done for evaluative judgements?

If reducing the contents of evaluative judgements to nonevaluative states of affairs would eliminate the evaluative element and so would distort them—as I think it is now widely agreed that it does—it does not immediately follow that they are not judgements that are either true or false, or that we cannot take "cognitive" attitudes like assertion and belief towards them. In fact, just the opposite would be true if the way we recognize the failure of reductionism is by seeing that an evaluation could be true even if its proposed nonevaluative equivalent were false, or vice versa. We would be relying on our understanding of the evaluative judgement in question—on our knowledge of the conditions under which it would be true or false—in resisting what we recognize to be a distorted reductive account of its meaning. I think dispositional theories of an object's colour can be seen to fail in this way.

To anyone armed with a prior conception of an exclusively nonevaluative reality, it will seem that there could be no such conditions under which evaluative judgements would be true or false. But that is only to say that they cannot be reduced to a nonevaluative base. Given that irreducibility, it is only to be expected that their contents, or the conditions under which they would be true, cannot be stated in exclusively nonevaluative terms. That means that no one can *say* what an evaluative judgement asserts without using some evaluative term. But that in itself shows nothing suspect about such judgements or about our attitudes involving them. The contents of judgements about the colours of things cannot be fully expressed without using colour terms, and they are not reducible to a noncolour base. But we can believe and even know such judgements to be true. I think the same holds for modal notions like causation and necessity.

Granting the irreducibility, a would-be unmasker of evaluative judgements would need some other grounds for denying that they have intelligible "cognitive" contents that are either true or false. The fact that they go beyond anything available in an exclusively nonevaluative reality is not enough. But the judgements, and the fact that we make them, would have to be acknowledged and understood in some way. Here the evidence seems to be all in favour of our regarding them as true or false. We appear to assert them, to put them forward as true, as something we believe. We disagree with others about them and argue with others about which of the conflicting evaluative judgements are right, or are to be accepted. We make inferences from one evaluative belief to another and can explain the validity of those inferences in terms of the impossibility of the second's being false if the first is true.

All of this must be acknowledged, and somehow accounted for, by any would-be unmasking. I think it is fair to say that it has not so far been shown that that can be done, on the assumption that our evaluative attitudes are something other than asserting and accepting evaluative contents as true. This is one pressing issue in the study of evaluative judgements. To concede that we treat them that way, that we unreflectively think of them as if they were true or false, and that we even make inferences that are best explained on that assumption, while insisting that that is only how we think of them or treat them, and that we are wrong or confused in thinking that they have any such contents at all, does not avoid the difficulty. It is simply to assert the apparently deflating conclusion which a successful unmasking is supposed to reach. The question is whether and how that conclusion can be consistently arrived at while attributing to us the thoughts it says we have in the evaluations we hold and express.

That would require making sense of what we think, and of our thinking it, whether its truth or falsity is ultimately seen as part of reality or not. And, as in the case of colours, there is a question whether the conditions of recognizing any such beliefs in the world can be fulfilled by someone who has no beliefs of that kind at all. If their contents are irreducible, there would be no possibility of explaining them as beliefs in combinations of states of affairs that could hold in the reality that a would-be unmasker already accepts. Some way of understanding and recognizing the contents of the judgements we make is required even of the kind of "dispositional" theory that says that in believing something to have a certain value we believe only that the thing is disposed to be valued in certain ways. The judgements that such an object is said to have a disposition to produce must be intelligible independently of the object's having that disposition. Only if that is so could the disposition in question be identified, and the contents of judgements which mention it be explained.[3] The psychological facts of evaluation must be acknowledged and understood in some way or other.

I have argued that only someone capable of making judgements about the colours of things could understand the contents of beliefs about the colours of things and hence could come to recognize other people as holding them. If that is right, it means that a completely general unmasking of the colours of things cannot consistently be reached. Whether a parallel obstacle arises for the general unmasking of evaluative beliefs obviously cannot be determined from that conclusion about colours alone, even if it is correct. The project must be tried out in that particular case in detail. But we can learn from the case of colours to pay special attention to what it takes for anyone to acknowledge the presence in the world of human beings' holding what he can recognize to be evaluative beliefs. If he needs some evaluative beliefs of his own to do that, he will never reach a conception of the world in which there is nothing corresponding to the contents of any of the evaluative beliefs he recognizes. No unmasking could succeed.

There is perhaps some reason to think that evaluative beliefs differ from beliefs about the colours of things in a way that makes an even stronger case against the possibility of unmasking them. Colour beliefs, I have argued, are unmaskable in general, even though they are not indispensable to any possible conception of an independent world. It is harder to believe that evaluative beliefs are dispensable even to the extent to which colour beliefs are. It is hard to believe that anyone could have any conception of an independent world at all if he could not see himself as acting in it and also see others as acting in the same world that he and they have beliefs about.

Making sense of people as acting intentionally in a world they understand would seem to require attributing to them judgements or be-

---

3. This is the parallel for evaluations of the defect in what I called the "hybrid" dispositional theory of the colour of an object at the end of chapter 6.

liefs about the relative values of the different courses of action they see as available, given their beliefs. Desires or impulses seen as mere pushes and pulls, understood nonintentionally, would not be enough to distinguish human beings from other things that move but have no beliefs and perform no actions. But if that is so, and some evaluative beliefs or other are indispensable to any human agent, and so are part of anyone's conception of the world, anyone who can recognize other agents in the world as holding evaluative beliefs would have to have some evaluative beliefs of his own. And if that were so, he could not consistently see others as making evaluations while holding that there are no evaluative states of affairs at all in the world that he acknowledges. The indispensability of evaluations in general is what would guarantee their unmaskability.

All this obviously raises huge questions for further inquiry. I simply point to some of them here. But even if the unmaskability of evaluative beliefs in general could be established or made plausible in this way, it would do nothing to show that values or evaluative states of affairs are really part of reality after all. It would simply leave us where we were at the beginning, before the metaphysical question arose, with everyday beliefs about one thing or one course of action or one way of life as being better or more advisable or more rewarding than another. It would not show that agreement among us as to the values of things is more widespread or more likely than we might have supposed. It would not show that we are right in all or some or even any of the evaluations we do agree about. It would not show that anyone is right about any evaluations at all.

Nothing about the truth or falsity of any particular evaluation would follow from the failure of the metaphysical project to unmask or to establish a subjectivist view of evaluative judgements. But it would follow that we could not consistently find the whole idea of one thing's being better or more valuable than another to be in general an illusion. We could not consistently find ourselves to be wrong in the very thought that some things or courses of action do have some value or are better than some others, while we continue to think of the world in the ways we do.

If we cannot lift ourselves completely out of the everyday world in that way and reach a reality in which nothing has any value at all, the evaluative disagreements that will certainly continue among us, perhaps forever, will still be seen as disagreements about what value, or how much value if any, the specific things or courses of action we are concerned with actually have. That is what we care about, and try to settle, in private and social life. But there is no nonevaluative talisman that can somehow settle such questions for us once and for all. We can always scrutinize and reassess some current evaluation, but only on the basis of other evaluations we still endorse, which in turn can themselves be reassessed. But in asking such questions, however momentous they might sometimes be, we are engaged in trying to find an evaluative answer. We would not be asking whether anything anywhere has any value at all, even though we cannot help thinking something does. The disengaged vantage point from which to ask that metaphysical-sounding question would still not have been reached.

Bibliography

Aaron, R., *John Locke*, Oxford University Press, Oxford, 1937.

Altham, J., and R. Harrison (eds.), *World, Mind, and Ethics*, Cambridge University Press, Cambridge, 1995.

Anscombe, G. E. M., "The Intentionality of Sensation: A Grammatical Feature", in Butler (ed.), *Analytical Philosophy: Second Series*.

Armstrong, David, *Perception and the Physical World*, Routledge & Kegan Paul, London, 1961.

———, *A Materialist Theory of the Mind*, Routledge & Kegan Paul, London, 1968.

———, "Perception, Sense Data and Causality", in Macdonald (ed.), *Perception and Identity*.

Austin, J. L., *Philosophical Papers*, Oxford University Press, Oxford, 1961.

———, "Unfair to Facts", in his *Philosophical Papers*.

Averill, E. W., "The Primary-Secondary Quality Distinction", *Philosophical Review* 1982.

———, "Color and the Anthropocentric Problem", *The Journal of Philosophy* 1985.

———, "The Relational Nature of Color", *Philosophical Review* 1992.

Ayer, A. J. (ed.), *Logical Positivism*, Free Press, Glencoe, Ill., 1959.

———, *The Central Questions of Philosophy*, Penguin, Harmondsworth, 1977.

———, "Replies", in Macdonald (ed.), *Perception and Identity*.

Ayers, Michael, *Locke*, 2 vols., Routledge, London, 1991.

Barrett, R., and R. Gibson (eds.), *Perspectives on Quine*, Blackwell, Oxford, 1990.

Bennett, Jonathan, *Locke, Berkeley, Hume: Central Themes*, Oxford University Press, Oxford, 1971.

Berkeley, George, *Berkeley: Philosophical Works* (ed. M. Ayers), J. M. Dent, London, 1975.

Bigelow, J., J. Collins, and R. Pargetter, "Colouring in the World", *Mind* 1990.

Blackburn, Simon, "Errors and the Phenomenology of Value", in Honderich (ed.), Morality and Objectivity.

———, *Essays in Quasi-Realism*, Oxford University Press, Oxford, 1993.

Boghossian, P., and D. Velleman, "Colour as a Secondary Quality", *Mind* 1989.

———, "Physicalist Theories of Color", *Philosophical Review* 1991.

Broackes, Justin, "The Autonomy of Colour", in Charles and Lennon (eds.), *Reduction, Explanation and Realism*.

Brown, R., and C. D. Rollins (eds.), *Contemporary Philosophy in Australia*, Allen & Unwin, London, 1969.

Burtt, E. A., *The Metaphysical Foundations of Modern Physical Science*, Routledge & Kegan Paul, London, 1950.

Butler, R. (ed.), *Analytical Philosophy: Second Series*, Blackwell, Oxford, 1965.

Byrne, A., and D. Hilbert (eds.), *Readings on Color*, vol. 1, MIT Press, Cambridge, Mass., 1997.

Campbell, John, "A Simple View of Colour", in Haldane and Wright (eds.), *Reality, Representation and Projection*.

Campbell, Keith, "Colours", in Brown and Rollins (eds.), *Contemporary Philosophy in Australia*.

———, "Primary and Secondary Qualities", *Canadian Journal of Philosophy* 1972.

Carnap, R., *The Unity of Science*, Routledge & Kegan Paul, London, 1934.

———, "Psychology in Physical Language", in Ayer (ed.), *Logical Positivism*.

———, "Testability and Meaning", *Philosophy of Science* 1936.

Charles, D., and K. Lennon (eds.), *Reduction, Explanation and Realism*, Oxford University Press, Oxford, 1992.

Cheng, C. Y. (ed.), *Philosophical Aspects of the Mind-Body Problem*, University of Hawaii Press, Honolulu, 1975.

Davidson, Donald, *Essays on Actions and Events*, Oxford University Press, Oxford, 1980.

———, *Inquiries into Truth and Interpretation*, Oxford University Press, Oxford, 1984.

———, "Radical Interpretation", in his *Inquiries into Truth and Interpretation*.

———, "Belief and the Basis of Meaning", in his *Inquiries into Truth and Interpretation*.

———, "A Coherence Theory of Truth and Knowledge", in Henrich (ed.), *Kant oder Hegel?*

———, "Three Varieties of Knowledge", in A. Phillips Griffiths (ed.), *A. J. Ayer: Memorial Essays*.

———, "Mental Events", in his *Essays on Actions and Events*.

Descartes, R., *The Philosophical Writings of Descartes*, 2 vols. (tr. & ed. J. Cottingham, R. Stoothoff, and D. Murdoch), Cambridge University Press, Cambridge, 1985.

Deutscher, M., "Mental and Physical Properties", in Presley (ed.), *The Identity Theory of Mind*.

Dummett, Michael, "Common Sense and Physics", in Macdonald (ed.), *Perception and Identity*.

Evans, Gareth, "Things without the Mind: A Commentary upon Chapter Two of Strawson's *Individuals*", in Van Straaten (ed.), *Philosophical Subjects*.

Frege, Gottlob, *Logical Investigations* (tr. P. T. Geach and R. H. Stoothoff), Blackwell, Oxford, 1977.

————, "Thoughts", in his *Logical Investigations*.

Geach, P. T., *Mental Acts*, Routledge & Kegan Paul, London, 1957.

Goodman, Nelson, "The Way the World Is", *Review of Metaphysics* 1960.

————, *Ways of Worldmaking*, Hackett, Indianapolis, 1978.

Hacker, P. M. S., "Are Secondary Qualities Relative?", *Mind* 1986.

————, *Appearance and Reality*, Blackwell, Oxford, 1987.

Haldane, J., and C. Wright (eds.), *Reality, Representation and Projection*, Oxford University Press, Oxford, 1993.

Hardin, C. L., "Colors, Normal Observers, and Standard Conditions", *The Journal of Philosophy* 1983.

————, "Are 'Scientific' Objects Coloured?", *Mind* 1984.

————, "A New Look at Color", *American Philosophical Quarterly* 1984.

————, *Color for Philosophers*, Hackett, Indianapolis, 1988.

Harman, Gilbert, "The Intrinsic Quality of Experience", *Philosophical Perspectives* 1990.

Harrison, Bernard, "On Describing Colours", *Inquiry* 1967.

————, *Form and Content*, Blackwell, Oxford, 1973.

Hellman, G., and F. Thompson, "Physicalism: Ontology, Determination, and Reduction", *The Journal of Philosophy* 1975.

Henrich, Dieter (ed.), *Kant oder Hegel?*, Klett-Cotta, Stuttgart, 1983.

Hilbert, David, *Color and Color Perception*, CSLI, Stanford, 1987.

Honderich, T. (ed.), *Morality and Objectivity*, Routledge & Kegan Paul, London, 1985.

Hookway, Christopher, "Fallibilism and Objectivity: Science and Ethics", in Altham and Harrison (ed.), *World, Mind, and Ethics*.

Hume, David, *A Treatise of Human Nature* (ed. L. A. Selby-Bigge), Oxford University Press, Oxford, 1958.

————, *Enquiries concerning the Human Understanding and concerning the Principles of Morals* (ed. L. A. Selby-Bigge), Oxford University Press, Oxford, 1966.

Jackson, F., and R. Pargetter, "An Objectivist's Guide to Subjectivism about Colour", *Révue International de Philosophie* 1987.

Jackson, Frank, "Do Material Things Have Non-Physical Properties?", *The Personalist* 1973.

————, *Perception*, Cambridge University Press, Cambridge, 1977.

Jardine, N., "The Possibility of Absolutism", in Mellor (ed.), *Science, Belief and Behaviour*.

————, "Science, Ethics, and Objectivity", in Altham and Harrison (eds.), *World, Mind, and Ethics*.

Johnston, Mark, "Dispositional Theories of Value", *Proceedings of the Aristotelian Society: Supplementary Volume* 1989.

————, "How to Speak of the Colors", *Philosophical Studies* 1992.

————, "Objectivity Refigured: Pragmatism without Verificationism", in Haldane and Wright (eds.), *Reality, Representation and Projection*.

Kant, I., *Critique of Pure Reason* (tr. N. K. Smith), Macmillan, London, 1953.

Kneale, W. C., "Perception and the Physical World", *Philosophical Quarterly* 1951.

Kripke, Saul, *Naming and Necessity*, Harvard University Press, Cambridge, Mass., 1980.

Landesman, C., *Color and Consciousness*, Temple University Press, Philadelphia, 1989.

Levin, J., "Physicalism and the Subjectivity of Secondary Qualities", *Australasian Journal of Philosophy* 1987.

Lewis, C. I., *Mind and the World-Order*, Dover, New York, 1956.

Lewis, David, "Psychophysical and Theoretical Identifications", *Australasian Journal of Philosophy* 1972.

————, "Dispositional Theories of Value", *Proceedings of the Aristotelian Society: Supplementary Volume* 1989.

Locke, John, *An Essay concerning Human Understanding* (ed. P. H. Nidditch), Oxford University Press, Oxford, 1975.

Lovibond, Sabina, *Realism and Imagination in Ethics*, University of Minnesota Press, Minneapolis, 1983.

Macdonald, G. F. (ed.), *Perception and Identity*, Cornell University Press, Ithaca, N.Y., 1979.

McDowell, John, "Values and Secondary Qualities", in Honderich (ed.), *Morality and Objectivity*.

————, "Aesthetic Value, Objectivity, and the Fabric of the World", in Schaper (ed.), *Pleasure, Preference and Value*.

————, *Mind and World*, Harvard University Press, Cambridge, Mass., 1994.

MacIntosh, J. J., "Primary and Secondary Qualities", *Studia Leibnitiana* 1976.

Mackie, J. L., *Problems from Locke*, Oxford University Press, Oxford, 1976.

McGinn, Colin, "Philosophical Materialism", *Synthèse* 1980.

————, *The Subjective View*, Oxford University Press, Oxford, 1983.

————, "Another Look at Color", *The Journal of Philosophy* 1996.

Maund, Barry, *Colours: Their Nature and Representation*, Cambridge University Press, Cambridge, 1995.

Mellor, D. H. (ed.), *Science, Belief and Behaviour*, Cambridge University Press, Cambridge, 1980.

Moore, A. W., *Points of View*, Oxford University Press, Oxford, 1997.

Moore, G. E., "Russell's Theory of Descriptions", in Schilpp (ed.), *The Philosophy of Bertrand Russell*.

Mourelatos, A. (ed.), *The Pre-Socratics: A Collection of Critical Essays*, Doubleday, Garden City, N.Y., 1974.

Nagel, Thomas, *The View from Nowhere*, Oxford University Press, New York, 1986.

Neurath, O., "Sociology and Physicalism", in Ayer (ed.), *Logical Positivism*.

Peacocke, C., *Sense and Content*, Oxford University Press, Oxford, 1983.

————, "Colour Concepts and Colour Experience", *Synthèse* 1984.

Perkins, M., *Sensing the World*, Hackett, Indianapolis, 1983.

Peterson, G. (ed.), *The Tanner Lectures on Human Values*, Vol. X, University of Utah Press, Salt Lake City, 1989.

Phillips Griffiths, A. (ed.), *A. J. Ayer: Memorial Essays*, Cambridge University Press, Cambridge, 1991.

Pitcher, George, *A Theory of Perception*, Princeton University Press, Princeton, 1971.

Presley, C.F. (ed.), *The Identity Theory of Mind*, University of Queensland Press, Brisbane, 1967.

Putnam, Hilary, *The Many Faces of Realism*, Open Court, La Salle, Ill., 1987.

Quine, W. V., *Word and Object*, MIT Press, Cambridge, Mass., 1960.

————, "Facts of the Matter", *Southwestern Journal of Philosophy* 1979.

Reid, Thomas, *Essays on the Intellectual Powers of Man*, MIT Press, Cambridge, Mass, 1969.

Ryle, G., *Dilemmas*, Cambridge University Press, Cambridge, 1956.

Schaper, E. (ed.), *Pleasure, Preference and Value*, Cambridge University Press, Cambridge, 1987.

Schilpp, P. A. (ed.), *The Philosophy of Bertrand Russell*, Tudor, New York, 1951.

Sellars, Wilfrid, *Science, Perception and Reality*, Routledge & Kegan Paul, London, 1963.

Shoemaker, Sydney, *The First-Person Perspective and Other Essays*, Cambridge University Press, Cambridge, 1996.

Smart, J. J. C., "Colours", *Philosophy* 1961.

————, "On Some Criticisms of a Physicalist Theory of Colours", in C. Y. Cheng (ed.), *Philosophical Aspects of the Mind-Body Problem*.

————, *Philosophy and Scientific Realism*, Routledge & Kegan Paul, London, 1963.

Smith, A. D., "Of Primary and Secondary Qualities", *Philosophical Review* 1990.

Smith, M., "Colour, Transparency, Mind-Independence", in Haldane and Wright (ed.), *Reality, Representation and Projection*.

Stebbing, L.S., *Philosophy and the Physicists*, Dover, New York, 1958.

Strawson, G., "Red and 'Red'", *Synthèse* 1989.

Strawson, P. F., "Perception and Its Objects", in Macdonald (ed.), *Perception and Identity*.

————, *Skepticism and Naturalism: Some Varieties*, Methuen, London, 1985.

Stroud, Barry, "Berkeley v. Locke on Primary Qualities", *Philosophy* 1980.

————, "The Physical World", *Proceedings of the Aristotelian Society* 1987.

————, "The Thought of Subjectivism", *Congreso Internacional Extraordinario de Filosofía*, Córdoba, 1988.

————, "The Study of Human Nature and the Subjectivity of Value", in G. Peterson (ed.), *The Tanner Lectures on Human Values*, vol. X.

————, "Quine's Physicalism", in Barrett and Gibson (eds.), *Perspectives on Quine*.

————, "'Gilding or Staining' the World with 'Sentiments' and 'Phantasms'", *Hume Studies* 1993.

————, "The Charm of Naturalism", *Proceedings and Addresses of the American Philosophical Association* 1996.

Tipton, I., *Berkeley: The Philosophy of Immaterialism*, Methuen, London, 1974.

Turbayne, C. (ed.), *Berkeley: Critical and Interpretive Essays*, University of Minnesota Press, Minneapolis, 1982.

Van Straaten, Z. (ed.), *Philosophical Subjects: Essays Presented to P. F. Strawson*, Oxford University Press, Oxford, 1980.

Von Fritz, Kurt, "*Nous, Noein*, and Their Derivatives in Pre-Socratic Philosophy", in Mourelatos (ed.), *The Pre-Socratics: A Collection of Critical Essays*.

Warnock, Geoffrey, *Berkeley*, Penguin, London, 1953.

Westphal, J., *Colour: Some Philosophical Problems from Wittgenstein*, Blackwell, Oxford, 1987.

Wiggins, David, "A Sensible Subjectivism?", in his *Needs, Values, Truth*.

———, *Needs, Values, Truth*, Blackwell, Oxford, 1991.

Williams, Bernard, *Descartes: The Project of Pure Enquiry*, Penguin, Harmondsworth, 1978.

———, *Ethics and the Limits of Philosophy*, Harvard University Press, Cambridge, Mass., 1985.

———, "Ethics and the Fabric of the World", in Honderich (ed.), *Morality and Objectivity*.

Wilson, Margaret, "Did Berkeley Completely Misunderstand the Basis of the Primary-Secondary Quality Distinction in Locke?", in Turbayne (ed.), *Berkeley: Critical and Interpretive Essays*.

———, "History of Philosophy in Philosophy Today: The Case of the Sensible Qualities", *Philosophical Review* 1992.

Wittgenstein, L., *Philosophical Investigations* (tr. G. E. M. Anscombe), Blackwell, Oxford, 1953.

———, *Philosophical Grammar* (tr. A. Kenny), Blackwell, Oxford, 1974.

———, *Remarks on Colour* (tr. L. McAlister and M. Schättle), Blackwell, Oxford, 1977.

Wright, C., "Moral Values, Projection and Secondary Qualities", *Proceedings of the Aristotelian Society: Supplementary Volume* 1988.

———, *Truth and Objectivity*, Harvard University Press, Cambridge, Mass., 1992.

Index